THE ULTIMATE
GAME OF STRATEGY

books for the future minded

Welcome to the next generation of business

There is a new world which we can look at but we cannot see. Yet within it, the forces of technology and imagination are overturning the way we work and the way we do business.

ft.com books are both gateway and guide to this world. We understand it because we are part of it. But we also understand the needs of businesses which are taking their first steps into it, and those still standing hesitantly on the threshold. Above all, we understand that, as with all business challenges, the key to success lies not with the technology itself, but with the people who must use it and manage it. People like you – the future minded.

See a world of business.

Visit **www.ft.com** today.

THE ULTIMATE
GAME OF STRATEGY

establishing a personal niche in the world of e-business

Peter Small

PEARSON EDUCATION LIMITED

Head Office
Edinburgh Gate
Harlow CM20 2JE
Tel: +44 (0)1279 623623
Fax: +44 (0)1279 431059

London Office:
128 Long Acre
London WC2E 9AN
Tel: +44 (0)20 7447 2000
Fax: +44 (0)20 7240 5771
Website:www.business-minds.com
―――――――――――

First published in Great Britain in 2001

ISBN 0 273 64999 X

British Library Cataloguing in Publication Data
A CIP catalogue record for this book can be obtained from the British Library.

Library of Congress Cataloging in Publication Data
Applied for.

10 9 8 7 6 5 4 3 2 1

Typeset by Land & Unwin (Data Sciences) Ltd
Printed and bound in Great Britain by Biddles Ltd of Guildford and King's Lynn

The Publishers' policy is to use paper manufactured from sustainable forests.

ACKNOWLEDGEMENTS

No book can be created by an author in isolation. This book is no exception. Indeed, the feedback from so many people during the draft stages of the writing was a major influence on the content. Listed below (in alphabetical order) are the people who in one way or another contributed to the evolution of this book.

Bassem Abdallah, Guy Anderson, Mark Baartse, Julian Baker, Perry Barile, Sheelagh Barron, Jonas Björkberg, Phil and Sorel Blomfield, Vaughn Botha, Paul Bradforth, Marcos Caceres, Yvan Caron, Tadeo Carrier, Cathy Chapman, Dora Chapman, Ian Clay, Damien Cola, Brian R. Davis, Jocce Ekström, Pete Everett, John Farrell, Nicholas Fish, Alexis D. Gutzman, Steve Howard, Bob Hughes, Vahe Kassardjian, Jackie Kleinschmidt, Maninder Singh Kumar, Janet Laidler, Barbara Lamar, Donald C. Lawson III, Simon Louis-Jensen, Matt Mansell, Robert Morris, Ted Panitz, Verne Pence, Elaine Phipps, Bryan Rieger, Tony Roberts, Eric Rosen, Giles Rowe, Blane Savage, Shawn Seabrook, Nick See, Anette Standfuss, Aubrey Stanley, Stephen Townsend, Darrel Wilkins, Dan Winchester, Andy Wilson, Matt Welch, Marcus Zillman.

Special thanks to Leonard Lewis.

Thanks also to the team at Pearson Education who commissioned and edited this book for the FT.COM series of books on e-commerce: Richard Stagg, Steve Temblett, Katherin Ekstrom, Annette Abel, Marilyn StClair.

Especially, I'd like to thank my wife, Dalida, and my two sons, Elliot and Oliver, who have had to make so many sacrifices to allow me the time to spend writing this book.

CONTENTS

PROLOGUE

olly's tool-box

Coming up to Christmas, my ten-year-old son, Olly, saw a tool-box in the window of an automobile accessory store. It contained over 200 different types of spanner. For some unfathomable reason he took a fancy to it and in the run-up to Christmas insisted that this was what he wanted for a Christmas present. As the tool-box was a clearance item and being sold off at a large discount, I bought it for him as an extra present to give him a little excitement for Christmas day.

What would a ten-year-old want with a set of automobile spanners? Well, for the first six months the tool-box lay around in the garage unused. Then one day a wheel came loose on one of Olly's skates. I tried to fix it but none of the spanners I had would fit. I'd forgotten about the tool-box but my son hadn't. He went out to the garage and came back with a collection of spanners, found one that fitted and fixed the wheel himself. Within a week or so, he was fixing things on his bicycle.

When his elder brother had trouble with the saddle adjustment on his bike, Olly got out his tool-box and fixed that. One day, the braking light on my car failed. The trouble seemed to be a contact switch that was hidden away in an inaccessible recess behind the pedal. Olly saw me sweating and cursing, trying to get at this faulty switch. Out he came with his tool-box, pushed me aside and promptly proceeded to reset the position of the contact switch. To my amazement, he got it working again.

Soon, Olly and his tool-box were called into service for a variety of different jobs. We began to wonder how we had survived so long without his handy little tool-box which always seemed to produce the right tool whenever one was needed.

The pay-off came about 18 months later. I saw him in the garage surrounded by a number of broken skateboards. He took them apart and out of all the components assembled one that worked. He took it to school next day and sold it to one of his friends – for more money than I'd paid for the tool-box.

This book is like Olly's tool-box. It isn't a 'how to' book. It is a tool-box. A set of tools consisting of conceptual models that can be applied to all kinds of e-business situations. The tools by themselves are of no use – their value only manifests when applied to a problem.

INTRODUCTION

when there is too much you need to know

Only a couple of decades ago, everything that was known about communication technology was teachable. The subject area could be neatly divided into categories and teachers could define any section to build a course around. Such courses concentrated upon 'need to know' concepts and methods, which provided students with enough knowledge and capability to get them immediately started on a career path.

This cosy state of affairs came to an end in the last decade of the twentieth century. The world of communication technology became increasingly complex and diverse. All knowledge and methodologies were continuously changing and evolving, taking the amount of 'need to know' information beyond the capacity of any human mind even to be aware of, let alone learn.

It wasn't just the increasing amount of knowledge causing the problem, it was the rapidly changing boundaries into which knowledge could be organized. In short, the knowledge base became unstable. Educational courses, in the field of communication technology, have now become little more than lucky dips into a seething ocean of knowledge; very small samplings of a gigantic whole that is impossible for any mortal to understand in its entirety.

It was this problem – of a knowledge base expanding beyond our capacity to comprehend – that was the main theme of the fore-runner to this book, *The Entrepreneurial Web*. It asked the question, 'What do you do, when there is too much you need to know and whatever you learn is out of date even before you've finished learning?'

> " EDUCATIONAL COURSES, IN THE FIELD OF COMMUNICATION TECHNOLOGY, HAVE NOW BECOME LITTLE MORE THAN LUCKY DIPS INTO A SEETHING OCEAN OF KNOWLEDGE "

Only one satisfactory conclusion was reached: if it is impossible to know all that is needed to be known, then it will be necessary to collaborate with other people: people who can fill in your knowledge gaps. In other words, success can only be achieved by people learning to communicate and collaborate.

The internet is the perfect environment to do just this, and game theory provides the most appropriate conceptual framework to make it happen.

a world of small niches

Somebody on an e-mail discussion forum once asked if it were possible to list all the niches involved in website design. Nobody could, there are too many angles, too many niches – it is impossible to grasp the full picture. As the Nobel prize-winning physicist, Richard P. Feynman, once famously remarked about quantum theory: 'If anyone says they understand it all, it's a pretty good indication they don't.'

Trying to look at niches in the world of the internet is like trying to look at shapes in a fractal. Each niche, upon closer investigation, expands into a plethora of new niches. Just like the knowledge base, the closer you look, the more you find – and the further the boundaries disappear over the horizon.

It hurts the brain to think about such staggering complexity. Even when you realize you have knowledge gaps and you need to collaborate with niche specialists, there is still the problem of which niche specialists to choose. It defies all logical thought processes. But this is where game theory comes in handy; if everyone is in this same state of confusion, you can be a winner just by being less confused than anyone else.

The trick is not to try to learn everything. Instead, you employ a strategy where you allow for there being large knowledge gaps – not only in yourself, but in everyone else you deal with. It may mean you can't always get things right, but you'll do a lot better than those who think they know it all.

In a web designer's discussion forum, a poster wrote:

1 'A good designer anticipates needs not expressed in the project's spec ...'

2 'A good designer anticipates the eventual needs of others'

3 'A good designer finds ways to discover what people need ...'

4 '... the things that underlie what they *think* they need'

5 '... the things that will eventually be needed by those in a relationship with the client'

These statements would seem to be truisms, but being in a position to know all these things isn't a practical reality. At best, any single designer will have only a partial picture. Any knowledge gaps will introduce bias. This is the problem. No single person, or even a group of people, can accurately predict what to design in volatile and highly competitive e-business environments. This causes the statements above, although appearing profound, to be a completely wrong way to look at the world of mass connectivity and rapid technological change. This advice handicaps designers, not helps them.

In the world of e-business, designs cannot be planned. Customer needs and expectations cannot be predicted. E-businesses have to take the form of flexible systems that can self-adapt to a rapidly changing marketplace. It is not the designers but the customers who drive this evolutionary process. The designers are no longer the seers and predictors. They do not calculate or decide what customers or clients want. Instead, they become initiators and responders: continuously offering clever options in response to customer feedback. Designers and customers combine into inseparable symbiotic relationships to form the basis of any realistically practical e-business model.

Overall design of an e-business then becomes a far more esoteric affair. It's not about designing a business or service, it's not about designing a website, it's not about smart marketing – it is about creating a system that is allowed to self-adapt to the unpredictable changes of the communication environment. This requires everyone involved to be dependent upon each other, yet, paradoxically at the same time, confined to their own particular niches.

a list of starting assumptions

Whether it is creating an e-business, establishing a personal niche or setting out on a career path, there has to be a starting place. This is always a mystifying process. What do you do? Do you go out and create opportunity or do you let opportunity come to you?

The seemingly obvious approach is to start by making a plan, but in a world of constant and unpredictable change, plans have little practical value. So, what is there that can be put in place of a plan? The answer is a strategy. A strategy is a list of rules that guide actions. It doesn't require you to think ahead, because actions take place in the present.

Such a thought would be anathema to the thinking of the conventional corporate world of the twentieth century. Action without planning or without thinking ahead would seem to be totally wrong. Yet, in the world of communication technology, where planning is unreliable, what choice have you got? This creates an enigma: how can you control your direction without a plan? This is where game theory is needed; it can provide a suitable framework whereby you can work with rules rather than plans.

> " THE SEEMINGLY OBVIOUS APPROACH IS TO START BY MAKING A PLAN, BUT IN A WORLD OF CONSTANT AND UNPREDICTABLE CHANGE, PLANS HAVE LITTLE PRACTICAL VALUE "

Rules would seem to suggest a mechanical approach to problem solving, but, with game theory, the rules are not fixed or absolute. They can change and evolve in response to situations and the environment. This is a difficult conceptual hurdle to overcome: understanding that rules are flexible and can become adaptive as a result of experience. The obvious question to ask is: 'Who sets or changes the rules?' Surprisingly, it is the environment that sets the rules and changes them when need be. The rules are a reflection of the environment and change when it changes.

This is a very big conceptual jump from thinking in terms of business plans. To make this jump, it is first necessary to appreciate what a business plan actually represents: it is a reasoned and calculated estimate of what is likely to happen during a future period of time. This estimate will take into consideration the past and the present and project these into the future with suitable allowances being made for uncertainties and errors of judgement.

As carefully as these business plans might be worked out, they can only be as accurate as the uncertainties inherent in the future period will allow. The more uncertainties there are, the less accurate becomes any model of the future (business plan). The problem with e-business is that it is conducted in such a new and fast-changing environment that estimates as to what will happen in any future period are likely to be widely inaccurate. The errors are unlikely to to be covered by even the most cautious of projections or the most far-reaching contingency plans.

This was one of the conclusions reached in the book *The Entrepreneurial Web*. It highlighted the problem by listing a number of initial assumptions that any planner in the e-business environment would have to make before setting out the details of a business plan. These assumptions were:

1 All potential clients or customers are constantly deluged and swamped with information.

2 Nobody knows all the answers.

3 The environment of the internet and the world wide web is beyond your or anyone else's ability to be able to understand completely.

4 Everyone is occasionally unreliable.

5 Everybody is mostly too busy for you to be able to get their attention.

6 Most people haven't the time to listen to what you have to say.

7 Whatever you know, there are many more important things that you ought to know but don't.

8 Nobody is going to cooperate with you unless they see there is something worthwhile in it for them.

9 Whatever you know, somebody knows it better.

10 Anyone you want to establish a communication relationship with has only a very limited number of people they have time to deal with.

11 Credibility and trust are very hard to come by.

12 Whatever you do, there are thousands of others trying to do the same thing at the same time.

13 Sudden and dramatic changes will occur constantly.

14 Whatever you do will be rapidly outdated by new technological developments.

15 Whatever you do or say will quickly be known to everyone else.

16 Whatever you do will be copied or bettered by your competitors.

17 All services and products will get progressively cheaper, as increased competition reduces costs and increased efficiency brings prices and profits down to a minimum.

18 Whatever you are offering, there will be a plethora of similar alternatives in the marketplace already.

19 Nobody can have more than one area of real expertise.

20 The solution you have to come up with is beyond your, or anyone else's, imagination.

21 Whatever technology, programs, tools, methods and techniques you use will rapidly become unsuitable or irrelevant.

22 Any final solution you come up with will have to be abandoned or radically altered within a very short period of time.

23 Everyone is going to distrust you until you have built up a relationship of trust with them.

24 Nothing is free, even if it seems to be.

These assumptions describe a situation of continuous and unpredictable change, rife with uncertainty, knowledge gaps and fierce competition. Even a flexible plan would be of little value under these conditions. Thus, with conventional business thinking, progress becomes a lottery with the odds heavily stacked against the planner.

The alternative is to view the situation in a completely different light. If it is a game of guesses, the best guesser will win. Game theory is about making better guesses.

super-charged game theory
The traditional way of creating a new business position is to carefully study case histories, look at past

successes and emulate their strategies and techniques. Forward thinking would be based upon market research, which uncovers customer or client needs and expectations. However, in this fast-moving world of e-business, such a strategy is likely to be counter-productive. What is happening in the present or what has happened in the past may be totally irrelevant to what is going to happen in the future. How, then, can one try to create a business when there are no precedents, no historical guidance, no solid foundations to build a business plan upon?

The only way out of this dilemma is to use a more appropriate conceptual framework. It stands to reason that most other people will be in this same situation, so, to be competitive, you don't have to know exactly what to do: you just have to have a better strategy for dealing with uncertainty than others.

Mathematicians and scientists have been dealing with the problems associated with conditions of uncertainty and competition for most of the twentieth century. The need for a solution has come from several main sources:

1   competitive pressures for governments in political manoeuvring and warfare;

2   business strategies;

3   financial decision making;

4   trying to understand the mechanisms of evolutionary biology.

Most solutions for dealing with uncertainty have been based upon probability. Various forms of decision theory allowed us to choose the best from a number of uncertainties. Game theory allowed us to structure this decision making to enhance competitive play in an uncertain and competitive environment. When technological progress began to expand at an ever-increasingly fast rate, decision theory became too unreliable and even a game theory approach proved inadequate. It needed something else, and that something else was found from the enigmatic processes of evolutionary biology.

It was realized that biological organisms were encountering similar kinds of problems to people trying to cope with the uncertain and unpredictable environment of e-business. They weren't using forward planning or predictive thinking to compete and survive, they were working blindly. Yet this blind process was achieving remarkable results as evidenced by the vast variety of life forms that we find on this planet. Mother Nature was working blindly, yet this blind process was solving all kinds of difficult problems.

The secret of this success was discovered in the 1980s by computer scientist John Holland, who took a radical new approach to artificial intelligence by copying some of nature's evolutionary techniques. What he found was that the whole complexity of the evolutionary process was being driven by a seemingly simple mathematical model: the genetic algorithm. This algorithm was giving Mother Nature the power to overcome seemingly insurmountable obstacles of uncertainty and competition. So powerful is this algorithm that it has been responsible for the design of not only the form of every individual and species on the planet, but also the human brain.

This book is about using this same power to enhance the advantages of using game theory to cope with competition and uncertainty in the world of e-business.

the creation of a conceptual tool-box

Dealing with a complex and volatile environment like the internet throws planning and management systems into total disarray. The procedures and methods of traditional business can't cope. In their place, we can use game theory and direct the strategy through the use of evolutionary processes.

In this context, game theory isn't used to deal with technology, or the details associated with the core business. It is used for something more fundamental: to deal with people – the people who know about the technology, the people who use the technology and most importantly the people who are the customers and clients.

Game theory can be used as a framework to build a network of collaborative associations. It can allow us to create systems of communication that link a variety of people together into self-organizing systems that solve problems. It can be used to create systems that adapt to and respond to customer needs, technological change or competitive moves.

Game theory; communicating with people; establishing collaborative associations – all require a special range of conceptual models: tools that can be used to build adaptive systems of mutual collaboration. This is what this book provides: conceptual tools that can be used to build the kind of personal communication networks that everyone must be able to construct if they are to successfully establish their own niche in the world of e-business.

the key to winning

The book is about establishing a personal niche in the world of e-business. Whatever niche this might be, it will involve contact with people. Contact with people will be needed for:

1   getting information to maintain proficiency in the selected niche;

2   using the niche speciality to make a living.

The internet provides a massive resource for making contacts. The snag is there are over three hundred million people connected to the internet to decide between – and it is only physically possible to strike up relationships with a very small number of them. The game is to choose the most suitable contacts from this overwhelming choice, then establish and maintain a trusting relationship with them. It is a game of vital, strategic importance, but it isn't an easy game to play.

There is a story about a man who spent his life searching for the perfect woman. When at last he found her, he wasn't her perfect man. This highlights an aspect of the problem that makes finding good contacts doubly difficult. You might find somebody who would make an extremely useful and valuable contact, but will they want you to be one of their special contacts?

How do you succeed in such a game? What is the measure of success? What are the goals? How do you win? Fortunately, everyone has a different idea as to what they consider to be success. Everybody has a different goal. This makes it possible for people to cooperate and collaborate because they needn't be in competition with each other to win. They can help each other if their goals are complementary.

The game, then, is not about competing with people to win money or rewards. It is a game about winning cooperation. This idea of mutual benefit holds the key to becoming a winner in this game.

BACKGROUND TO GAME THEORY

PART 1 INTRODUCES SOME OF THE BASIC
ELEMENTS OF GAME THEORY. NOT THE MOST
APPETISING WAY TO START A BOOK, BUT, AS A
RUDIMENTARY KNOWLEDGE OF GAME THEORY
IS GOING TO BE ESSENTIAL TO ANYONE USING
THE INTERNET FOR BUSINESS, IT IS BEST TO
GET THIS PROPELLER-HEAD STUFF OUT OF THE
WAY FIRST.

YOU MIGHT WELL ASK WHY GAME THEORY
SHOULD BE SO IMPORTANT IN E-BUSINESS. IT IS
BECAUSE GAME THEORY IS THE MOST
APPROPRIATE FRAMEWORK FOR DEALING WITH
UNCERTAINTY, UNKNOWNS, COMPLEXITY AND
COMPETITION. THIS IS THE ENVIRONMENT IN
WHICH E-BUSINESS WILL BE CONDUCTED. IT IS
AN ENVIRONMENT WHERE CONVENTIONAL
BUSINESS METHODS AND PROCEDURES ARE
SEVERELY COMPROMISED AND START TO BREAK
DOWN.

CONVENTIONAL BUSINESS IS BASED UPON
ELIMINATING UNCERTAINTY WHEREVER
POSSIBLE TO ALLOW REASONABLY ACCURATE
PREDICTIONS TO BE MADE. THIS IS FINE IF YOU
KNOW WHAT UNCERTAINTIES THERE ARE, BUT
IN THE FAST-MOVING WORLD OF
COMMUNICATION TECHNOLOGY THIS IS NOT
POSSIBLE. PREDICTIONS ARE THEREFORE
ALWAYS HIGHLY SUSPECT.

GAME THEORY IS BASED UPON THE ENIGMATIC
AND COUNTER-INTUITIVE EFFECTS OF THE
LAWS OF CHANCE AND PROBABILITY. THESE
EFFECTS DEFY LOGICAL EXPLANATION, BUT
THIS IS WHY GAME THEORY IS USEFUL: IT
WORKS WHEN LOGICAL REASONING CANNOT
COME UP WITH THE RIGHT ANSWERS.

1

STARTING WITH THE BASICS

business acumen In any competitive situation, the competition
divides competitors into two categories: success or failure. It cannot
simply be a matter of chance as to which category a competitor goes into.
Something more than luck must account for the difference.

Fortunately, there is a branch of mathematics that has evolved during the
course of the last century that allows us to deal with this kind of
problem. It is called game theory, a conceptual framework for studying
competition in environments where there are many unknowns, constant
change, uncertainty and competition. This describes the environment of
the internet and the world wide web, so game theory should help us in
determining the differences between winners and losers in the serious
game of e-business.

Game theory approaches the problem of uncertainty by looking for best
decisions rather than right decisions. Strategies are devised that consist of
sets of 'rule of thumb' guidelines to decision making. This ensures that
although decisions may not always be correct, the number of right
decisions is always more than could be obtained by relying on luck. In

other words, game theory is a way of making intelligent guesses. In business this might be called 'business acumen'.

It may seem that business acumen can be learned by studying successful business people, seeing how they create business opportunities and build successful businesses. Ah! If only it were that simple. Business acumen isn't about what people do, it is about how people think.

As we can't get into people's heads to take a peep inside, we have to do it the hard way and learn to think correctly ourselves. We have to acquire a set of conceptual tools that will give us a competitive edge. This is what this book is about. It is about building a tool-box of conceptual tools – that can be used to make us more successful competitors in the world of e-business.

Don't be frightened off by the somewhat abstract approach. It is being able to manipulate abstraction that is the secret of being successful. Let others work with buzzwords and bullet lists. We want to get at the fundamental reasoning.

the enigmatic nature of probability
The concepts of chance and probability are so common in our everyday life that most people assume they understand them completely. This is far from the truth. Probability and chance are the most mystical concepts in science and fall far short of any rational explanation.

Yet, for all the mystery surrounding probability and chance, it has been the single most important concept to account for the rapid advance in science, technology and civilization in general throughout the twentieth century.

My first serious encounter with probability came as a preliminary to lectures on the physics of semiconductors. It was explained to us that the flow of electrons over an energy gap was through a proportion of the electrons randomly acquiring sufficient energy to cross a voltage barrier. The higher the voltage, the greater became the number that could randomly acquire sufficient energy to jump the gap.

To my student mind, what happened inside a transistor was far less interesting than the implications of the theory. It was telling me that I could make sense out of apparent disorder and by so doing create my own luck.

It didn't take long for me to start applying this concept to everyday events. Straight from the lecture, I produced a pack of cards to create a simulated horse-racing game. The idea, as I explained to my fellow students, was that this theory could be used to win money. I shuffled the deck and then started to deal out the cards, placing hearts in one row, spades in another and the diamonds and clubs in other rows. 'The first suit to produce a line of 10 cards would be the winner,' I announced.

As the cards came out, the rows corresponding to the various suits changed in relative lengths. First the row of clubs was in the lead, then it was overtaken by the hearts, but in a late spurt the spades suit produced 10 spades to become the winner of the race.

Now came my cunning money-making plan. I'd understood that the way in which probability and chance worked was to even things out. It had been explained to us that if the chance of something happening was the same for all objects, then after a sufficient number of chance happenings, the event would happen to all objects about the same number of times.

It seemed obvious to me that if spades had won the first race, all the other suits would catch up as eventually they would end up with an equal number of wins owing to the law of probability. Logical reasoning then told me that the chances of the spades winning in subsequent races must be less than for the other suits. With this conviction in mind, I gave odds of four to one on spades and only three to one on the other suits: encouraging the students to place bets on the suit I saw as having the lesser chance of winning.

All the other students, going purely by the statistical probability of each suit having an equal one chance in four, placed their bets upon spades. Spades won.

Not particularly alarmed, I then invited the students to let their winnings ride and I increased the odds on spades to five to one. I chuckled when they all placed their money on spades again, but the smile swiftly left my lips when spades won for a third time in a row.

Panicking that all the students might want to cease playing and demand payment, I raised the odds on spades to 20 to one. Everyone stayed in the game and to my relief all of them staked their winnings on the spades.

To my absolute dismay, spades won for the fourth time in a row. 'One more time,' I cried, and raised the odds on spades to 50 to one. By this time, the students had realized that I owed everyone so much money that I wouldn't be able to pay them anyway so they let their winnings ride once more on the spades. To my discomfort, and to the merriment of the other students, spades came up for an unbelievable fifth time.

Fortunately, all the students took it in fun and didn't insist on being paid, otherwise I'd still be paying them off today.

the mystery

That experience made a deep and lasting impression on me. Like most experiences in life, you learn more from failures than from successes. Where had I gone wrong? Spades shouldn't have lost all those times in a row. A quick calculation told me that the chance of spades winning a race was one chance in four. Winning twice in a row would be one chance in four multiplied by four, 16. Winning three times in a row would be one chance in four times four times four, 64. Winning four times in a row would be one chance in four times four times four times four, which equalled 256.

I concluded that I must have just been very unlucky and had been hit by a 256 to one improbable situation. I then pondered on the chances of this streak of bad luck continuing. The chances of spades coming up five times in a row worked out at 1,024 to one against. Surely I'd be justified in offering odds of 500 to one if I'd have continued the card racing game? The difference between getting four spade wins and five spade wins in a row were 1,024 minus 256; surely that meant there was less chance of spades coming up than any other suit?

Yet the mathematical theory told me that there was no great counter in the sky. Each new race started with each of the suits having an exactly equal chance, one chance in four, of winning the race and it didn't matter that any particular suit had won a sequence of races before. As far as probability theory was concerned, the memory of any previous events was completely erased.

I didn't believe it. That night I sat up the whole night dealing out cards and running suit races. To my satisfaction, after hundreds of races had been run, the suits had each won an almost equal number of races. There had to be some great counter in the sky, exercising an influential force to slow the winners down and speed the losers up. Yet, logic and the mathematics told me that there was no mechanism for memory in place: each race started with the same odds for each suit winning, whatever sequence of events had gone before. It was very perplexing indeed.

war games

These first encounters with probability theory occurred when I was attending lectures at a college situated in the middle of a British Government research establishment. Part of this five-year course involved every student spending three-month periods in various of the research establishment laboratories.

Not long after my card suit races experience, I was assigned to a laboratory where they were testing electronic components under various environmental conditions. Batches of components would be left for hours on shaker tables. They'd be left for days in humid ovens or in deep freezes.

Before and throughout the different environmental exposures, the components were tested to see if the extreme environmental conditions caused any failures. By testing one hundred similar components at a time, the number of failures gave a direct indication of the probable failure rate for the type of component being tested.

A probability of failure was measured in this way, for every type of component used in a piece of equipment installed in a fighter plane. It was then possible to use probability theory to work out the overall probability that one or other of the components would fail during a critical mission. Such a failure would render the equipment inoperable, so this calculation was vital to the strategic use of aircraft in a war operation.

The chief scientific officer in charge of this laboratory took the trouble to explain the logic of these tests and calculations. He explained that, for some pieces of critical electronic equipment, there were so many components that although the failure rate of any particular component was low, adding them all together would result in the probability of a fatal failure occurring within as little as two hours. 'It is something like a chain being as strong as its weakest link,' he explained. 'The first component to experience a random failure would result in the failure of the whole equipment.'

He further explained that missions expected to last for longer than two hours would have to arrange for spare equipment to be taken along to allow substitution if and when failure occurred (note: the piece of equipment being tested at the time was a radio set, and this was at a time before transistors and microchips; when notably unreliable thermionic tubes were used in all electronic equipment).

Being acutely conscious of my recent experience with the card suit races, I pointed out that an unfavourable run of luck could see equipment failing much sooner than two hours and in some cases even the backup equipment failing as well. 'Surely,' I asked, 'to ensure that the mission would not fail, there would have to be many duplicate backups to allow for a bad run of failures during a particular mission?'

Patiently, the scientific officer explained that the probability of double failures would be taken into consideration. They could calculate, using probability theory once again, the likelihood of double equipment failures and so predict how many of a squadron's planes would likely be out of action through this effect. The mission would thus be planned with more planes than were necessary to allow for those that were expected to become inoperable through random failure of components.

He then proceeded to explain how this anticipation of probable failure rate allowed a mission to be planned to ensure that a correct number of planes would be in operation over a target area, even though the target might be many hours of flight time away.

predicting the future with probability

When this war scenario was explained to me, I had one of those eureka moments, when a paradigm shift happens and suddenly an insight or a new way of thinking occurs.

It was readily apparent that being able to use probability to make a fairly accurate assessment of a future development within a scenario would be of great advantage in a competitive environment. Being able to build in sufficient redundancy, to take care of uncertainties, would be a major competitive advantage.

Before reading on, perhaps the reader might care to take a moment to look back to the introduction to the list of 24 initial assumptions that have to be made before designing an e-business strategy. Notice how many of them involve uncertainty. If probabilities can be used to lessen the effects of these uncertainties, then they might be used to significantly enhance an e-business strategist's ability to compete (this also explains why I've chosen to start this book with an examination of probability theory).

As any publisher will be quick to point out to an author, starting a book off with an arcane theoretical treatise is a certain turn-off. Theory is boring and only becomes interesting when it can be used to practical advantage.

This is the problem I had when creating the CD-ROM book *How God Makes God*. In that work – despite the cryptic title it is about game theory and business strategy – the whole subject matter was dependent upon having an intuitive understanding of probability and, as probability is largely counter-intuitive, this presented a real challenge.

My own intuitive understanding of probability hadn't come about through the lectures in probability theory I attended. Neither had it come as a result of those interesting conversations I'd had in the component-testing laboratories of the research establishment. A true appreciation of probability came after I'd left college. It happened through being the proprietor of a gaming club and subsequently spending some time as a professional poker player.

The theory certainly helps to put probability and chance into perspective and provides a sound basis for calculation, but this is far short of true understanding. An instinctive awareness of the variety of different ways probability can take effect can only be obtained through the long-term observation of empirical results: the experience of using probabilities in real-life strategies. Gaming and poker tables gave me a unique opportunity to do just this.

I could look at a game of roulette in operation for a short while and make a pretty good estimate as to how much the house was profiting each hour. I could watch a gambler at one of the tables and be able to estimate how much he or she would lose over an evening's play. To most of the players at these tables, the practical certainty that the house always wins is not obvious, even though they may have had every opportunity to predict such results themselves from the theory.

Knowing, from my own long experience with probabilities, how difficult it is to understand probability, even when in possession of all the mathematical formulae, I had to come up with an unique way of explaining the concept to the readers of the CD-ROM book.

It then struck me that with a CD-ROM it was possible to give the readers the same practical experience of probability that had given me an intuitive understanding. I could create a roulette wheel and let the readers play games of chance to experience for themselves how probability can take such esoteric and deceptive forms.

I presented them with a fully functioning roulette wheel and a table upon which they could place bets. I provided them with a stack of money and invited them to try to work out a winning system. The simulation was such that the readers could slide money onto the table to make the bets, click a button to start the wheel and then a random number between 1 and 37 would be generated to simulate the functioning of a real-life roulette wheel.

When the random number came up, the computer program would calculate the winnings and losses of all bets, and then deduct or add the sum result from or to the player's money.

After being given the opportunity to try for themselves to create a winning system, I then told the readers that I would give them the secret of the most effective roulette system possible, and offered a $10,000 reward for anyone who could come up with something better.

The reader was then presented with a scene set in a nineteenth-century railway carriage, where two passengers are on their way from London to a channel port where they could board a ferry to the European continent.

Here is the conversation they had that contains a description of the optimum system for playing roulette:

a free holiday in monte carlo

Are you taking the boat train to France?

I am, but I'm going on to Monte Carlo.

How exciting. I should love to go there to see all the fine hotels and the casino.

I go there every year.

You must be very rich.

No. I go there for a free holiday every year.

A free holiday?

Yes, I have a system for playing roulette and my winnings pay for my holiday.

How marvellous. Is your system a closely guarded secret?

No, I'll tell you what it is if you want to know.

Yes please. I should love to be able to have a free holiday in Monte Carlo.

It's very simple really. I don't play to win a lot of money, I just play each day for the cost of the next day's living expenses.

How much is that?

Ten guineas. That pays for my hotel, three decent meals, some good wine plus a little extra for entertaining the ladies.

And you do this every day?

Every day of my holiday, and sometimes I stay there the whole summer.

What is your system then?

Every evening, I take a cab to the casino. On the way there, I write down a sequence of seven reds and blacks which I think will come up as the first sequence of seven spins in the evening's play.

Surely you cannot guess that?

Of course not, that is the key to my system. If I guess wrongly I win.

I don't understand?

When I go to the casino I get 1,270 guineas' worth of chips.

I haven't got that amount of money.

Neither have I, but I borrow it from a friend.

I suppose I could do that if I had a foolproof system. How do you proceed once you have borrowed the money and then thought up this sequence for the first seven spins of the wheel?

For my first bet, I look at the first item of my sequence. If it is red, I bet ten guineas on the black. If black comes up, I win my ten guineas straight away, cash in my chips and leave for the day.

And if a red comes up?

I look at my sequence again and bet 20 guineas on the opposite colour of the second in my sequence. If I win I get back the money I have lost, plus ten guineas' profit.

And you can finish for the day again?

Yes, and if it loses I bet 40 guineas on the opposite to the next in my sequence.

What do you do if the zero comes up?

I treat it as the opposite colour to the colour I have bet on.

I see, every time you lose you double up on the next in the sequence, but if you win just once you can leave with the next day's expenses in your pocket?

That's right, I'm not greedy. I quit as soon as I've had one win.

A single win?

That is why my system is so successful. I need to win only once in an evening.

But you could lose all of your money if you lost seven times in a row?

Yes, but what is most likely, me being able to guess the first seven spins of the evening or me winning a single bet?

So it isn't very likely you can lose?

No, it isn't very likely and I am such a bad guesser of those first seven spins of the wheel that I get a free holiday in Monte Carlo every year.

But you could guess right one day and lose?

Yes. I would lose a friend.

What friend?

The friend who lends me 1,270 guineas every year to go to Monte Carlo for my holiday.

I don't think I would use your system. I would prefer to put all of my money on one single bet on the red.

After describing this optimum system for playing roulette, the reader of *How God Makes God* is then presented with the simulation of the roulette game and invited to try the system out for themselves and also try to work out a better system and so be able to claim the reward of $10,000.

2

THROUGH THE LOOKING GLASS

when Lewis Carroll sent Alice through the looking glass, she encountered a world where things were different and all the rules had changed.

Chapter 1 was the view of the world as seen from the conventional side of the looking glass. In this chapter we are going to go through the looking glass of the conventional world of rules and values to encounter a strange new world where nothing is as it seems.

We'll begin by taking a more professional look at the roulette system described by the man on the train.

borrowing money to play roulette In the CD-ROM *How God Makes God*, the dialogue that described the optimum roulette strategy was followed by a scene of a man going to a money lender to try to borrow money to play roulette and get free holidays in the same way as the man on the train. This is the start of the dialogue:

Can you lend me 1,270 guineas?

What for?

I've discovered an infallible roulette system that will get me free holidays in Monte Carlo.

Why do you need to borrow money if you've discovered an infallible roulette system?

Because it will need a substantial amount of money in order to make it work.

Have you tried out this system yet?

How can I try it out without any money?

By using a computer simulation.

How can I do that?

You write a program to simulate a roulette wheel.

Can you do that?

Yes, all computers can be made to generate random numbers so you just get the computer to deliver random numbers between 1 and 37.

I see, each number corresponds to a slot in a roulette wheel.

Yes, 1 to 36 for the numbers and the 37th for the zero.

I think I will try that.

While you are at it, you might as well program the computer to make the bets for you.

Do I need to do that?

Yes, because it will allow you to run thousands of bets in just a few minutes. You can emulate playing roulette for weeks, months or even years without having to risk any money at all.

But my system is complicated. I think of a sequence of seven reds and blacks and then bet on that sequence not coming up.

I know that system, you double up after every bet you lose.

That's right, but the clever part is that I finish for the day after any win and, although I don't stand to win a lot of money, I earn a day's free holiday for every day that I play.

That's easy enough to program into a computer. I'll show you.

On the CD-ROM, the reader is then presented with a program that can be used by the reader to simulate going to a casino and trying out the system. Clicking on a button will start an automatic sequence of betting that takes the reader through a continuous series of bets using the exact system described by the man on the train and clocking up not the winnings but the number of days of survival.

the analysis of a roulette system
The next scene on the CD-ROM shows the would-be system player insisting that the computer simulation has confirmed the validity of the system. He'd tried it out several times and been able to survive for a free, one-week holiday almost every time he'd run the program.

The money lender told him that, to be able to borrow money on such a system, he'd have to show conclusively that the system was infallible. When asked how to prove this infallibility, the money lender offers to create a computer program that will analyse the results of 5,000 people going to the casino to play this system to try to win free holidays.

The reader of the CD-ROM is then presented with a program that simulates 5,000 players going to the casino and using the system to win 10 guineas a day for an indefinite period. In other words, each of the 5,000 players stays playing until the day comes when the first seven spins of the roulette wheel correspond to the random sequence they'd thought up that day on the way to the casino.

In this simulation, as each player makes daily bets, the results are recorded in a variety of ways. Not only is a record kept of how many days they survive before losing their money, but also the total number of bets and the amount accumulated. These values are displayed in fields on the screen. Further fields show the combined totals of all players' bets and amounts staked.

The money lender has run this program before the would-be borrower returns to his office (Figure 2.1 shows his results). The dialogue goes like this:

Did you get that computer program finished?

Yes, and I left it running for several hours and have got the results of 5,000 players playing your system.

What does it show you?

Here, take a look (see Figure 2.1).

Zero = lose

Number of players	5000
Average number of days won	103
Average cost of each day's holiday	12.3301

Lasted	1 week	4647	1 month	3685		
	3 months	2050	6 months	865	over 1 year	160

Total number of spins	1065406
Total amount bet	39840050

Average spins per day	2.0569
Average bet per spin	37.3942

FIG 2.1 The result of 5,000 people playing the roulette system. Zero counts as a loss for the player

There, what did I tell you? My system does work, 4,647 out of the 5,000 lasted more than a week.

Yes, but it also means that 353 lost their money in the first week. That's about 7 per cent of them: one in every 14 players.

Then it isn't a perfect system?

No. In the long run, no system can succeed because the casino has an edge: it has the advantage of the zero in its favour.

But how does this small advantage stop systems from winning?

It's due to the law of averages.

How does that apply?

With the zero in its favour, the casino averages winning one 37th of all spins. If this is averaged out over a large number of spins, the casino wins one 37th of the total value of all bets made.

I still don't see how this advantage stops systems from working. Aren't systems supposed to overcome the house's advantage?

Take a look at the computer simulation results and tell me the average number of days' holiday the players won.

One hundred and three.

Yes, but if they had each used their 1,270 guineas to pay for their holidays at ten guineas a day they would each have had 127 days' holiday.

Oh! I see. They have averaged out having less holidays by using my system?

That's right, they have each spent 1,270 guineas and averaged only 103 days of holiday which works out that the average cost of each day's holiday using your system is over 12 guineas a day.

I see now why you have included the average cost of each day's holiday in your simulation.

Yes, it comes out on this simulation at 12.3301 guineas for every day of holiday won by gambling, making your roulette system an expensive way to pay for a holiday.

How is it, then, that my system makes the holidays more expensive?

Take a look at the total number of spins that were bet on by the 5,000 players.

Your results show they bet on a total of 1,065,406 spins.

Yes, over a million spins. Now look at the total amount of money that they bet on those million spins.

Your results show 39,840,050 guineas, that's almost exactly 40 million guineas.

Now if you divide the total number of spins by the total amount bet.

You get 37.3942 guineas.

Yes. Because of the doubling up they have had to do, their average bet on each spin is about 37^1/$_2$ guineas. If we apply the casino's average take to this figure, that is one 37th, we should expect the casino to win an average of one 37th of this amount for every spin.

Let me work that out: 37.3940 divided by 37 gives 1.010655 – about one guinea a spin.

Yes, the casino gains an average of just over a guinea per spin and, as you can see from the results, the players average just over two spins per day so the casino gains just over two guineas a day from each player.

So this is why the holidays are costing over 12 guineas a day with my system?

That's right. You cannot win with any system because the casino always wins approximately one 37th of every bet you make.

But using a system is better than no system at all.

No, using a system like yours makes things worse.

Why?

Because the doubling up used by your system increases the total amount bet, so the casino will win one 37th of a larger amount.

I don't understand that.

If you look at the simulation results again and divide the 40 million guineas bet by 5,000 you can work out that each player placed bets averaging a total of 8,000 guineas. The casino takes one 37th of this, which amounts to over 200 guineas per player.

So what is the best way to play roulette? What is the optimum system?

The way that minimizes the total amount bet. This means that the optimal way to play is to make one single bet of all your money, rather than spreading it out over a number of bets.

You mean there is no better system than going into a casino and placing all of your money on a single red?

Exactly. That is the optimum roulette system and there is a reward of $10,000 for any system that can beat it.

But it cannot win?

Of course it cannot win. No system can win. Betting all your money on the red in a single bet simply loses less money over the long term.

I don't believe this.

I'll prove to you how much better it is to bet all of your money on the red rather than using the money to play your system.

How can you prove it?

I'll write another computer program to show what happens to 5,000 players when they play to win holidays using this optimum single bet system.

You mean you are going to run a simulation of 5,000 players, each going to Monte Carlo with 1,270 guineas and playing to win or lose all with a single bet on red?

That's right, each one will either win enough for 254 days' holiday, or lose everything and have to go home without having had any holiday at all.

The next scenario sees the would-be borrower returning, after this new computer simulation has been run:

Did you create that computer program to show what happens when players put all their money on the red?

Yes, I ran it for 5,000 players again. Have a look at the results (see Figure 2.2).

There are more losers than winners, I notice.

Yes, but look how many holidays they averaged.

124 days each.

Yes, that compares with the 103 days of holiday the players averaged using your system.

How did the single bet system produce better results?

Well, look at the total amount that was bet by the single bet players.

Just over six million.

That's right. Now, do you remember how much the 5,000 players bet using your system?

Almost 40 million, wasn't it?

Zero = lose	
Number of players	5000
Average number of days won	124
Average cost of each day's holiday	10.27
Number of winners	2434
Number of losers	2566
Total number of spins	5000
Total amount bet	6350000
Average spins per day	1
Average bet per spin	1270

FIG 2.2 Results of 5,000 players going to the casino and using all of their money to make a single bet on red. Zero counts as a loss for the player

Yes, using your system the casino gained one 37th of almost 40 million, but when players have just the one big bet on the red, the casino gains one 37th of only 6,350,000.

Very clever. So you seem to have proved your point, a single bet on the red is better than my system.

I'm afraid so. Whatever system you come up with could never be better than the single bet system.

Of course, in Chapter 1, you had probably realized that it wasn't the man playing roulette for a free holiday that was describing the optimum system for playing roulette. It was the other person, who, in the last line of the dialogue, spoke of preferring to make a single bet of all the money on red. No system of roulette, however complex, can better this strategy. It doesn't win, but it loses less than any other.

relating roulette to business

System play in a game of roulette may not immediately strike you as having much to do with business strategy, but at an abstract level there are many useful conclusions that can be drawn. This becomes apparent if the game of roulette and business strategy are examined in the context of game theory.

Game theory differentiates between two different types of game: a zero sum game and a non-zero sum game. Zero sum games are those games where the winners win what the losers lose, such that the total winnings of all winning players, minus the total losses of all losing players, equals zero. Hence the description as a zero sum game.

Non-zero sum games, on the other hand, are games where winnings do not add up to the same value as the losses. At the end of the game, there could be more money won than is lost, or more money lost than is won. Winnings minus losses do not come to a zero sum.

Roulette is a typical zero sum game because the players win from the house or lose to it. At the end of every roulette session, if you sum the winnings and losses of all players together, it will equal the amount won or lost by the house. Although, almost invariably, it is the house that wins because they have that edge: the percentage in their favour due to the zero slot.

There is, however, a different way of looking at a game of roulette that can turn it into a non-zero sum game. That is to consider the players to be playing against each other and the amount going to the house being an overhead charge, paid to the house for providing the playing facilities.

With this paradigm shift, the players can be seen as playing against each other (for the total they bet minus the amount taken by the house). The practical certainty that the house always wins makes this a realistic way to view the game, thus making the game between the players a non-zero sum game (because there will be more losses than winnings for the players: a negative non-zero sum game).

Looked at in this way, the game can be likened to a competitive game of chance with an overhead charged on turnover. However, as we have seen, winning and losing is not determined solely by chance because the strategy used by the players will have a direct bearing on how much the house takes as an overhead: a single bet strategy loses less to the house than a system. This will ensure that some players will lose more than others according to the way they play.

This can be seen by looking at the relative costs per day of the holidays: according to whether they played the sequence of system seven or the all-in-one bet system. The all-in-one bet system players are getting their holidays cheaper than those who play the sequence of seven system. They are faring much better than the system players in the game.

the source of profit

A comparison of roulette systems with business strategies would have been irrelevant in the formalized and reasonably stable business world of the twentieth century. In the time before the rapid advance of computers and digital communication technology, strategies could be based upon formalized plans where uncertainties are mostly eliminated.

Business is quite different in the twenty-first century, where there is massive connectivity, rapid technological change and information overload. Uncertainties and unknowns are unavoidable. Strategies have to be employed, not to try to eliminate them, but to be able to cope with them better than competitors. This makes the ability to understand and use probabilities an essential requirement for anyone involved in e-commerce or e-business. This is why the game of roulette is of interest to us.

Up till now, though, we have considered roulette only as it is played in a conventional way. This is not applicable to e-commerce or e-business because, as we have just seen, it can be viewed as either a zero sum game with a disadvantage to the players, or as a non-zero sum game where losses are always greater than winnings.

As the idea of business is to make a profit, such a scenario doesn't seem to be a particularly apt model to use. To resolve this problem, let's stop for a moment to examine the nature of profit and define what we mean by it.

> BUSINESS IS QUITE DIFFERENT IN THE TWENTY-FIRST CENTURY, WHERE THERE IS MASSIVE CONNECTIVITY, RAPID TECHNOLOGICAL CHANGE AND INFORMATION OVERLOAD

Taking another scene from *How God Makes God*, there are a group of people sitting around talking to each other about the nature of making money. Here is a snatch of their conversation:

What type of game is 'money making'?

It has to be a zero sum game because if you make money it has to come from somewhere, and that somewhere has to be from somebody else.

How do you reason that out?

If you bought something, and then sold it for a profit, you would gain either at the expense of the original owner, who could have sold it for more, or at the expense of the buyer who could have bought it for less. By being clever enough to be in the middle of a buying and selling operation you could perhaps gain from both of them.

Doesn't that disturb you?

What?

Making money at someone else's expense? That is like stealing or trickery.

Is it really true that to make money you must take it from someone else?

Think of the different ways in which people make money. Employers make profits; where does that money come from?

Obviously they make profits by not paying their employees all the money they are earning. The employers are keeping some of it for themselves. Surely that is cheating?

Are you saying that all employers cheat their employees?

'Exploit them' is a better way of putting it.

Let me tell you about our local butcher. He has a Rolls Royce and lives in a grand house.

Capitalist!

Do you think he got all his wealth by charging his customers too much for their meat?

Of course. He must have done, otherwise he wouldn't be so rich.

It seems logical, except that everybody went to his shop because he gave better value than any other butcher for miles around. Every reputable business that I know makes money in this same inexplicable way: at the expense of others who do not seem to mind.

How very odd.

It seems that in all forms of successful business enterprise, the people involved, whether buyers or sellers, all seem to think they are gaining from the business they do together. Nobody seems to think they are losers. How do you explain that?

But how can everyone be gaining? Where does the profit come from?

To know that is to know the secret of creating wealth.

It is truly surprising how many people confuse making money with the creation of wealth. They are not the same. You can make money without creating wealth and you can create wealth without making money. The concepts are totally different.

Making money without creating wealth is the characteristic of the zero sum game. The winners win from the losers. Making money by creating wealth is to play the non-zero sum game, where if the wealth creators cooperate with each other and don't let in any of the zero sum players they can all win.

The mystery surrounding the creation of wealth disappears if you look at business enterprises as creating benefits. Although there are innumerable ways to describe benefits they all boil down to one single principle: increase in efficiency.

If you can supply somebody with something they need at a better value than anyone else, you have improved the efficiency by which their needs are satisfied. If you come up with a superior service it must, by definition, have provided a more efficient service than other alternatives. A better price, a quicker delivery, a more attractive or superior product. Each of these represents to the recipient an improvement in the way they live or work. This is the source of wealth creation. It is the act of adding to the efficiency by which others can lead their lives.

66 IT IS TRULY SURPRISING HOW MANY PEOPLE CONFUSE MAKING MONEY WITH THE CREATION OF WEALTH 99

going through the looking glass

Pinpointing the source of wealth creation provides a good starting place when looking for a profitable niche in the world of e-business. Instead of having to consider a limitless number of possibilities and examine the techniques and strategies of other people or firms, it is far easier to look for some way in which you can use your own special skills, experience or situation to increase other people's efficiency. This sounds trite, but it is a highly practical starting point.

It may seem that there is more scope in taking the zero sum game route. Every day, you probably hear of people making money this way: using blatant zero sum strategies to provide very little value for great sums of money. But you also hear about people winning lotteries and vast amounts on television quiz shows, so it doesn't necessarily mean that this is a sensible strategy to pursue.

Ethics aside, it may be worth an investigation to compare the strategies of a wealth creator to those of a zero sum game player. This can be done using the roulette model.

We have already seen the results of zero sum game playing on the roulette wheel. We saw how using a complex system of betting fared worse than a simple strategy of one single gamble. In the former case, the strategy produces an average cost per day of holiday gained of 12.33; the latter did considerably better by reducing the average cost per day of the holiday to 10.27.

To change the nature of the game to a positive non-zero sum game between the players, all that is necessary is to arrange for the house to accord a win when the ball falls into the zero slot. In this way the house is adding one 37th to the players stakes' rather than taking it away.

This emulates real-life trading, when the effect of the trade is to increase efficiency. Value or wealth is introduced into the game which, in this case, is like increasing the players' efficiency by one 37th (just under 3 per cent).

If we now repeat the computer simulation of 5,000 players, with the zero giving wins to the players, rather than to the house, we obtain the result shown in Figure 2.3.

Zero = win	
Number of players	5000
Average number of days won	131
Average cost of each day's holiday	9.73
Number of winners	2570
Number of losers	2430
Total number of spins	5000
Total amount bet	6350000
Average spins per day	1
Average bet per spin	1270

FIG 2.3 Results of 5,000 players going to the casino and using all of their money to make a single bet on red. Zero counts as a win for the player

Immediately, we see that the average number of days won by each player has increased to 131. This is more days' holiday than they would have been able to have with their money if they hadn't gambled. This means the actual cost per day of the holiday has decreased from 10.27 to 9.73. On average, taking a risk is seen to pay when the odds are in the player's favour.

Now, given the choice between playing in a game where the house is winning on the zeros and a game where the house is paying out on the zeros, which game would you choose to play in? Quite obviously you'd choose the latter, so, when contemplating what kind of e-business to go for, it makes sense to ensure that you are playing in a game where efficiency is being increased by the business activity.

This is the major attraction of the internet for people who want to make money. The increase in efficiency that can be achieved by using digital technology has the same effect as a casino paying out on the zero.

> THE INCREASE IN EFFICIENCY THAT CAN BE ACHIEVED BY USING DIGITAL TECHNOLOGY HAS THE SAME EFFECT AS A CASINO PAYING OUT ON THE ZERO

This conclusion may be fairly obvious, but the effects of varying a playing strategy are not. Look back to see what happened when a complex strategy of doubling up was replaced by the strategy of the single bet. The single bet strategy was far superior, resulting in a far lower average cost per day of the holidays. What do you think will happen if the system strategy is employed when the house pays out on the zero?

Figure 2.4 shows the result of another simulation, with the doubling-up strategy being used by 5,000 players. This time it is with the zero being in the favour of the player.

Zero = win

Number of players	5000
Average number of days won	152
Average cost of each day's holiday	8.3553

Lasted	1 week	4769	1 month	4042		
	3 months	2739	6 months	1550	over 1 year	464

Total number of spins	1485782
Total amount bet	49609000
Average spins per day	1.9472
Average bet per spin	33.3892

FIG 2.4 The result of 5,000 people playing the roulette system. Zero counts as a win for the player

As you can see from Figure 2.4, a far greater number survived in all time periods. Only 231 failed to survive for at least a week. This is only two-thirds of the number that failed in the first week when the zero was in favour of the house. This raises the one-week survival percentage to over 95 per cent.

The average number of holidays has also increased quite dramatically, with a corresponding decrease in the average cost per day. These are both better results than the average the players would have got by paying for their holidays directly without taking any risks.

More significantly, these results show that using a strategy of many small bets and doubling after a loss is far more profitable, on average, than making single bets of all the money on the red. This reverses the situation of the normal game where the optimum strategy is to make a single large bet of all the money.

what does it mean in the real world?
All this may seem perfectly obvious and the conclusions only those to be expected, so what relevance does all this arcane roulette stuff have to the nitty-gritty world of real e-business?

This is a trick of scientists and entrepreneurs. The real world is too cluttered with specific detail to be able to get at the underlying fundamental issues. So, it is necessary to construct abstract models that isolate and concentrate upon only the important considerations. In other words, scientists and entrepreneurs will try to create a simple model that covers the broad concepts that are not obscured by irrelevant detail.

Changing technology, unknowns and competition create conditions of uncertainty and risk. These are the problem areas and the key determinants of outcomes in the world of e-commerce. Thus, before getting down to work out an appropriate niche speciality, we need to make sure we can properly cope with risk and uncertainty. Once we are clear on this fundamental level, we can then move on more confidently to consider specific details.

implications of the roulette results
The roulette simulation implies two clear guidelines. Firstly, the starting place for deciding which niche speciality to choose is that of making sure that the niche speciality

will provide some real benefit to someone. It must effectively create wealth by increasing efficiency somewhere. If your niche speciality cannot do this then you put yourself in a zero sum game situation, which the roulette simulation so neatly pinpoints.

Secondly, the implications of the roulette wheel simulation are that the many little deals scenario is a more profitable strategy than the big deal. But how does this translate into an e-business strategy?

To me, it hints at a preference for using a tit-for-tat strategy. This is the classic game theory strategy where relationships and partnerships for business associations are approached gradually and cautiously to allow a mutual understanding of trust to build up.

The general idea is that on an initial encounter with somebody you show them trust, do them a favour or give them something of value. They can either say 'Thank you very much' and not return the favour, or they can return a favour back. On subsequent encounters, you copy the response of the other person at the previous encounter: if they returned a favour, you respond with another. In this way, what may start as a risky relationship with a stranger can be developed gradually until the element of trust and the reciprocal favours can be highly beneficial to both parties.

Such an association between the results of a roulette game and a strategy to build up a relationship may seem highly dubious and tenuous. But, at a more abstract level, they are both concerned with making increasing commitments in a risky situation and increasing that commitment until it pays off. In a zero sum game, or a game where there are more losers than winners, this is not a good strategy, but in games where wealth is being created (the zero wins for the players) it can turn out to be the optimum strategy to provide the best chance of success.

Such a conclusion may not be of any consequence to a business strategist used to the stability of an Industrial Age scenario where risks are largely eliminated (by using references, track records and experience of similar situations – all of which are of questionable value in the rapidly changing environment of the internet). But, in the uncertain and unpredictable conditions of an e-business environment, this is a very important observation to make. Credibility and the difficulties associated with establishing relationships of trust over the internet are major barriers to creating a successful e-business.

The inference is that in situations where there are substantial elements of risk, many small dealings are likely to be more profitable than large deals: suggesting that breaking up large risks into a collection of smaller risks might be an essential part of any e-commerce strategy.

This is in sharp contrast to the zero sum player's best strategy. Those who do not add value by increasing the efficiency of a business activity might find greater advantage in playing for the big deals.

Stepping outside of this artificial environment of the simulated roulette game, it is not hard to see how this accords with everyday experiences in the real world. The cowboy website builders who provide plenty of glitz but no real value for their clients' businesses always go for the big deal, whereas the real value providers prefer to work with many different clients and build up stability through providing satisfaction through a larger number of smaller deals.

a seemingly impossible problem to solve
Time to pause here, to see what has been covered so far in the book and work out where it is going.

We started off in the introduction with the proposition that although the internet seems to offer unlimited e-business opportunity, the reality is that success is not going to come easily. The 24 assumptions, which are by no means a fully inclusive list, give an indication of the difficulties to be overcome.

It would have been easy to have started off this book with some real-life examples to illustrate the problems and show how these problems can be overcome. However, a little thought will soon tell you that this is not a practical approach, because there are so many possible ways of creating e-businesses that taking any single choice will lock you into a niche speciality region that will produce unique problems that apply only in that area.

Not only that. By examining real-life examples we'd be confining ourselves to the known; and the known is crowded out with competition. Far better to be able to look beyond what is already happening on the web today to be able to get into a position to establish new initiatives. In this game it is going to be the leaders, not the followers, who will be most successful.

To the pragmatist and the more practical minds, the stuff about game theory, chance and probabilities may seem to be a lot of airy-fairy nonsense. Who but some daft academic, without any real-life experience of the nitty-gritty world of making a living, would think of business in these terms? Let's see.

In Chapter 1, there was a dialogue that claimed to contain the optimum system for playing roulette. As you read that claim, you might have assumed that by optimum it meant a winning system. You would have immediately been sceptical, because common sense would tell you that if there were a winning system, there wouldn't be any casinos left in business for you to be able to play the system.

This represented a paradox; an anomaly was detected that needed resolving. Understanding that the optimum system was not a winning system, but merely an optimum system in the sense that it lost less than any other system, made it believable. The paradox was resolved and the anomaly disappeared. Arcane and seemingly irrelevant theoretical modelling often provides the means for resolving such paradoxes and dispelling anomalies.

Let's apply this thinking now. The inference of this book is that the author can create a successful e-business. For an author to make such a claim surely stretches the reader's credulity to the limit. Isn't it everyone's dream to be able to say, 'Oh, I think I'll start a successful e-business today.' What sort of credibility could be given to anyone who made such a statement?

What if this person were asked what was the substance of the business they had in mind and they answered, 'I don't know, but it would have to be something that nobody is doing yet.' Would this increase or decrease their credibility?

Now imagine somebody coming up to you and saying, 'Think of an object or an idea. It can be tangible or intangible. It can be anything you like. Whatever it is, I've got a strategy where I'll be able to work out what that object you have in mind is.' Would you think that possible? There would be millions of possibilities for a thought that was in your mind. What possible strategy could be used to single out that one particular object?

The person might then say, 'I'll need your cooperation a little here, I want you to answer 'yes' or 'no' to 20 questions I'm going to ask you.'

Immediately, it is seen how this one chance in millions of guessing the answer is changed into a a reasonable chance of success. This is evidenced by the well-known game of Twenty Questions. It is this very simple strategy that is at the heart of game theory.

Now take the proposition that I intend to create a successful e-commerce business by the time this book is published. At first this seems a fatuous statement to make, but it is no more fatuous than the idea that somebody could guess exactly what you had in mind when you randomly thought about some object. The trick is to ask enough intelligent questions to be able to reduce the list of possibilities down to a single one, or at least a manageable few possibilities.

The seemingly irrelevant concern with the roulette system is an example of using an abstract model to generate such intelligent questions; using them to eliminate some of the possible options available for creating an e-business.

There must always be a question as to whether it is better to play a zero sum strategy – where you win by taking away business from competitors without providing any increased value (as might be the case where a high-powered advertising or sales pressure technique is used) – or go for the more difficult non-zero game strategy which involves creating real value in the form of increased efficiency.

Looking at the abstraction provided by the roulette system helps us make this decision. From the seemingly irrelevant computer simulation, it would seem that creating value is a more profitable way to proceed than trying to succeed using solely advertising or selling skills. Deciding this is the way to go eliminates a large proportion of the massive number of possible options available (in a choice as to which type of business to go for).

Of course, this choice may be wrong. It might be wrong, for instance, to a speciality team of sales people who have not the technological under-standing to be able to create superior value or increase efficiency. They might be far better off opting for the zero sum game, which would give them a different set of options to eliminate from their range of possibilities.

The question 'Should I go for a game of winning from my competitors or creating a situation of increased efficiency?' can thus be given an answer. The question 'Should I go for a business that risks a large sum or go for a business consisting of many small risks?' can also be answered. The strategy has begun – and so has a start been made in acquiring e-business acumen.

dealing with unknowns and uncertainty More pertinent,
though, is where a question is posed (in order to eliminate options) that has a degree of uncertainty attached to it. This can be represented in the Twenty Questions model by the person answering the questions being unable to answer a straightforward 'Yes' or 'No' to a question. The answer might be 'I think it is yes, but I'm not sure.'

In the game of 'Twenty Questions' the answer to a question answered in this way might be ignored, but what if every question were answered this way? Then, to have any chance of arriving at a solution, a probability has to be assigned to each answer.

This may seem to negate the strategy, or at best give it a very dubious conclusion. But this isn't necessarily true. This is best explained by a game that was very popular in the 1970s called, amongst other names, Mastermind.

This game consists of a peg board with six rows of holes with a dozen holes in each row. There are also a number of pegs of six different colours. The idea is that one player writes down a combination of six colours (some of which could be the same) in a particular order and then the other player works out what this combination is by making guesses through placing six coloured pegs at a time into the holes in the peg board. As there were 12 columns (of six rows) the player could have a maximum of 12 guesses in which to discover the code.

The first try would have to be a complete guess of six pegs chosen at random. These will be placed into the first column. Then the person who has set the code tells the guesser how many of the pegs are of the right colour and how many are in the right position. There is no indication given, though, as to which of the pegs are correct and which are incorrect: the guesser is simply given the two numbers.

When I was working in Copenhagen on one occasion, my 14-year-old daughter came to visit me. To keep ourselves amused one rainy after-noon, we decided to play this game of Mastermind. It wasn't long before both of us got the hang of it – which was to use the information given in an accumulative way to progress towards the solution.

Soon, we were both able to guess each other's code within no more than six guesses, at which time the game began to get boring. Then we decided to make it more difficult by making a rule that each of us could tell one lie when providing the information as to how many of the pegs were of the right colour and in the right position.

This made the game considerably more difficult because there were many possible alternative solutions, the correct solution having to be found by a process of elimination. Despite this handicap though, we were eventually able to guess each other's code within eight or nine guesses.

At this point the game became boring again, so we decided to let each other tell two lies when declaring the numbers of right colours and right positions. This more than doubled the complexity of the elimination process, but eventually we reached a stage of being able to consistently guess each other's code within the allowable maximum of 12 guesses.

This game proves quite elegantly that uncertainty can be overcome if a suitable strategy is employed. The trick was to give each peg position a probability of being right, then test the most likely solution to see if the uncertainty could be eliminated. The net result was that solutions could be found just as surely as when the information was accurate – it just took a few more guesses.

This is the way game theory is used to eliminate uncertainty. It doesn't trust answers to questions, but counters this problem by asking additional questions to cover the possibility that some answers may be wrong.

This can be modelled by imagining the game of Twenty Questions being played where you can ask several different people about the same unknown object. Then, when a person answers a question with 'I'm not sure whether the answer is a "Yes" or a "No"', there will be other people to ask and perhaps one of them might be able to answer with more certainty.

Where there might be conflicting answers, with some answering 'Yes' and some answering 'No', the ratio of 'Yeses' and 'Noes' could be used to give the answer 'Yes' or 'No' a probability of being the correct answer.

Staying with this same model, it would only be common sense to assign some sort of weightings to the answers given. For example, if the question involves the person having to have a certain amount of technical knowledge to answer correctly, an answer from a person who is known to have such technical knowledge would carry far more weight than an answer from a person who is known not to have any such knowledge.

Taking all this reasoning into consideration, the idea that you can make an optimum choice from amongst a limitless number of choices does not seem such a hopeless task as it would first appear. It simply involves devising a suitable strategy where uncertainties can be eliminated by:

1   asking appropriate questions;

2   asking several people the same question;

3   giving weightings to the answers.

A game theory strategy might then be summed up as:

1 finding suitable questions to ask;

2 finding suitable people to provide answers;

3 making sure that the questions can be posed to a number of different people.

Such a strategy is ideal for highly technical environments where there is so much to know that everyone can be expected to have substantial gaps in their knowledge.

One final point of note. The game of Twenty Questions does not rely on being able to ask exactly the right questions. Different combinations of quite different questions can be posed, which might still lead to a correct solution. In this way, lack of knowledge can be bypassed. It is not necessary to have to know all the questions that could be asked, as long as a suitable strategy is employed to eliminate the uncertainties.

Now take a quick glance back to the introduction, at the list of the 24 initial assumptions that have to be made before embarking upon an e-commerce venture. Do they seem quite as formidable as when you first looked at them?

3

CHOOSING IN CONDITIONS OF UNCERTAINTY

feedback from the café As each chapter of this book is written, copies are sent to a virtual café. This virtual café consists of about six tables of readers who each get e-mailed a copy to read. More will be said about this virtual café later, but suffice it to say at this time that the readers provide valuable feedback and inspiration for subsequent chapters.

Two responses to the first two chapters need to be addressed before we carry on. The first was from Mark Baartse:

My understanding is that at a very simple level, decision theory is basically a tree diagram. You map out different possibilities, different outcomes, etc., in a tree. As you can imagine, with lots of options and lots of outcomes, the tree can get pretty complex.

Branches are created as an activity to do this or do that: basically, a potential 40% chance we get the deal with x and 60% we don't. You also attach values to each event or activity (e.g. decision: we do a TV campaign for 5m or a radio campaign for 1m). At the end, you will have multiple (potentially dozens) of options with a value attached to each which allows you to create the best decision.

My question is: what is the advantage of game theory over this tried and tested system that's been taught in business schools for decades? Why doesn't this system work in e-business?

Sure, there are a lot of possibilities and possible outcomes, and yes, you often make a best guess (60% you'll get the deal? a bit subjective), but isn't it quite similar to game theory – you're picking the one most likely to be profitable based on information at hand?

Although the method described by Mark may seem to be very similar to the technique of selecting an appropriate e-business niche – described in Chapter 2 – it is not suitable for environments where there are unpredictable uncertainties. This is because the method relies on a reasonably accurate estimation of the probabilities involved in a problem. This confines the method to reasonably stable environments – such as those found in much of the business environment during the second half of the twentieth century.

Game theory uses a different kind of conceptual framework, which can deal with situations where calculations of probabilities are not always reliable. The difference is subtle, but critically important. If you look at Mark's description of qualitative analysis, he begins: 'You map out different possibilities, different outcomes, etc...'.

In a reasonably predictable world, where you can use a structural top-down approach, you are able to isolate a range of options, complete with information relating to possible outcomes, and use a statistical approach to choose between them. In the world of e-business, not only is it virtually impossible to calculate probabilities, but some of the best options often emerge only after projects are under way.

> EVENTS MOVE SO FAST IN THE WORLD OF E-BUSINESS, THAT WHATEVER HAPPENED IN THE PAST DOESN'T NECESSARILY HAVE ANY BEARING ON WHAT HAPPENS IN THE FUTURE

Events move so fast in the world of e-business, that whatever happened in the past doesn't necessarily have any bearing on what happens in the future. Think how many businesses were planned around charging for internet services. The idea of creating a customer base, of several thousand people paying a few hundred dollars a year each for an internet link, seemed an attractive basis for a viable business enterprise. Many entrepreneurs bought hardware and designed software specifically to cater for this potentially lucrative market.

Unfortunately for these early start-ups, there were so many people setting up internet services with the same idea that competition soon forced the charges down to around one hundred dollars a year. This diluted the profits, but the situation was still viable. So the rise in the number of internet service providers (ISPs) continued, keeping up with the exponential growth of the internet.

Then, a few large companies realized that these surfers would be spending money on the internet. A back-of-the-envelope calculation soon revealed that the cost of supplying people with internet service would be a mere fraction of what they would likely be spending buying goods and services through their internet connection. To gain access to these millions of potential customers, and their combined buying power, it seemed economically sensible to provide them with an internet service for free. As subsequent equity issues proved, the market places a very high value on what was then seen to be a captive audience of receptive buyers who had the means to purchase at the touch of a button.

The many thousands of start-ups, who had based business plans on gaining revenues by supplying internet connection services, were left with egg on their faces. Their lucrative market disappeared overnight.

The more adaptable saw the potential for providing web space for people and businesses. Very soon, most of those who'd lost or were losing their ISP customers to the free services were including free web space in with their ISP services. It didn't take long for the big companies to work out that the relatively small cost of providing web space for their customers could also be offset by their buying potential. They then began offering free web space to all their customers.

NOTE there are many types of portals and there is as yet no single agreement as to exactly what the term means, but in this book the term will be used to mean a point of entry for many people to access an organized sector of the web. We shall be dealing with portals more specifically later in the book.

To compete against the free services being offered by the giants, the smaller hosting services began designing special server-side software so that they could keep and attract customers by offering better service and specialized facilities. This spawned a host of software development companies supplying this server-side software to everyone. It wasn't long before these specialized services were also being offered for free by the larger companies, who were by then aggressively competing with each other to build the largest portals.

With free, or next to nothing, web hosting available, hordes of people were attracted into e-commerce. Multitudes of website design companies grew up to serve this massive potential market. At first it provided a lucrative business for web designers. It attracted hundreds of thousands into the business. Even high-school kids were jumping onto the bandwagon to cash in on the gold rush.

Competition soon started to drive down the cost of web design and construction. Once again, the envelopes came out and the more savvy web designers figured out that it would pay to design an initial website for free – as this could provide them with a stable base of satisfied customers who would most likely turn to them when they wanted to improve their site or expand their web-based businesses.

Professional website authoring packages then started to come into their own. Complex websites could be designed within the environment of these authoring tools, cheaply and efficiently, by anyone who took the trouble to learn how to use them properly. Templates could be made from sophisticated website designs, making it easy and inexpensive for similar sites to be produced *en masse*.

The cost of customizing these clones for different clients became minimal. Pretty soon, eTailing sites – which had started out costing clients hundreds of thousands of dollars to be designed specifically for them – were being offered for a fraction of their original design costs to all and sundry.

As entrepreneurs realized the potential of hosting e-business sites – complete with their customer bases – out came the envelopes again. These valuable clients could be captured. It didn't take long for the software mechanisms involved in e-commerce to be offered for free: together with free web space. There were minimal costs involved in customizing these eTailing sites for individual businesses, so it made economic sense to offer eTailing sites free of charge. Soon, there was a flurry of activity as companies raced each other to create virtual malls, providing traders with free eTailing sites – complete with shopping carts, ordering systems, inventory controls, back-end database management – all completely free of charge.

Now, how can a decision theory approach deal with this kind of situation? How can any future plans be based upon experiences in the past? This is a great enigma for Industrial Age strategists who are used to planning in a predictable universe. How can they plan and organize projects where there can be no clue as to what is going to happen in the future? This is why the Information Age strategists are now turning to game theory.

Game theory assumes that the future is uncertain and unpredictable so, unlike decision theory, which starts by making a list of probable solutions, it starts with all possibilities – however unlikely and bizarre – and gradually pares this infinite choice down using broad principles and taking calculated risks.

The difference then, between decision theory as described by Mark Baartse and game theory as applied in Chapter 2, seems to be that decision theory works by means of intelligent selection whereas game theory works by intelligent elimination.

As we shall see later, game theory can be interpreted and applied in many different ways.

NOTE This may seem to be a strange way to interpret game theory because game theory is usually discussed in terms of rules and pay-off matrices. But, an elimination is in fact a rule that takes the form: 'If such and such condition holds true, do that or don't do this.'

This contrasts subtly with decision theory, which takes the form: 'Do this in preference to that,' which is a selection procedure, rather than a method using rules based upon conditionals.

many small risks or one big one?

The second interesting response to the first two chapters came from Yvan Caron, a systems analyst working in Canada. He identified what would seem to be a paradox. He'd been following a discussion on an internet advertising listserve discussion forum, where a question had been posed by a restaurateur who'd wanted to know what percentage of his gross revenue he should risk on web advertising. After supplying a copy of the restaurateur's post, Yvan Caron wrote:

Let's analyze this restaurateur's problem in terms of the roulette game where the Gambler *has* the *Advantage*.

Suppose you've checked a wheel and discovered that through a *bias* you have a mathematical advantage over the casino. We know from Chapter 2 that everything changes almost from black to white.

From the standpoint of capital requirements, we have two choices: do we minimize our risk or maximize our gain? As you may begin to guess this relates to the question: 'What percentage of my gross revenues should I dedicate to my web strategies?'

What we seek is a compromise between the extremes of minimal (long-term) risk and maximal (short-term) gain. We need a wager optimally combining the greatest safety with the greatest growth rate of our capital or bankroll.

Given this, what should be our bank-to-bet ratio? What do you bet?

Yvan's problem highlights a typical gambler's problem. Do you play safe by spreading risk, or do you go for broke in order to make a substantial gain?

This was a problem that came home to me when I spent a year in the City of London writing an educational course on Investment and Finance. To make the course interesting, I proposed that students give themselves an imaginary amount of capital and during the 12 weeks of the course, pretend to be buying and selling equities with this imaginary money at the prices prevailing each day in the *Financial Times*. This would allow them to get some experience of market conditions without risking any real money.

With the students, I joined in this imaginary game, with the hope that the methods I was describing would produce a handsome profit at the end of the 12 week period.

The methods I'd outlined in the course were the traditional methods that had evolved from hundreds of years of stockbroker experience. This involved trying to get what is known as a technical valuation of the investments (based upon the anticipated earnings per share of the equities: comparing the ratio of earnings to equity price with the current prices being quoted for fixed annual incomes, i.e. annuities).

Of course, there is no straightforward comparison that can be made between the relatively safe and certain income from annuities and the uncertain income that can be derived from equities; all kinds of risks and uncertainties have to be discounted. But they can give a rough guide, which often exposes anomalies.

Using a game theory approach, a fundamental investment strategy rule was established that gave preservation of capital a top priority. To satisfy this rule, the investment of the capital had to be split up as much as possible so as to spread the risk – just in case any of the investments failed. This gave an overall investment result that was effectively the average gains and losses of many different separate investments.

To my disappointment, the result of this investment strategy produced very little improvement on the average for all equities in the market. Any deviation to try to invest more heavily in volatile offerings compromised the safety of the capital. It was a problem I never resolved and led to my abandonment of investing in the stock market as a route to riches.

The reader might like to ponder here on the similarity between playing the stock market and playing the game of roulette as discussed in the last chapter. In a rising market, the game is the same as if zero wins for the players. In a falling market, it is as if zero wins for the house. Notice too, that playing the stock market is really a zero sum game. There is no value introduced by the investors; they are merely winning from one another (minus the stockbroker's fees).

Playing the stock market, however, is quite different from the situation where investors invest in a company by taking up equity to provide a company with working capital. This is a game where the capital can be put to profitable use and so create real wealth to make it a win-win, non-zero sum game. It is this second way of investing in equities that can be more appropriately related to the strategies discussed in this book.

When I later applied game theory strategy to entrepreneurial business situations, I came up with a similar problem to that pinpointed by Yvan Caron. Do you go for high gains by concentrating all your resources on favoured projects, or spread the risk by dividing available resources between as many different options as possible?

The reader might consider here that the term 'resources' does not necessarily relate to capital. It applies as much to time. In many cases time might be an even more critical factor, maybe even the only one to many under-capitalized start-ups. In which case the problem revolves around 'Do I invest all of my time in one favoured project, or spread the risk by dividing my time between several?' This is a critical decision for all entrepreneurs where projects involve risk.

This is also true for anyone involved in e-business: even subcontracting experts and specialists run a risk with their time, just as much as any entrepreneur. How many specialists are there that have devoted months, even years to a particular niche speciality (authoring package, hardware, database system or computer platform) only to see that speciality area be superseded or disappear altogether?

When Yvan Caron came back with his own answer to the problem he'd posed, this was his post:

Hi All,

Remember the question that came from a local restaurateur where he asked: 'What percentage of my gross revenues should I dedicate to my web strategies?'

Then I told you that what we were seeking was a compromise: between the extremes of minimal (long-term) risk and maximal (short-term) gain. What we seek is a wager, optimally combining the greatest safety with the greatest growth rate of our capital or bankroll. Given this, what should be the bank-to-bet ratio?

So here is my second part to this post ...

I did not invent this strategy, but took it from an old book on my book shelf. I must confess though, that I don't know exactly how we could apply it to the web.

One of the scholars of proportional betting is an American mathematician, John L. Kelly, Jr., who proposed an optimal ratio in 1956. In simplified form the Kelly system states that, when the game is *favourable to us* (whether on red or on one or more numbers), at every spin we should wager an amount equal to our current bankroll divided by a number based upon the amount of risk involved.

Simple isn't it?

Mathematicians consider the Kelly proportional betting system the best mathematical strategy, constituting, as it does, the perfect compromise between betting, in relation to our capital, too little (overly time-consuming) versus too much (overly risky).

In explaining the Kelly proportional betting system, for simplicity I used an even chance (say red), but it's just as valid for any kind of investing enterprise.

The problem here, is that I have not yet resolved how to know or evaluate business advantage to be able to give a value to the constant multiplier.

NOTE probabilities are usually expressed such that one (1) equals certainty and nought (0) equals absolute impossibility. Anything in between is expressed as a decimal fraction of one (1) e.g., a 50 per cent chance of success would be expressed as a probability of 0.5; a 10 per cent chance of success would be expressed as a probability of 0.1; an 80 per cent chance of success would be expressed as a probability of 0.8.

This problem of what proportion of available resources to allocate to a risk is not something that can be formalized in the real world of business. There is no optimum or universal percentage that can be applied because all risks in business come with different probabilities of success. There is also the problem that business risk is usually impossible to estimate. This was pointed out by another reader in the café, Bonnie Austin, from Texas, USA.

Bonnie wrote:

In my experience, with my own businesses and from discussing strategies with other business owners, determining one's present position, including probabilities of various outcomes, is the most difficult (and often impossible) task for the entrepreneur.

I can't think of any example in the real world where a person can say with certainty, 'The probability of my getting the job I'm bidding on is .2.'

Rather, there's more like a range of probabilities. The best one can do is to say, 'Well, I think I have a pretty good chance of getting the contract.' Meaning that the probability is somewhere between .15 and .3.

If an entrepreneur has several irons in the fire (that's an old Texas expression meaning that a person's working on several possibilities at the same time) it gets easier to say that there's a certain probability that at least one of the deals will work out. Even so, one has to keep in mind that a model is not a perfect representation. Sometimes, I say that the entrepreneur calls upon intuition to bridge the gap between the model and reality; but, maybe there's a large element of luck.

As Yvan Caron's post pointed out, a high-risk situation will warrant risking a lower proportion of available resources than a less risky situation. But how can this rule be applied if the risk is difficult or impossible to estimate? This conundrum makes a game of roulette an inappropriate model with which to consider this problem. A more appropriate game might be the game of poker – even though this is a pure zero sum game.

I spent a short period of my life as a professional poker player. This involved the continuous use of strategies that allocated sums of money for bets according to perceived risks. The need to keep in the game, surviving over the course of many losing hands, necessitated that bets were made with due consideration to the amount of money available to play with. After a winning run, and with accumulated winnings, higher bets could be made – and bets made on riskier situations. After a losing run, when funds were low, bets were smaller, less frequent and made with much more care.

However, whether winning or losing, the basic betting strategy remained more or less the same: bets were always only a small fraction of my capital if I was playing just to stay in a hand and where I was not particularly hopeful of winning (I'd be staying in the hand for a small bet because there was always a chance for a favourable fall of the cards to turn the hand to my advantage).

I'd play in many hands where the cards wouldn't fall my way, but as soon as a hand came along where the cards turned in my favour, I'd up the stakes, increase the amount of my bets and play to the limit of my capital.

a range of possibilities

Translating the poker-playing strategy into a business scenario, it can be described as making many small investments in risky situations, waiting for one of them to show promise (become relatively risk free) and then going for broke. Sometimes I went broke, but over the long term this strategy enabled me to create some outstanding successes – sufficient to ensure that overall the strategy was a lot better than pursuing a regular career.

THE HYPOTHETICAL MAN IN CHAPTER 3 Because this book will be read by many different kinds of people it will be impossible to cover individual niches. However, game theory strategies, whoever uses them and for whatever purposes, will have many fundamental similarities.

For this reason it will be convenient to invent a hypothetical businessman who will be the focus of attention. This the reader is asked to identify with, even if at times this person will not exactly coincide with their own personality or relate directly to their own unique situation.

Ladies, please excuse the choice of gender, but I'm sure you will understand that to keep having to refer to 'businessman or businesswoman' every time would be highly inconvenient. As 'businessman' is shorter to write than 'businesswoman' I opted to make the hypothetical business person a man. But I'm sure you will understand.

This person will seem at most times to have an entrepreneurial viewpoint. This is not meant to imply that this book is only for entrepreneurs. It's just that entrepreneurs are more likely to be associated with freedom of action, which is what this book is about.

In fact, most people will make decisions of an entrepreneurial kind in the world of e-business so it shouldn't make much difference. Where there are obviously differences in strategies (say for employees, or contractors) the differences in strategy will be covered.

This hypothetical 'businessman in Chapter 3' will now be introduced. We will be developing his strategy as we progress through the book.

In poker, this principle of staying in hands to wait for a favourable break is known as 'open play'. It allows a player to make big wins when the breaks come. In business, this strategy is used to 'get into the game'. By being in a business, even when it is not profitable, one is more likely to encounter a profitable situation when it comes along than by waiting safely on the sidelines.

The cost of spreading risk in a start-up situation is illustrated in this fictional scene, where a man is visiting a friend who is trying to start up a new business after a recent business failure:

I see you are back in business again?

Not yet, all I have is this office. I have yet to decide what business to go into.

Have you got any ideas?

Yes, I have made a short list of possible business ventures to go into.

So you have to decide which on this short list to go for?

No, I shall probably have a go at them all.

All at once?

Yes. Why not? They all seem quite good ideas and I see no reason to pick any particular one.

But wouldn't it be more efficient to go for just one of them?

Certainly, if I knew which of them would be successful.

But you said they were all good ideas.

Yes, but I know from experience that even good ideas have no better than one chance in six of getting off the ground.

So how many ideas have you got on your list?

Six.

So trying out all six will make it certain that at least one of them will get off the ground?

No. The odds of succeeding are improved, but success is not certain.

What are your chances of getting one of them off the ground then?

Each idea has five chances in six of being unsuccessful so the probability of all six being unsuccessful is (he then draws and makes a few calculations on a sheet of paper) about one chance in three of all six ideas having to be aborted. So I would say that there are two chances in three of one of these ideas getting off the ground.

What are you going to do if none of the ideas work out?

Put together another list of six.

Again with two chances in three of succeeding with one of them?

That's right, and the chances of failing with two lots of six is one-third multiplied by one-third.

Giving you a nearly a 90 per cent chance of getting something off the ground?

Yes, so there seems to be a reasonable cause for hope.

In this scenario, the businessman has assigned a value for dividing up his risk. From his past experience of business start-ups, he has observed that when he has a good business idea it only seems to come to fruition about one time in six. He therefore allocates about 13 per cent of his resources to each project.

If his resources were in terms of a fixed amount of investment capital, then it would be a simple case of spreading the investment risk across a number of risky situations. However, if he is starting from a square-one position, with little or no capital, the resources would be in the form of a continuous but limited amount of time he could allocate.

In these terms the businessman could choose to allocate roughly 13 per cent of his available time to each of the six projects. This is similar to the poker player allocating small bets to hands that he is not very confident of winning. However, it is unlikely that the probabilities of success of each project would remain constant. Just like the hands the poker player plays in, they can each develop differently. It is most likely that work on some projects would reveal hidden flaws that would cause them to become less viable and there would be others where situations would emerge to manifest a higher probability of success.

With the various projects beginning to prove more or less likely to succeed, it would be obvious that the businessman would reallocate his time accordingly. Most likely, at some stage one of the projects would emerge as being highly likely to succeed and then the businessman might feel it expedient to drop all the other projects to concentrate on that single one. In a game of poker, when a poker player feels confident that his hand can beat all the others he will be inclined to bet to the limit of the total money he has available – known in poker circles as 'going all in'. Of course, there is no certainty that this final choice will win, but, as with the poker player, there is always another day.

It is also worth noting that at the beginning of the chapter, Mark Baarste had described decision theory as selecting from a list of likely possibilities. With that technique, probability is used to choose between them, i.e. make the best choice. The game theory technique is to say there is insufficient information to be able to make a choice, so all options must be treated as equally likely to succeed. This being the case, all possibilities are tried together without making a choice of any particular one. Unpredictable, emergent events are left to determine which of the possibilities ends up as the final choice.

Because e-business involves so many unknowns and uncertainties, this provides us with an important fundamental rule to use in e-business strategies: *never make rational choices between alternative options; always make sure that a variety of options are being tried out at the same time, letting the developing situations determine the final choice.*

but it is possible that you can never win
The single most difficult concept to grasp in probability theory is that of calculating the probability of success. It requires a way of thinking that is 'counter-intuitive'; that is to say, it produces conclusions that cannot be arrived at by applying common sense.

In the doubling-up strategy of the roulette system, the weakness was that there was a very real chance of failure. Averaging out over many players, one player in 14 would fail. Similarly, the man dividing his time between six projects, then failing and trying six more, then failing again and choosing another six, can never be certain that he will ever succeed – however many times he tries. Just as it is possible for an exceptionally large run of reds to occur at some time during the history of a roulette wheel, so it is possible for even the smartest business person in the world to have such a run of bad luck that he or she never succeeds.

It is this very real possibility of never succeeding that causes most people to shy away from risk, particularly if it involves the possibility of losing all of their money, their job or their health. Game theory deals with this problem by using compromise.

clearing up a paradox
This chapter has been about dealing with the uncertainty involved in choice. In the complex environment of e-

> " THE SINGLE MOST DIFFICULT CONCEPT TO GRASP IN PROBABILITY THEORY IS THAT OF CALCULATING THE PROBABILITY OF SUCCESS "

business it isn't possible to make decisions based on rationalities because there are too many unknowns in the equations. The only viable strategy therefore is to allow a range of options to take their course and wait for unfolding events to point to a clear leader.

There seems to be an anomaly here, though, because even though the final decision of choosing between the options is determined by the unfolding of events, the options have to be chosen beforehand. Surely these initial options have to be arrived at through rational choice?

Here we come to the crux of game theory. The range of options is arrived at in the same way as the game of Twenty Questions arrives at a conclusion: it's a process of elimination. Rules are applied to all possibilities so as to eliminate all but a few remaining possibilities.

There is one difference though. In Twenty Questions there is only one correct solution. In games there can be many. Game theory isn't about choosing the perfect solution, but choosing a solution that satisfies certain criteria. Solutions can therefore be easier or harder to come by depending upon how particular you are with the criteria. The trick then, in being able to get solutions most efficiently, is to choose sensible criteria and place pragmatic values on them.

This is more easily explained by the process of mate selection. For everyone, somewhere in the world there is somebody who would be the best possible match for them. But, as there are over six billion people in the world, nobody would ever settle down with a mate if they had to interview three billion people to find the ideal one for them. So they are forced to adopt a strategy that is a compromise. They will apply a set of rules or standards to help narrow down their search. They will confine their search to a practical geographic search area. They'll probably arrive at a range of possibilities and make cautious exploratory investigations by dating them.

Out of the process, a most suitable choice is likely to emerge. It is unlikely to be the best in the world, but it is a solution that is acceptable. How near this might be to a perfect choice is a combination of chance (luck), standards set and length of time available for the search. As is readily observed, this process may start out with high standards when there is plenty of time available for the search, but standards quickly drop if no results are forthcoming and time is running out.

This easily translates into business scenarios: a choice of business; a niche speciality; an employee; an employer; a partner; a client; a contractor or a subcontractor; even an area of study. All of these have to be chosen in the same way as people choose their mates: a compromise – where the optimum results are determined by the time available, the efficiency of the search process and the selection criteria imposed. This is what game theory is about: devising an optimum strategy to reach the best compromise in conditions of uncertainty and competition.

It is only in light of such a strategy that the importance of the internet can be appreciated. A person seeking a mate is severely restricted in choice through the limitations imposed by geographic location. Imagine now being connected to millions of others through the internet. Certainly, a person couldn't make a final choice through the internet, but an efficient search strategy to arrive at a number of alternative starting options could use a far more rigorous set of criteria than if the search was restricted to a local social scene. This is what e-business is about, taking advantage of the fact that everyone can use the internet to set higher standards for their explorative search strategies. This is where we are going now.

DEALING WITH COMPLEXITY AND INFORMATION OVERLOAD

PART 1 DEALT WITH CHANCE AND PROBABILITY.
THIS IS A KIND OF UNCERTAINTY, BUT IT IS THE
KIND OF UNCERTAINTY THAT CAN BE HANDLED
WITH MATHEMATICS TO BRING ABOUT SOME
DEGREE OF ORDER AND PREDICTABILITY. ONCE
YOU ASCERTAIN PROBABILITIES, DECISIONS
CAN BE MADE. HOWEVER, IT IS NOT ALWAYS
POSSIBLE TO ASCERTAIN PROBABILITIES. SOME-
TIMES, IT ISN'T EVEN POSSIBLE TO KNOW WHAT
IT IS YOU HAVE TO GET THE PROBABILITY OF.

IN THIS SECTION WE ARE GOING TO DEAL WITH
QUITE A DIFFERENT TYPE OF UNCERTAINTY,
WHERE MATHEMATICS CANNOT HELP AT ALL. IT
IS THE UNCERTAINTY AND CONFUSION THAT IS
CAUSED BY COMPLEXITY AND INFORMATION
OVERLOAD. IT IS THE UNCERTAINTY CAUSED BY
HAVING TOO MANY PERSONAL KNOWLEDGE
GAPS AND KNOWING THAT EVERYONE ELSE HAS
KNOWLEDGE GAPS AS WELL.

THIS IS THE REAL WORLD OF E-BUSINESS,
WHERE IT IS NOT ABOUT KNOWING WHAT IS THE
BEST ACTION TO TAKE BUT DECIDING WHAT TO
DO WHEN YOU CAN'T POSSIBLY KNOW WHAT IS
THE BEST ACTION TO TAKE.

MATHEMATICS CAN'T HANDLE THIS KIND OF
PROBLEM. BUT A GAME THEORY FRAMEWORK
CAN.

SHOULD A SINGLE GREAT BUSINESS IDEA HEAD AN E-BUSINESS VENTURE?

the value of a business idea

The businessman in the dialogue in Chapter 3 is shown as having six alternative options. He assumes that his chances of any one of them being successful is one chance in six. We have already seen how, in the uncertain world of the internet, it would be impossible to differentiate between them, and he would have to treat them all equally until emerging events highlight a favourite.

The scenario still begs the question, though, as to how the man arrives at the number of options as being six – this is supposedly based upon his past experience that only one in six of his business ideas become viable. Why one chance in six? Can you make that kind of assumption in the world of e-business where there is practically no previous experience or historical data to draw upon?

If we look at the list of initial assumptions in the introduction we see they include:

2   Nobody knows all the answers.

3 The environment of the internet and the world wide web is beyond your or anyone else's ability to be able to understand completely.

18 Whatever you are offering, there will be a plethora of similar alternatives in the marketplace already.

20 The solution you have to come up with is beyond your, or anyone else's, imagination.

22 Any final solution you come up with will have to be abandoned or radically altered within a very short period of time.

Game theory is about applying rules to reduce or eliminate alternatives. If we are to take the above assumptions seriously, then they must be applied as rules to any business idea we come up with. Clearly, applying such rules *to discount the uncertainties and unknowns in any great business idea we'd find we'd have to discount so heavily that the value will drop to a point where the success probability of the business idea is hardly any better than that of a random guess.*

Such a pragmatic assessment will cause any carefully thought out business idea to be hardly worth the bother of trying to put it into operation. This is a startling conclusion and a radical paradigm shift from the conventional business approach used in the bricks and mortar world of the twentieth century.

The businessman in Chapter 3 has whittled his options down to six possibles, but if these options are e-business ideas and we apply the e-business assumptions to each of those ideas they will all be virtually worthless. This will totally negate the value of his approach because six worthless options will be equal to a worthless total, whichever way you want to look at it.

Developing this thought further, it becomes obvious that any scheme based upon great business ideas will suffer the same fate. This is not dissimilar to the situation with roulette systems. The underlying probabilities determine the average outcome and this will not change however the bets are arranged.

This counter-intuitive conclusion presents an enigma: *a strategy to find a successful e-business cannot be based upon a business idea.*

This seems ridiculous, but game theory is actually telling us something very subtle. It is telling us that if we start without a business idea in an unpredictable environment we will be at an advantage to those who do. Those with fixed ideas will be confined by them. Without a fixed idea you can look for opportunities over a very much larger range of possibilities.

This is the way the master game strategist, Sherlock Holmes, might have looked at it. He worked on the assumption that if the probable is eliminated and you are left only with the improbable, then the solution must lie amongst the improbable. It is there we go now.

making your own luck

The conclusion reached in the last section is somewhat perturbing. It's not only that the obvious first step in creating a business strategy has been eliminated, the even greater problem is that it leaves us with a bottomless pit of all the other less probable approaches to investigate. It is this kind of quandary that brings to an abrupt halt any progress towards creating a business. This problem is illustrated by the following dialogue:

I would like to set up my own business and make money for myself.

You'll need to have the right mental approach.

I have the right approach. I have spent quite a bit of time working in various business offices making money for other people. In fact I am quite experienced.

It doesn't matter how experienced you are at working in an office. People who work for someone else cannot conceptualize the world in the same way as people who work for themselves.

I don't see why.

If you work for someone else, employed to make money for them, there are always implied or specific goals.

I'm quite good at setting my own goals.

Ah! But when you work for yourself you are fully in control of your own life. This means quite literally that you can do absolutely anything you like.

How is that a problem?

It is very hard for people who don't have this problem to realize what a problem it is. The brain cannot cope with over-choice and simply refuses to perform rationally when there are too many options available. Just think, if you could do anything, have unlimited choice, be able to choose from amongst an infinite number of possibilities, what would you choose to do?

But I am perfectly capable of deciding what to do and what not to do and also working out what I want and what I do not want.

Then why not just go out and start your own business?

This dialogue encapsulates the crux of the problem most people have in trying to choose an appropriate niche in the world of e-business. There is so much choice, there are so many possible ways to set up in business. How do you choose between the vast number of possibilities and how do you allow for the fact that there are many other possibilities that might be ideal for you but of which you are completely unaware?

> YOU LEAVE THE PROBLEM TO SOLVE ITSELF: THROUGH RANDOM EVENTS AND LUCK

Game theory suggests you don't try to solve this problem. You leave the problem to solve itself: through random events and luck. However, the kind of luck used in game theory is the luck you make for yourself by employing a suitable strategy. This can be explained with the aid of another dialogue:

How do you get into a money-making business?

It just happens.

You mean it's luck?

In a way it is, but luck is something that happens only in the present. To make money, you have to be concerned about what the future is going to bring and arrange things so that luck is on your side.

Can you influence luck?

Of course you can.

How do you do that?

Simply by creating favourable odds for something good to happen.

How do you go about doing that?

Well, you have to go out and about to find out what is going on in the world, meeting different people so that you are exposed to as much information, chances and situations as possible.

This improves your luck?

Of course it does. You are arranging the conditions to allow many opportunities to occur. From a sea of information, waves of opportunity appear.

How do you take advantage of these waves of opportunity?

Try to think of yourself as a surfer. Surfers have to rely on catching the big waves that occur erratically and unpredictably in a sea full of little waves. Surfers don't rely on luck to catch the right waves: they go to the right beaches and wait at the right places on those beaches where they figure it most probable that big waves are likely to occur. In this way, a surfer uses a strategy to make it more likely that he will be in just the right place at the right time.

I see, in the same way that a big wave turns up for a surfer, the right situation can come along for me if I get out and about to expose myself to the right sort of people and take part in suitable events and activities?

That's right, you just have to be ready to seize the opportunity when it comes along.

But you cannot be certain of succeeding when an opportunity comes along.

You are missing the point. Events are happening all the time – you don't have to rely on any particular opportunity. A surfer doesn't pack up and go home if he misses a wave, he simply waits for another to come along and tries that. You have to think of yourself as being like the surfer: when an opportunity comes along you can take it or leave it and if you take it and it does not work out you are not finished. You are still free to wait for another opportunity and take another chance; if necessary, you can wait for another and another and another until an opportunity turns into a profitable reality.

Is that what you mean by making your own luck?

Yes, because when a suitable opportunity does eventually come along and you do make money – perhaps after many failed efforts – someone is bound to tell you how lucky you were to have been in just the right place at just the right time.

This mental model describes a typical game theory approach to solving the kind of problem we have here in trying to find a suitable e-business niche (or a number of niches) – a blind approach that waits for something to come along. The trick is to be able to continuously monitor and observe all the unfolding events so that you can measure each of them against a set of heuristic rules. These rules will eliminate the unsuitable and highlight the suitable. This process can be used to recognize a number of different possible solutions.

It is not an intuitive approach. It doesn't seem sensible to embark upon a blind venture into e-business without any clear idea in your mind as to what business you would like to be in. But it is an inverse form of Twenty Questions, where you know what all the questions are and you measure all the objects you come across to see if they are a match for the questions. A suitably fuzzy set of questions will allow a range of solutions.

If business possibilities are found in this way, you can find several of them so that you are not dependent upon any particular one succeeding. This subtly changes the scenario of the man with six options in Chapter 3. He doesn't start with six business plans or ideas: he puts himself in a position to recognize six possibilities as they emerge out of the information environment he places himself in.

With a little thought, it becomes obvious that this is a better strategy because any predetermined idea is going to take some time to investigate. Plans have to be made; market research has to be carried out; suitable skill sets have to be acquired or hired. All this uses up time and resources, greatly limiting the number of opportunities that can be investigated. Using the technique of recognizing emerging ideas as they arise, much of this preparatory work will already have been done.

Game theory, then, is about using a suitable strategy to be in the right place at the right time and to have an appropriate set of rules to apply to be able to recognize the right kind of opportunities when they rise. This removes the problem of how to choose from an infinite number of possible alternatives.

BECOMING PART OF A SYSTEM

In Chapter 2 we came to the conclusion that the best type of business to become involved in is one where efficiency is creating wealth. This makes sure that we will be playing in a non-zero sum game where everybody involved can become a winner.

At first thoughts, this seems at odds with the conclusions we've just reached. Surely, to create a situation that is going to provide increased efficiency we would need pre-planning? But this is a very Industrial Age attitude and not applicable in e-commerce. In a continuously changing unpredictable environment such as the internet, planning isn't possible and that includes planning for increased efficiency. However, this doesn't preclude waiting around for an opportunity to increase efficiency presenting itself.

The more practical game theory approach is to look at the world of e-business and see it as a self-organizing, dynamic system that you have to fit into rather than view it as a static environment where you have to create some new invention or initiative. A self-organizing system creates voids and needs as it writhes this way and that in chaotic attempts to reach states of equilibrium. It is the ability to slip into

these openings as and when they arise that is the key to establishing a successful e-business niche.

The key to seeing how this helps to recognize business opportunities when they come along is in understanding that the elusive state of equilibrium – which a dynamic complex system is always searching for – is the state of minimum energy expenditure. In other words, a fundamental characteristic of all such systems (and this includes the internet environment) is that they tend towards a state of maximum efficiency.

The trick, then, is not to try to get the system to do something, but to do something the system forces you to do. You go with the waves rather than be like King Canute and try to control them. (In fact, King Canute didn't try to control the waves; he used this as a demonstration that no mortal, even a king, can control natural forces.)

Realizing that the game is about becoming part of a dynamic system puts yet another different perspective on the conclusions reached in Chapter 3. There, it was easy to visualize eliminating different possible business ideas to arrive at a short list to concentrate upon. It was quite easy to see how working away at several different ideas at the same time would give an opportunity for one of them to emerge as a clear favourite to become the one to concentrate all resources upon. But what do we do when we start thinking in terms of system instabilities rather than ideas?

If we are contemplating a dynamic, self-organizing system, which is constantly undergoing chaotic change, we will have to work with enigmatic and intangible entities rather than concrete business ideas (those that might seem to have stability and substance). How do we even recognize a system instability, let alone arrive at a short list of them? How can we judge the relative merits of instabilities in a dynamic system to see which of them is emerging as the best opportunity? Clearly, working in an e-business environment will need quite a different mindset from that used in the conventional world of bricks and mortar.

the big picture

To understand and appreciate the kind of instabilities that need to be recognized, we need to look at the big picture, beginning with an idea of the size of the internet and the web. Several websites have been set up to record current statistics, but, for our purposes here, there are two websites in particular that between them give some idea of the size, scope and complexity of the e-business environment.

The first of these sites was set up for The Censorware Project (http://censorware.org/web_size/). Michael Sims' essay on this site lucidly explains the impossibility of the task faced by any organization trying to censure the web's content. He points out that a scientific article in 1997 had estimated the size of the web as being somewhere around 320 million pages. By February 1999, he notes, the well-respected magazine *Nature* had estimated the size of the web as being 800 million pages, with 15 trillion bytes of textual information together with 180 million images using a further 3 trillion bytes of web space. These figures covered only the publicly available websites that were readily available through search engines. It did not include the vast amounts of data available within intranets and other private internet domains.

Sims then displays within the body of the essay a continuously updating number of statistics that show the current estimate of the size of the web, which, on 9 February 2000, were as follows:

1,610,000,000 pages;
30,200,000,000,000 bytes of text;
363,000,000 images; and
6,050,000,000,000 bytes of image data.

In just the last 24 hours, the web has added:

3,280,000 new pages;
61,400,000,000 new bytes of text;
737,000 new images; and
12,300,000,000 new bytes of image data.

In his essay, Sims points out the rapid expansion of the web revealed by these figures. By some estimates, he tells us, the web is doubling in size every year (it might be an interesting exercise for the reader to visit this site at the time of reading to see how much it has changed since 9 February 2000).

Despite the claims of some web search engines to be able to satisfactorily cover the web, Sims explains the practical impossibility of such a task. He quotes the reputable web search engine company Alexa's assessment that the average life of a web page is only 44 days. From this he deduces that every day 36,700,000 pages and 8,250,000 images are changed. Just looking at these would require downloading nearly a trillion bytes a day and that's if you could find the ones that have changed.

Even the most efficient and powerful of search engines cover only around 20 per cent of web pages and their ability to keep up with page changes is perfunctory to say the least. It is into this environment that a business or a personal website is placed.

The exact figures are irrelevant; it is the sheer scale of the web that is remarkable. The size is unimaginable, yet, despite this, many people treat their websites as advertising billboards or even more naively as broadcasting stations.

Common sense tells us that any website put into this environment cannot rely on any kind of casual browsing. Any visitors to a site will have to be specifically routed there by one means or another. With such a vast number of pages competing with each other for eyeballs, those who succeed will need an exceptional strategy and this must involve specifically communicating with visitors before their visits.

The second of the websites I'm using to provide a snapshot of the big picture is that of Nua Ltd (http://www.nua.ie/surveys/ how_many_online/ index.html). Nua Ltd was officially formed in September 1995 by three people, Niall O'Sullivan, Antóin Ó Lachtnáin and Gerry McGovern. Together with its sister company, Local Ireland – an Irish portal for everything Irish, Nua employs (as at February 2000) upwards of 100 people. In 1999, *Fortune* magazine rated Nua among the top ten internet strategy companies in the world, while in the same year, Nua founder and CEO, Gerry McGovern, released a major book on the internet entitled *The Caring Economy*. Nua gained worldwide prominence though sending out a regular newsletter – in February 2000, going to 200,000 subscribers – which summarized various important trends and statistics relating to the evolving internet and web.

In February 2000, Nua put these statistics of the number of internet users on its website:

World Total **275.54 million**
Africa **2.46 million**
Asia/Pacific **54.90 million**
Europe **71.99 million**
Middle East **1.29 million**
Canada & USA **136.06 million**
South America **8.79 million**

Whether these figures are accurate or not (and they are likely to be quite different by the time you read this book) is not a critical issue. What they do, though, is give a rough idea of the order of magnitude of the number of people who are accessing the web.

With statistics like these, it is very tempting just to skip over them and not bother to wait for the significance to sink in. After all, ever since early school days we've been exposed to population counts of one type or another and they never seem to make any significant difference to our lives. This time it is different, though: because you can instantly be in direct contact with all of these people, at any time. The people in this particular population are as intimately connected to you and each other as if you were all next-door neighbours.

It is hard to imagine having a house next door where you can see and talk to several hundred million people, but this is one of the stark realities of the internet, which is why the full potential hasn't even begun to be realized.

At first thoughts, you might scoff at this simile because you cannot see the other hundreds of millions of people on the internet. Surely, it would seem, this situation is not very different from the situation we have already with the telephone. The telephone has been universally in existence for many decades and you might think the internet provides little improvement on this: it is still the same kind of mass connectivity via a telephone connection.

But it is different: very different. People cannot congregate into groups by means of the telephone, they cannot easily form special interest forums or bounce ideas around within a peer group on the telephone in the same way that they can in internet discussion forums. The telephone doesn't make it possible to instantly obtain a wide variety of feedback on ideas, or provide a mass concentration of experts always on hand to help you with your problem solving. This is the difference and the power of the internet. The internet gives everyone immediate access to an unlimited number of useful people.

The overwhelming advantage of the internet over the telephone is that you can so easily join groups and make friends with strangers. You can join in a group discussion or listen anonymously in the background. You can ask questions and test your own knowledge by answering the questions of others. In this way the internet becomes a place where you have a chance to meet like minds and together join forces to help each other to learn and progress.

This is not just some Utopian dream of mutual altruism; this is actually

66 THE OVERWHELMING ADVANTAGE OF THE INTERNET IS THAT YOU CAN SO EASILY JOIN GROUPS AND MAKE FRIENDS WITH STRANGERS 99

happening now – and in a massive way. The people who are in these communication groups and forums are enjoying a tremendous advantage over those who aren't – and it is very hard for those who are not connected to the internet to realize this.

islands in a sea of randomness

The biggest handicap of the telephone as a communication medium is the lack of a visual element. Voice tones and speech mannerisms add extra dimensions to a discussion, but a wealth of visual communication aids are not available. Facial expressions, eye contact, posture, physical appearance and clothes all provide important clues that add or subtract weight to or from what a person says. These are not evident during a telephone conversation.

The internet appears to be an even less reliable medium for establishing credibility than the telephone. Not only are communicators invisible to each other, they cannot even hear each other to be able to gain from auditory clues. This is readily apparent when communication is by way of internet chat groups (where people communicate with each other in real time). Such chat groups are based around a common server that e-mails all messages, as they are received, to everyone who is currently logged on to a server.

Such real-time chat groups are often frequented by teenagers who can say lots of rude and insulting things to each other using fictitious names. In these chat forums, people can pretend to be whomever they like and it isn't uncommon for men to assume the identities of women and vice versa. Chat is also used on adult sites to provide viewers with a sense of being there without any real identities being exposed. More sophisticated versions of real-time chat environments allow participators to adopt visual images (known as avatars) and let these images interact with each other – sometimes even in three-dimensional environments.

Although these real-time chat environments can be quite fun and often form the basis of serious role-playing adventure and fantasy games, they have very little application in e-business. What serious application there is, is limited mainly to providing novelty forms of customer service so that customers feel they are communicating with a real person rather than a robotic machine.

On the face of it, this inability for people to be able to establish credibility using e-mail communications would seem to be a fatal flaw for e-business e-mail communication purposes. In any form of business, reliability, truth and credibility are essential requisites. However, for serious business purposes, real-time e-mail chat isn't the only option, as e-mails can also be sent to a group of people without them needing to be online. This works by means of the server having a list of subscribers: a copy of any e-mail coming in from any of the subscribers is sent to everyone on the list.

In this way, a form of group interaction can be arranged that has no parallel outside of the environment of the internet. People can take their time over what they say to others in a group. There is no obligation to make immediate responses. Time can be taken over reading e-mails before answering them, allowing more thought to go into the understanding and interpretation. One subscriber can start up a topic and others join in the discussion. A subscriber can ask a question and that question will go out to all subscribers for them to respond if they know the answer.

Such e-mail discussion forums, known as listserves, can become stable centres of interaction with subscribers forming personal and group bonds just as they might in any group in the world of bricks and mortar. They can be of any size from a handful of people to several thousands and become a stable feature of the internet environment. Over periods of months and even years, regular subscribers to these listserves can become respected personalities and earn the respect and trust of other subscribers just as people might within long-standing stable groups in the real world.

Upon realizing the existence of these e-mail discussion forums – and there are tens of thousands of them covering a multitude of different subjects, topics and themes – the big picture of the internet takes on a new form. It is not a vast mass of randomly interacting individuals. There are patterns there, patterns not too dissimilar to the patterns of weather that might be observed looking down on earth from a spaceship. These patterns are patterns of people, assembling into groups for specific communication purposes. They may wax and wane like areas of high and low pressure in weather systems, but they are always present. They are islands of stability in what would on first impressions seem to be a featureless unorganized environment.

It is these e-mail discussion forums, the islands of stability, through which the immense power and potential of the internet can be realized. Anyone can go to these islands to make friends, find business partners, get information, help and knowledge. These can provide the workshops in which to create and refine ideas. Within these enigmatic communities, gaps in the fabric of the self-organizing process of the internet can be recognized and identified.

We started off this chapter by becoming aware of the uselessness of a single great idea or a predetermined business plan. It seemed impossible that any rational approach could be used to embark on any kind of e-business venture. But these islands of stability offer a solution; by frequenting these e-mail discussion forums, paying attention to what is going on, joining in the discussion and asking questions, it will be like the surfer going to the right kind of beach, arranging to be at the right place to wait for suitably large waves to appear.

E-business solutions are not planned off-line, but manifest online as a dynamic consequence of human interaction and communication. It is being in these listserves, paying attention to what is going on and being able to spot opportunities to increase efficiency, that replaces the concept of the great business idea in the world of e-commerce.

the new paradigm shift

We are now in a position to update the Chapter 3 model of the businessman with his alternative options. It is not practical for his options to be in the form of plans or predetermined business ideas, but it is practical if his options are defined in terms of emergent opportunities to create efficiencies that have been recognized by him through his interaction with people on the internet.

We can now think of this businessman not as some brilliant thinker and planner, but as a person who spends much of his time within internet discussion forums looking for opportunities to fill gaps in the emerging system. These act as extensions of reasoning and thinking processes. Everyone has a limited knowledge, but through the internet discussion forums they can gain access to knowledge that is far beyond their own ability to learn and understand. In this way internet discussion forums can act as knowledge bases and tools for anyone who wants to become successful in e-business environments.

When an emergent situation is identified, it will most likely require a particular mix of resources, knowledge and skills to be able to take advantage of any opportunity offered. In all probability, this would require resources, knowledge and skills beyond any single person's allocation or capability. Almost certainly then, the identifier of an e-business opportunity would need to work with others, where between them they have a full complement of appropriate resources, knowledge and skills. This will necessitate skilful communication with others.

This changes the nature of the game. Being successful in e-business is not a question of gaining greater knowledge and understanding, but is about being able to communicate successfully with people. How then do we communicate successfully with people? This is not a problem that can be satisfactorily handled through rational thinking – it is a problem best handled through the framework of game theory.

5

THE PROBLEM OF KNOWLEDGE GAPS

coping with technology The scariest thing for most people contemplating setting up an e-business is the vast amount of technology involved. Creating an e-business involves putting the right technical elements in place and getting them to function properly. How can this be done if most of the elements are a complete mystery and are far too complex to understand or to see how they fit together?

So, how much technology is involved? Is it reasonable to expect a CEO or an entrepreneur to have sufficient grasp of all the technical details involved in the creation of an e-business? What about professional solution providers or management project leaders? Should they be able to cope with all the technical issues involved in deciding and putting together a complete e-commerce package?

On a website I came across (http://dsite.net/webdevskills/) a New York student – Dora Chapman, who is contemplating making a career of web development – had sensibly tried to make an assessment of all the areas she would need to cover to become suitably proficient. By searching through all the job opportunity websites, she had made a list of most of the chief educational or experience requirements listed for website design-related positions. Her aggregate list came to over 200 speciality areas of knowledge, any of which would need six months to two years of study and experience to become truly proficient.

Obviously, no mortal could be truly proficient in anything but a fraction of the specialities included in Dora Chapman's list. The best that could be hoped for is that a web master had sufficient awareness of the various areas of knowledge and sufficient understanding to be able to bring in specialists when and where they are needed. However, even that assumes that somebody is sufficiently knowledgeable to be able to know how, when and where to apply the appropriate technology; this would necessitate the competent web master needing also to be skilled and knowledgeable in business and marketing.

This creates the central problem for any e-business. It is just impossible for any single person to know all there is to know. This glaringly self-evident fact will necessitate that the successful creation of any e-business system will have to depend upon the efficient interaction and cooperation of a number of quite different types of people.

> **THE SUCCESSFUL CREATION OF ANY E-BUSINESS SYSTEM WILL HAVE TO DEPEND UPON THE EFFICIENT INTERACTION AND COOPERATION OF A NUMBER OF QUITE DIFFERENT TYPES OF PEOPLE**

This is more than just stating the obvious; it presents a problem unique to the Information Age. In the old economies of the twentieth century, technological aspects of a solution could be specified and partitioned off into neat little areas that could be allocated to appropriate specialists to deal with the problems in relative isolation. This is not possible in the fast-moving world of digital communications. Any e-business strategy would need to be intimately linked with all ongoing changes in competition and many different kinds of evolving technologies.

This is not a problem only for the business strategists; the experts and specialists themselves will have a similar problem to deal with within their own niches. They will each have to be intelligently aware of the changing competitive strategies of e-business to ensure that they are keeping up with the most appropriate technology. It is as easy for a specialist or technologist to waste precious time and resources pursuing a dead-end technology as it is for an entrepreneur to lose money and time on an unsuccessful venture.

The seemingly obvious solution is for business people and technologists to work closely together to develop e-business solutions and strategies between them. But this is easier stated than put into practice because it involves culture clashes that are not easily resolved.

What is happening in many instances is that this need to combine business acumen with technology is producing hopelessly inefficient ad hoc arrangements where costs and dependencies are killing many e-business ventures in the water. Major companies that are trying hard to break into the e-business field are often held to ransom by overpaid web masters who have created a screen of mystery over their activities in order to build impregnable power bases within the organizations.

It is not just the fault of the web masters. In their hectic scramble to get into e-business as fast as possible, companies have been seizing the 'bright young things' with knowledge of servers and networks and building businesses around them. It is not just the web masters who have created their own ivory towers – the companies usually build ones for them. What web master wouldn't want to remain in this protected position where they are treated with respect and awe?

The web masters are not fools. They are quite aware of their own limitations and in most cases are fully aware that they haven't complete knowledge. However, few will admit this. They will do everything within their power to ensure that their Achilles' heels are not exposed and will confine the technical scope of the company's activities to within their own limited range of knowledge, throwing up smoke screens all around to avoid being rumbled.

NOTE there is an excellent article by Michael Schrage on this subject of inappropriate dependency on technologists (ISSN 0015-8259, Vol. 141, No. 2, page 154, On The Job- CLMN- Brave New Work). It was put onto the web by Northern Light Technology Inc at:
http://library.northernlight. com/PN200001132400001 25.html?cb=13&sc=0#doc

A similar situation exists with the specialist. The world of the expert programmer is becoming like the world of professional sports where prima donna programmers are switching in and out of teams, offering their services to the highest bidder. The sad fact is that many of these programmers are competent only within a narrow area, and because their craft is regarded by non-specialists as something akin to the black arts they are accorded inappropriate respect which give many of them a heightened sense of their own abilities.

There is a well-known axiom of successful business strategy that says that if any person within an organization becomes indispensable, they should be sacked immediately. This very sensible philosophy seems to have been reversed in many instances, with some companies entering the field of e-business seeming to go out of their way to create such dependencies.

At a meeting I attended at the European headquarters of a major multi-media software house, a team of web design specialists were putting on a demonstration. They were only young men, hardly out of college, and they were demonstrating a front-end to a website. The graphics were beautiful, the design novel and ingenious; the only problem was that it was totally impractical and in effect gave every visitor to the site a complicated puzzle to solve in order to find out how to use the facilities that were on offer. The whole complex arrangement had apparently taken them three months to design, yet it did no more than a simple clickable list of options would have done – far more efficiently and effectively.

I thought no more of this until I was investigating the strategies of venture capital companies. Their latest fad (early 2000) was the concept of incubation. This is where the venture capitalist provides not only working capital but also management expertise and business premises. It seemed highly altruistic until I found several companies doing something similar and realized that there was more to this arrangement than immediately meets the eye. The venture capitalists were setting up these arrangements because they wanted to have a team of web design specialists in-house so that they could tap into their expertise to make judgements on venture capital decisions, the logic being that this expertise on hand could pay for itself by taking on outside contractual work.

It was with some surprise then that I discovered that the team of naive young web developers I'd seen at the multimedia company's headquarters had been selected for the incubator of a venture capital company. It made me wonder as to the quality of the investment decisions that would be coming out of that symbiotic arrangement. As far as e-business strategy was concerned it was very much the case of the blind leading the blind, even though it must have seemed to make economic sense to all concerned.

The fundamental difficulty in getting a match between business and technology is that each does not appreciate the world of the other. The non-technical business person holds the knowledge of the technical expert in too much awe and the technical expert is often so enamoured of their own importance that they feel they can make business decisions better than the experienced business people. This problem has a parallel in psychology studies.

BEING ABLE TO APPRECIATE INDIVIDUAL LIMITATIONS Incomplete knowledge is a factor that has to be specifically allowed for if any e-business strategy has any chance of being successful. However, it may be relatively easy to recognize and make allowance for limitations and knowledge gaps in others, but far more difficult for people to recognize and make allowances for their own. For this reason, it may be worth looking at some academic investigations that have been made into personal self-appraisal.

Such a study is outlined in an article on the web entitled 'Unskilled and Unaware of It: How Difficulties in Recognizing One's Own Incompetence Lead to Inflated Self-Assessments' (http://www.apa.org/journals/psp/psp7761121.html) by Justin Kruger and David Dunning from the Department of Psychology, Cornell University. This interesting document offers some clues as to why it might be difficult for us to be able to allow for our own deficiencies in game theory strategies.

Kruger and Dunning cite several papers that have found widespread evidence that people seem to be inaccurate in appraising themselves and their abilities in environments where they have little experience. Quoting Charles Darwin (1871), who over a century ago noted, 'ignorance more frequently begets confidence than does knowledge,' they point to several studies that have revealed what is called the 'above-average effect'. This is the tendency for most people to believe they are above average, when asked to give their opinion as to their own capability compared to the capability of their peers. People tend to think they have more leadership qualities than the average, are able to get along with people better than the average, be better business managers or shrewder judges than their peers. This of course is not logical because half of people must, by definition, be below average.

Studies seem to suggest that the tendency toward inflated self-appraisals is strongest amongst those who are the

> ❝ THE FUNDAMENTAL DIFFICULTY IN GETTING A MATCH BETWEEN BUSINESS AND TECHNOLOGY IS THAT EACH DOES NOT APPRECIATE THE WORLD OF THE OTHER ❞

least competent: novices overrate their abilities far more than experts. Also, in certain areas that involve logical reasoning, some individuals seemed not to have sufficient mental ability to be competent. Such individuals might then have a double whammy in as much as the ability needed to acquire competence is the same ability that is needed to judge their own competence against others – the observation summed up by the old adage 'where ignorance is bliss'.

While testing their hypotheses by setting up experiments with students, Kruger and Dunning made two other observations that have relevance to the effects of knowledge gaps in e-business. Firstly, the students who came out best in the tests had a tendency to underestimate their own abilities. They assumed that others had a similar degree of competence as themselves and therefore tended to rate themselves as modestly above this wrongly perceived average.

Secondly, it was found that where a lack of ability or knowledge was patently obvious – such as where competence involved a demonstrable competitive skill, or an obvious natural ability – there was no attempt for people to over-estimate their abilities. If anything, such people tended to underestimate their abilities when there were clear-cut reality restraints. This is perhaps why so many people don't try to grasp the basics of certain key technological subjects: because they think them beyond their ability to comprehend.

These may be the conclusions from arcane academic experiments with students, but, if mapped across to the world of e-business, they compound the problems associated with knowledge gaps because often many knowledge gaps are unrecognized or get distorted.

the resolution of a paradox

If we take the results of Kruger and Dunning's tests and observations at face value, they might go some way towards explaining some of the attitudes and behaviours in the present-day world of e-business. We do find experienced, middle-aged executives standing aside, or being pushed out of the way to make room for technical wizards who are novices in terms of business acumen. We do find the technical experts and specialists seeing themselves as streetwise and experienced business people.

Examples of overestimations of commercial prowess abound in most technical e-mail discussion forums, where young technicians, fresh out of college, dispense with fundamental principles of sound business practice to propound great ideas that, while having great appeal to their peers, are commercially ludicrous. How many websites have been created with lavish graphical interfaces that are a real inconvenience to use? How many websites drive visitors to distraction with a confusing array of flickering, animated banners that have no relevance to the purpose of the site's core business? How many websites have a vast complexity of unnecessary JavaScript programming that totally confuses and irritates the user?

It doesn't take much surfing around the web to see how much incompetence is in control. Yet, if you look at the successful sites, the ones that are actually performing well commercially, they are usually devoid of all gimmickry and artistic design. They seem to be thriving on technical naivety.

After reading this chapter, one of the reviewers at a table in the virtual café, developer and designer Bryan Rieger, wrote:

I found this chapter really had a lot of relevance in my own e-business/web experience over the past five years. This chapter is a MUST read for any businessman who is thinking of getting into e-business. Especially if they are not technically inclined themselves.

'In their hectic scramble to get into e-business as fast as possible, companies have been seizing the "bright young things" with knowledge of servers and networks and building businesses around them.' I couldn't agree more. Before going off on my own I worked for several companies who were led by individuals who had no knowledge of the industry they were getting involved in – they heard that it was where things were happening and they were looking to get rich quick.

They hired based on 'buzzwords' rather than credentials and would trust these 'bright young things' to build their digital empire – while they watched. Business decisions were also made with other business people – without ever consulting the technical staff. 'Sure we can build you a hyper-ghadzoontit-warble-blaster, we've built three already.' Then they go back to the staff that either say 'Sure – we can do it...' (and have no idea what they just agreed to) or say 'What the hell are you doing?.' The last comment usually results in mass-migration as the business owner decides to find 'skilled' people who know what they are doing. ;-)

'Young web professionals' aren't interested in hearing 'functional, simple and intuitive'. In my experience these individuals are only interested in making the 'phattest, most rad, mind blowing experience one could ever have...' I always try to explain that we're selling electrical equipment for our client, not LSD. What's cool and what's required are two very different things – and getting young developers to realize this is a major undertaking.

The other problem with running an e-business is trying to run it like any other company. With the demand for internet 'professionals' growing by the day – employees have 'the world at their fingertips'. As soon as an employee feels that they are not being listened to, appreciated or advancing fast enough they'll start surfing the 'monsterboard' on their lunch break. And chances are they'll have an interview by end of day.

This entire 'employment frenzy' is only made worse by educational institutions and the media hyping the growth in the industry and telling recent graduates that they should come out of a six-month program and be making 60K per year doing HTML and data entry.

This problem is compounded by the 'quick and dirty schools', the media and bosses putting inexperienced employees in an ivory tower. On one occasion, I came to work for a company that had been around 6 months – where the owner of the company made young man of 21 responsible for the strategy, development and design of several blue chip clients. I might add, he just recently graduated as a graphic designer and this was his first job. You can imagine what happened at client meetings when after six weeks of development time all he had to show them (and he thought this was good) was three screen shots mounted on an illustration board.

There are parallels in the world of bricks and mortar. In the early 1970s a hippy fashion market came into prominence in Kensington High Street, London, UK. It attracted a wide variety of artisans and designers who could set up small units to sell their creations. This market also attracted many Asian traders because it was at a time when the newly independent African countries were throwing out all the Asian business people (because they were running all the shops and businesses, it was assumed that this was through unfair monopolies rather than commercial skills).

At first, the immigrant Asian traders were scorned by the artists and designers because of their lack of taste and appreciation of currently trendy ideas of design and beauty. These Asian traders were constantly accused of bringing down the tone of the market and were harassed for not creating tasteful displays and giving attention to the aesthetic appearance of their units.

It wasn't long, though, before it began to dawn on the people trading in the market that these Asian traders, with their open-fronted units and clothes spread out to cover every part of the decor, were taking more money than the cutely designed units with tasteful, arty displays. One by one, the artistic fascias, the cleverly designed shop fronts and the stunning displays were abandoned in favour of the open and more practical but unsightly displays used by the experienced Asian traders.

This is the kind of problem that is hampering the commercial success of many e-businesses. While the designers and the technicians are in control, e-businesses are being designed and judged on the basis of peer group pressures. Eye candy, clever technical tricks and innovations are the criteria for judgement, while the business strategy and commercial results are conveniently ignored. The experienced, older business executives, who might immediately spot gross errors of design and strategy, are more often than not left out of the picture; their opinions are regarded as dated and irrelevant.

It is the realization that the marvels of the new technologies have to be tempered with the pragmatism of sound business principles that will be the key to commercial success in the Information Age, but to get these two disparate elements working together in harmony is going to need some seriously clever strategies.

jigsaw puzzling
It is easy to see how web masters, graphic designers, programmers and other technologists can be described as experts or specialists. They have a particular area of speciality knowledge

> " EYE CANDY, CLEVER TECHNICAL TRICKS AND INNOVATIONS ARE THE CRITERIA FOR JUDGEMENT, WHILST THE BUSINESS STRATEGY AND COMMERCIAL RESULTS ARE CONVENIENTLY IGNORED "

in which they can become particularly proficient. Such knowledge usually has a tangible form that can be seen or experienced; it can be described and formulated in books, magazines and on websites.

In sharp contrast, the expertise of the strategist, the skill of the street-wise, the acumen of the business person is far more nebulous. No game of strategy can ever be formularized or defined because, if it could be, it wouldn't be a game of strategy at all: it would be a problem solvable with algorithms.

Game strategists deal in mental models and abstract representations. They use heuristic rules to probe, search and prune a problem space. They extract the essence of previous experience and apply it to the present and future, generating potentially fruitful new conclusions.

More specifically, the game strategist is an expert at the art of deferral: the leaving of part of a solution until more evidence or information comes to light. In this way, solutions are constructed as loosely connected modules that start out as incomplete and indefinite structures. Initially connected by supposition and intelligent guesswork, these roughly tacked-together solutions are then put to the test to reveal the weaknesses.

Modules forming the basis of such structures are not pre-planned. Their inclusion is not anticipated. They arrive by chance and circumstance. The process can be likened to a strategy to solve a jigsaw puzzle. This is not solved by means of an algorithmic plan but by a series of associations. The puzzle is not solved by starting at one edge and building across the puzzle; it is best solved by identifying certain characteristics and building little islands of matching pieces. As the islands grow, they start to meld together into a main picture and it then becomes easier to identify the missing pieces to fill in the gaps.

The mental trick for the e-business strategist is to see the development of an e-business as something similar to putting together the pieces of a jigsaw puzzle. But the pieces are not matching pieces of wood or cardboard: they are ideas, information and people. Think of these ideas, information and people as being scattered around the internet and the game is to find the matching pieces and put them all together to create a sensible-looking picture.

To find the pieces to create one particular puzzle would be difficult. This is the equivalent of trying to start an e-business based upon a set plan or a single great idea. A far better strategy is to imagine that there is not a single puzzle, but many puzzles, where the pieces are all mixed together in many giant heaps. A search for matching pieces will then not be restricted to finding a single solution, but would allow any of many possible solutions to emerge.

Now, imagine these heaps of puzzle pieces being the object of a game, with several players each trying to be the first to complete one of the puzzles. This will be a fair representation of the kind of game that is played in the world of e-business. The pieces are ideas, information and people, the heaps, where they are to be found and matched together, are listserves.

It is in viewing the game of e-business in this light that a suitable strategy can be visualized. This allows us to now see the strategy of the businessman, portrayed in the dialogue of Chapter 3, as a person building little islands of matching parts, constantly growing them from components derived through participating in listserves.

His options are not in the form of ideas or plans, they are in the form of partly assembled puzzles consisting of different mixes of matching ideas, information and people. Each option is developed piece by piece through chance and opportunity until one of the options starts to form a complete and clear picture.

The strategy then is not to look for the pieces of a single particular puzzle, but to keep an open mind so that one of many possible solutions can emerge. This makes full sense if you understand that many puzzles have missing pieces and to go for just a single puzzle could see you running into a dead end where the puzzle has no practical solution.

6

UNDERSTANDING AND COPING WITH KNOWLEDGE GAPS

about this chapter

This chapter reads something like an arcane college textbook. No apologies. Although it appears to be explaining about learning, in reality it is considering something far more relevant to the world of e-business: the inability to learn all that needs to be known.

Whatever niche is filled in the world of e-business there will be so much essential knowledge needed that it will be impossible to learn it all. Even if anyone tried, it would probably be out of date by the time they came to put it to use.

This is not a reason for despair or apathy, it just calls for a different attitude towards learning and acquiring knowledge. The people who will succeed are not going to be those who try to learn everything – but those who realize they (and others) have knowledge gaps and figure out a strategy to get around the problem.

> A CONNECTION TO THE INTERNET [...] IS A ROUTE INTO A COMPLETELY DIFFERENT KIND OF ENVIRONMENT

The need for a few fundamentals

A connection to the internet is more than just a connection to another source of information, it is a route into a completely different kind of environment where the rules and conventions of the world of bricks and mortar no longer apply. To understand and be able to make the most of this new world requires a type of thinking that is often at odds not only with conventional business practices, but also with emotions and common sense.

This will be particularly true in two important areas: obtaining knowledge and facilitating collaboration, where the required paradigm shifts are exceptionally difficult to make because they are counter-intuitive.

In this chapter we shall start to explore some of the unique opportunities offered by internet discussion forums (listserves). There is no historical precedent for this phenomenon, so, to escape from the confining concepts of conventional communication techniques and strategies, let's begin with a few fundamentals. If the reader is impatient with theoretical modelling, please bear with this for a while, as it may help to avoid later misunderstandings.

paradigm shifts

A paradigm shift is an elusive concept. Look at the box-like shape in Figure 6.1. Keep staring at it until the angle you are viewing it from suddenly changes. One moment you are looking down on to this shape and at another moment you are looking up at it. Keep looking, and for no apparent reason the angle of viewing will change again. This random flipping between the two views will happen continuously all the time you are looking at the figure and the change from one view to the other will be very difficult to control consciously.

Any inputs from the body's sensors (i.e. the eyes) cause the brain to go into some form of chaotic activity while the neural mechanisms try to match the inputs with some correspondence in memory. Almost instantaneously, the neural activity stabilizes around something that makes sense: in this case a box-like shape. In this example, the brain has two equally probable interpretations. Not having any clues as to which is the more accurate perspective, the brain's activity will more randomly from one to another. There is no in-between state; the brain flips from one perspective to another.

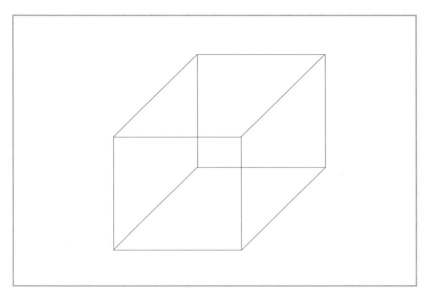

FIG 6.1 Visual example of a paradigm shift

In his book *Dynamic Patterns: The Self Organization of Brain and Behavior (Complex Adaptive Systems)* (Reprint edition, March 1997, Bradford Books, ISBN 0262611317), J. A. Scott Kelso describes the mathematics of how these effects arise through islands of stability forming in the chaotic fluctuations of brain cell activity. He explains how this mathematically based activity of brain cells provides an extremely efficient method for the brain to transfer from one complex stem of brain activity to another. One of many examples he provides is the brain activity transitions a horse will have to go through to change its speed of locomotion. It doesn't go through a gradual change from walking to trotting to galloping. It changes in distinct jumps from walking to trotting and then to galloping, corresponding to three quite different patterns of brain cell activity. He shows by means of graphs that these changes from one kind of movement to another occur by temporarily destabilizing the system of brain activity to allow it to find a new stability which brings into play a completely different set of muscle-controlling neurons.

The brain can be trained to create these islands of stability to allow specific patterns of physical activity to be called upon without having to think about the details of the complexity. This is quite evident in observing how babies learn to coordinate movement: learning to focus their eyes and grasp objects, learning to crawl and then to walk. In this way, people are able to coordinate their movements unconsciously: instantaneously assigning groups of physical and mental activity whenever there is a need, without being slowed down by conscious decision making.

Probably, the best remembered example of this process in operation is the experience of learning to ride a bicycle. One moment it seems impossible to balance and ride a bicycle and the next finding yourself cycling along and wondering to yourself how you ever thought it could be difficult to learn. Learning to swim and learning to drive a car are similar experiences. Once the appropriate patterns of neural activity are established, they become permanently fixed as stable unconscious patterns of behaviour to which the brain's chaotic activity can revert whenever the need arises.

Jumping between different stable states of neural activity can be triggered by external events. You can think of a jockey's whip as being a trigger that momentarily destabilizes the pattern of a horse's brain activity, prompting the activity to settle down into a different steady state that evokes a higher speed of movement. This will not happen for any touch of the whip, but will occur only when the tap of the whip exceeds a certain severity.

Such an efficient method of changing the way in which brain activity instantly reconfigures in response to external stimuli is a product of evolution. We have evolved similar mechanisms that allow our brains to reconfigure our activities instantaneously when a potentially hazardous signal is received from the environment. The sudden appearance of a lion at close quarters would rapidly transform us from being in a relaxed, contemplative mood to a state of hypertension where all systems are primed to take immediate evasive action.

The important considerations here are, first, that there is no rational or conscious transition: we automatically transform from one state to another. Secondly, this change will happen only if the trigger exceeds a certain threshold (i.e. the same reaction would not occur if the lion were spotted a mile away).

Something similar happens with our thinking processes. We don't progress from one way of looking at things to another as a gradual process. It is a sudden jump, from one conceptual model to another, with no conscious transition between the two. When such transitions occur for the first time, they are often called eureka moments: sudden realizations, sudden insights – non-logical jumps in thought that bring about a different understanding.

This experience is most often encountered with paradoxes, when seemingly contradictory statements suddenly make sense when the paradox is resolved. Much humour is based upon stories giving one impression and then the punch line creating a paradigm shift that gives a whole new interpretation to whatever has been said before.

If new thoughts, new ideas and influences could easily change the steady state of the mental models we use for contemplating and analysing the world around us, we would not have a very stable system of judgement and decision making. To provide stability, it seems that our brains have evolved to be able to ignore or reject most of the intelligence we receive from the outside world: responding only when information causes an overwhelming need for a change in thinking.

This same mechanism that gives us mental stability also prevents us from readily accepting new ideas: it causes us to reject and fight against any information that challenges our established mental models. Unfortunately, this instinctive trait that has served our species so well in past generations is proving a handicap in our attempts to come to grips with the new realities of the digital communication age. It makes it hard for us to make the necessary mental adjustments that are needed to cope with the new environment of mass connectivity.

Understanding that there is such a barrier in place, handicapping our efforts to understand new and unfamiliar situations, will help us to over-come them. This we can do by keeping an open mind and being ready to consider ideas that seem to contradict our instinctive judgements or conflict with common sense.

learning in the environment of e-business Many of the

reviewers reading the last chapter made comments on the dilemma the student had found herself in – when she realized that she was faced with an impossibly large range of knowledge requirements applicable to her intended career as a web master. Several pointed out that web masters could and did perform quite satisfactorily with only a subset of this list. However, this was missing the point; the student would have to make some kind of decision as to what subjects she was going to learn and there were no obvious right choices.

One of the readers, Steve Howard, had been saved from this educational choice problem by being educated in computer technology before the multimedia and information technologies had taken off. His education hadn't been confused by the myriad of different niches that have sprung up to overwhelm the subject area. His education had been limited to only the fundamental principles that provide the foundations of computer technology. He'd had a 15-year gap between learning these basics and plunging into the deep end of this technological revolution just as it exploded into a maelstrom of different directions. But his fundamental knowledge stood him in good stead to tackle any niche speciality that came his way. Here is part of Steve Howard's post commenting on the student's situation:

There is every likelihood that any tools selected for study today will be obsolete in four years' time. I would suggest that aiming for an education that gives a sound foundation to the market niche you plan to specialize in would be a better strategy. With a little forethought, a course that covers enough of the niche with sufficient spread across the basics of related technologies would, IMHO, produce a more employable graduate.

‹snip›

Dora's study plan concentrated almost totally on modern 'popular' tools, with no consideration whatsoever for 'first principles'. Most modern tools, especially the 'visual' tools, seem to try hard to hide the inner workings of the software and hardware from the user and the developer. I think that this creates developers who have a limited understanding of what is happening in their code. A limited understanding equates to a stunted ability perhaps?

I'm not suggesting all young programmers are inept – most of them are probably more skilled than I am – but what I am suggesting is that someone trying to take Dora's course plan seriously might well make themselves inept, by trying too hard to get a grasp on high-level tools without spending enough time on low-level understanding. Lay good enough foundations, and you can build anything on top...

Steve Howard nicely pinpoints the solution to Dora's problem. She shouldn't decide to go for any of the narrow speciality areas because for one thing she would be unlikely to get sufficient depth in any of them for the learning to make her professionally proficient; besides which, the limited choices she would have to make would stunt her development (much the same as a body builder might stunt his body if he relied upon just a single exercise).

The sensible advice for Dora must be for her to get a fundamental education that avoided all the speciality areas but would put her in a good position to learn any speciality after she had finished college. This begs the question, 'How is Dora going to learn the appropriate speciality skills that will enable her to apply for a well-paid job after she has completed her university education?'

Here is where a paradigm shift is needed, to be able to take a fresh look at education to see how best to acquire knowledge in a field where there is an impossibly large range of choice and too much to learn. For this we need to look at some of the more forward-looking learning strategies that are being proposed by some of the educators who are beginning to get to grips with this problem.

Rather than trying to explore the whole field of education in a search for ideal solutions, I've chosen a single educator, who seems to have come up with just the right answer at just the right time: Dr Theodore (Ted) Panitz, professor of mathematics at Cape Cod Community College, W.

Barnstable, MA, USA. Dr Panitz explains his philosophy on education in detail on his website at http://www.capecod.net/~tpanitz/tedspage, but here I'll just give a brief outline, sufficient for the purposes of this book.

His starting premise is a proposition put by John Dewey over 80 years ago: 'Education is not an affair of "telling" and being told, but an active and constructive process.' In explaining that the acquisition of knowledge is more than simply the transference of information from one head to another, Dr Panitz makes a critically important distinction between cooperative and collaborative learning. He defines cooperation and collaboration as follows:

Cooperation is a structure of interaction designed to facilitate the accomplishment of a specific end product or goal through people working together in groups.

Collaboration is a philosophy of interaction and personal lifestyle where individuals are responsible for their actions, including learning to respect the abilities and contributions of their peers.

At first sight, these definitions would seem to be saying much the same thing, or, at most, they involve a considerable amount of overlap. Dr Panitz's insight shows them to describe two totally different mindsets. Just as the box-like shape in Figure 6.1 can exist in two perspectives, there is a paradigm shift involved here where it is easy for the conscious mind to get stuck in one of them and to be totally oblivious of the other.

The old paradigm for teaching and learning was that the knowledgeable should teach the unknowledgeable: those with knowledge should pass this knowledge on to receptive students who accept and absorb the knowledge in a passive way. More modern educators are dropping this approach in deference to much research that has shown knowledge isn't learned parrot fashion, but involves individual processing by the students – who construct their own internal ordering of any knowledge or information they receive.

This newer wisdom says that knowledge learned by students isn't simply put into some kind of neural database to be withdrawn on demand, but is used to build cognitive structures that can apply the knowledge in novel situations. In this way, knowledge is thought of as building blocks that not only create new cognitive structures but also modify and extend existing ones.

In this paradigm, the teaching is not simply a matter of transferring information but assisting students in the dynamic process of creating internal mental models. As each student will have individual abilities, capabilities, brain structures and prior knowledge, no two individual cognitive structures will be identical, so no two students can make identical use of any information or knowledge they receive.

Given that learning is very much an individual process, it is incumbent upon each individual student to test out their own mental structures to ensure that the mental models they are building for themselves are viable and will lead to rational predictions and decision making. For this purpose, modern educators will encourage students to interact and communicate with each other, so that they can use each other to test, modify or reinforce the cognitive structures they are building during the learning process.

With the teacher also becoming involved in this interaction the knowledge of the teacher will gradually propagate throughout the group, in some cases by direct transference of knowledge and information, but also indirectly as students learn from each other.

This paradigm, then, sees learning as a combination of a personal and social activity where teachers have to be able to build positive relationships with students and create the conditions within which students can establish caring and committed relationships with each other.

cooperative learning environments

Based upon the understanding that learning is a dynamic process, many educators create cooperative, team-based organizational structures within which they can transfer their knowledge to students. The emphasis is on social inter-action, group structure and methods by which group members combine and unite in the processes of creation, analysis and application. Fundamental to this approach is that there should be group managers or team leaders, with the teacher instigating and directing the activities.

Cooperative encouragement is based upon interpersonal factors and a joint aspiration to achieve a significant goal. It is assumed that cooperative efforts are powered by motivations to receive recognition or rewards. Focus is on relational concepts, dealing with what happens among individuals rather than what happens within them. The approach concentrates upon the organizing of social interaction and relationships, usually involving prescribed behaviour at each step. Significantly, the concept of the structure is divorced from the actual activity, such that the same organizational structures can be applied to any task.

These organizational structures are then put into practice, by assigning groups of students to work as teams on various projects, allowing them to practise and refine their team-working skills. In this way, team member strengths can be fully utilized and weaknesses compensated for, as team members learn to complement each other's skills and knowledge to create a combined unit that can achieve much more than the sum of its parts.

Cooperative learning methods concentrate on social skills; developing self-esteem, responsibility and respect for others. It is concerned with social status and the management of conflict and the division of tasks into various roles. Leadership and management are defined and formalized.

limitations of the cooperative learning environment

Dr Panitz refers to the writings of Ken Bruffee in observing that cooperative learning is most appropriate when dealing with foundation knowledge: defined as the fundamental areas of knowledge that all agree upon. With cooperative learning, people are encouraged to come together in groups, where they interact with each other in order to accomplish a specific common goal or develop an end product.

But Dr Panitz also draws attention to Ken Bruffee's concern with non-foundational knowledge. This is the knowledge that deals with uncertain knowledge and questions which have dubious or ambiguous answers. This knowledge does not come from agreed and accepted principles but through reasoning and judgement.

In teaching non-foundational knowledge, it is necessary for students to be taught how to question and doubt facts and information. Even the teacher's authority, knowledge and judgement mustn't be taken for granted. This removes the teacher from the centre of the educational process and sees him as just another participant in a process of enquiry: as much of a student as the students themselves.

Removing the authority, the leader or centre of focus of a group completely changes the nature of the group itself. The rules which define the all-important structure of a cooperative learning environment no longer apply. Who is to be the determinant of what is right and what is wrong? Who should respect whom? Whose opinion is most valid in a situation where opinions differ? What common ground can the group members focus on to achieve group adhesion?

Clearly, the uncertainties and ambiguities, the lack of a central authority, the dearth of fundamental agreed principles will be devastating within a structured cooperative environment. This is the problem that Dr Panitz sees being tackled more appropriately using a strategy of collaboration rather than cooperation.

collaborative learning
To deal with non-foundational knowledge – where there are no certainties of fact or opinion – there cannot be a leader or central authority, so there has to be a transition from a closely controlled, teacher-centred system to a student-centred system, where the teacher and students share authority and control of learning.

This collaborative learning shifts the responsibility for learning away from the teacher and on to the student. The student is seen as being responsible for the results of his or her own learning, knowledge construction and organization. Learning is seen as a process of interdependence where solutions and answers are possible only through accessing the opinions and knowledge of others.

Students are seen as each having a boundary of individual knowledge and opinion. They have to negotiate at that boundary with others, who also have boundaries. Groups are not formed through conventions, rules and protocols, but by a melding of these boundaries to produce a common boundary that brings people into association.

In this way, each student draws from a distributed pool of knowledge, taking from it their own needs to build their individual cognitive models that they can use to make their own unique judgements and decisions. There is no compulsion for these models to be identical or even similar; there is simply the restraint that they must be compatible or complementary with others in the group.

The role of the teacher in this situation is simply to provide the right atmosphere and ambience for students to interact in a way where information, ideas, knowledge and opinions are freely exchanged and the students are able to test out their cognitive models on each other.

The essence of this process is that nobody tries to convince or influence others. Disagreements occur where there is a conflict of opinion, but the pressure is not on trying to change the thoughts of others: disagreement is a signal for self-reflection and a reappraisal of one's own knowledge base and methods of reasoning. This is in sharp contrast to the cooperative learning process, where uniformity of thought and thinking processes is important and the pressure is for people to be brought into common alignment.

This way of learning requires a radical paradigm shift because it is counter-intuitive. Instinctive reactions to a differing of opinions would see a struggle for the proponents to convince each other of the error of their ways. With collaboration there is a respect for differing opinions and they are regarded as something to learn from and associate with rather than to change.

Disagreement and intellectual conflict in a collaborative learning situation are thus seen as desirable features of a group learning exercise. It forces individuals to consider new information and to be able to apply their cognitive understanding to new settings. It brings exposure to different points of view to allow students a more objective examination of an environment and offers the opportunity to see perspectives other than their own.

collaborative learning on the internet

It is only a short step to transfer the collaborative learning environment of the college classroom to the internet. In a virtual world where communication is by e-mail the classroom environment can be simulated as a listserve. As the teacher in a collaborative learning environment is not distinguishable from the students, there is no need for any controlling authority. In fact, any of the students can become a teacher and any teacher can become a student.

This is exactly the environment that is created in internet e-mail discussion forums and special interest groups. These have formed spontaneously as self-organizing groups that function specifically for the purpose of the subscribers to collaborate in learning. There is no controlling organization. There is no pressure for everyone to have the same knowledge or express the same opinions. Each person in the group is responsible for building their own cognitive models and extracting their own knowledge from each other.

It is highly significant that the teaching strategies advocated by experienced educators have come up with exactly the kind of learning environment that has evolved naturally on the internet. But thanks to their analysis (and to Dr Ted Panitz's in particular) we can view these listserve learning environments in an edifying perspective.

It also solves the problem for the New York student, Dora Chapman; she can choose her subjects on the grounds of getting a fundamental education in foundation knowledge and then supplement or extend that knowledge in specific areas of niche speciality in the listserves. These have now taken on a role that complements the functions of colleges and universities.

Not only do listserves and educational establishments have complementary roles, they are now becoming interdependent. This is evidenced by the increasing number of teachers and university lecturers who are participating in the collaborative learning environments of the e-mail discussion forums. For them, it is increasingly becoming the most effective way to extend their own knowledge and keep up with the trends and changes in their own particular spheres of speciality knowledge.

WHEN THE
MANAGED TEAM
DOESN'T WORK

FUNDAMENTAL TO ALL INDUSTRIAL AGE
BUSINESS THEORY ARE THE CONCEPTS OF
PLANNING, COOPERATION AND THE MANAGED
TEAM. THE PROBLEM FOR ORGANIZERS AND
MANAGERS, SWITCHING OVER TO E-BUSINESS
FROM A CONVENTIONAL BUSINESS
ENVIRONMENT, IS THAT THESE CONCEPTS ARE
NOT ALWAYS VIABLE OR PRACTICAL IN A
MASSIVELY CONNECTED WORLD.

PART 3 EXPLAINS WHY THESE CONCEPTS ARE
HIGHLY SUSPECT AND WHY THEY BREAK DOWN.
IT OFFERS ALTERNATIVES THAT ARE MORE
RELIABLE.

THIS PART OF THE BOOK WAS INTENDED TO BE
A SINGLE CHAPTER, BUT THE DISBELIEF AND
THE RELUCTANCE TO ACCEPT THAT PLANNING,
COOPERATION AND MANAGED TEAMS ARE
INFERIOR ORGANIZATIONAL CONSTRUCTS IN
THE INFORMATION ENVIRONMENT HAVE
NECESSITATED STRETCHING THIS SECTION OUT
TO FOUR CHAPTERS. AS A CONSEQUENCE,
THERE IS MUCH REPETITION IN THIS THIRD
PART OF THE BOOK AS THE SAME POINTS OF
VIEW ARE APPROACHED FROM DIFFERENT
ANGLES.

THIS APPROACH TO THIS PARTICULAR ASPECT
OF E-BUSINESS IS ONLY NECESSARY BECAUSE
IT IS ESSENTIAL FOR ANYONE USING THE
INTERNET FOR BUSINESS TO BREAK AWAY
FROM THE CENTRAL DOGMAS OF
CONVENTIONAL BUSINESS. IT IS NOT THAT THEY
ARE WRONG, IT IS JUST THAT THEY DON'T WORK
THE SAME WAY AS THEY DO IN THE WORLD OF
BRICKS AND MORTAR.

7

A COOPERATIVE TEAM VERSUS A COLLABORATIVE TEAM

blind spots can inhibit understanding New knowledge can suddenly open up doors to new thoughts and ideas. The corollary of this is that knowledge gaps can keep us trapped in a blinkered mindset that handicaps progressive thought. This is best explained with a few examples.

Generally acknowledged as one of the best movies ever made, the movie of the year in 1973 was *The Sting*. It was a story about a young scam artist, Johnny Hooker (played by Robert Redford), whose partner is killed by a ruthless New York racketeer, Doyle Lonnegan (played by Robert Shaw). Seeking revenge, Johnny Hooker enlists the help of an experienced, old-time con artist, Henry Gondorff (played by Paul Newman), to run a gigantic scam on the racketeer.

With a brilliant script, this is movie magic at its best. Every line, every scene builds on what comes before. With twists and turns all the way through, the final ending is breathtaking in its ingenuity and audacity as the racketeer is fleeced of a huge sum of money.

The audience is also conned because the plan is so complex that at times it seems as if the action is far removed from the main theme of cheating the racketeer. It is only in the final moments of the film, when the racketeer hurries away after being fleeced, that all the machinations of the plot are exposed as clever smokescreens: to ensure that not only would the racketeer be cheated but he would also be completely unaware that he'd been a victim of a scam.

Yet, if the audience had been observant, the reason for all the complexity of the plot was revealed right at the beginning of the movie when the experienced Gondorff had explained to the novice Johnny Hooker that the secret of pulling off a really great scam is for the victim to remain totally unaware that he has been cheated. If you'd have missed the significance and importance of that remark (and it was deliberately played down) most of the movie would have been perplexing. However, seeing the film a second time – and thus knowing the reasoning behind all the complex arrangements – all the pieces fit logically together.

This is an example of the kind of paradigm shift that can occur only if a particular piece of knowledge is known. Without that knowledge there is a lack of understanding; with that knowledge there is an understanding. It is through such knowledge gaps that people can easily be led astray in the world of e-business.

the need for a new kind of thinking
The last chapter stated that a connection to the internet leads into a world where all normal business rules are changed – and it will require quite a different kind of thinking from that employed in conventional business environments to be able to succeed in e-business.

At one of the tables in the virtual café of readers reading the draft chapters of this book there was an immediate protest against this statement, claiming it was unfounded. Someone else complained that the section on learning strategies was irrelevant and had little to do with e-business. As is often the case within groups, and is borne out by many examples in the virtual café, a first opinion is often accepted and adopted by all. There followed a flurry of posts from others at that table, agreeing with the view that the book was losing its focus by going off at a tangent into learning strategies.

At another table there was quite a different reaction. Bryan Rieger wrote:

Well, I've just finished Chapter 6 for the third time. The first two reads it just didn't do anything for me, but on the third read the penny dropped.

‹snip›

... collaboration is more like an organic structure – with each cell operating independently but within a whole. When one cell evolves, other corresponding cells will also evolve, possibly making a more efficient piece of the whole.

This analogy not only works in education, but is also very relevant to business. I find it much better to work with many 'like-minded' individuals learning, and evolving their ideas – than with specialists that only fit within one specific framework.

Also, cooperation tends to operate by 'rules' or 'recipes' and imposed structures – while collaborative environments are a little more chaotic, modelling ideas from their acquired knowledge base.

It's also interesting to point out that most of the people I know that tend to work in a collaborative manner tend to have grown up with building blocks, modelling or Lego. When given an objective, they draw upon their knowledge base and exposure and apply their current tools accordingly. Everybody will build the same thing a little differently – but they will all reach their intended objective.

‹snip›

... many people I have worked with view their knowledge as proprietary and do not wish to share it with others – the basis for this idea being that they will no longer be required if somebody else knows what they know. It's very difficult to get people to abandon this way of thinking – especially in an economy where knowledge is money.

Bryan Rieger had accepted the proposition that the world of e-business would require a different type of thinking. Although the reason hadn't been explicit, he'd gleaned from the previous chapters that the world of e-business would contain much more change and greater uncertainty than conventional business in the world of bricks and mortar.

He'd been able to see that the section about learning was more than just about learning *per se*: it could also be applied to any situation where there is much uncertainty and ambiguity. He'd abstracted the essence of the learning situation and transferred it to a business environment. As a consequence, far from the learning section being irrelevant to e-business, the findings of Dr Panitz could offer a conceptual breakthrough in being able to think more constructively about how e-business solutions can be organized.

the limitations of a managed team

Applying the methods, techniques and concepts of the relatively stable world of bricks and mortar to the fast-changing world of e-business can throw up many strange anomalies and unpredictable failures that are difficult to correct. Without a suitable mindset, the problems seem perplexing because the solutions require the abandonment of many fundamental principles usually associated with successful business enterprise.

> **MANY PEOPLE FOUND IT ALMOST IMPOSSIBLE TO ENVISAGE SETTING OUT ON A BUSINESS VENTURE WITHOUT A FORMULATED BUSINESS PLAN**

In the book *The Entrepreneurial Web*, there were a number of issues that caused much controversy when the relevant draft chapters were given out to the readers for their comments. The first of these was when it was proposed that the conventional practice of working with a structured and predictive business plan would be totally unrealistic given the nature of the chaotic environment of e-business.

Despite the fact that it was patently obvious that continuous techno-logical developments and rapidly changing competitive strategies would make a mockery of any forward-looking planning, many people found it almost impossible to envisage setting out on a business venture without a formulated business plan. Here was an example of an established and deeply seated dogma being retained, even in the face of overwhelming evidence that it is a nonsense.

By examining in explicit detail the fundamental assumptions upon which such plans are based, the majority of the readers overcame their resistance to the idea of working without a plan and managed to make the paradigm shift to be able to see how businesses could be grown rather than planned. They saw how planning could prove to be a handicap in the Information Age and the competitive advantage would go to the businesses that employed bottom-up strategies, where customer feedback dictated the evolution and structure of the business models.

The second major controversy was when, by the same reasoning, it was proposed that the concept of a managed team would not be an appropriate organizational structure to use in any approach to set up an e-commerce or e-business solution. To some, this proposition was unthinkable and, despite all rational argument, they clung to the notion that nothing could ever replace the organizational construct of a managed team. They were stuck in this paradigm and no amount of persuasion could trigger a paradigm shift.

Paradoxically, many of the main supporters of a managed team approach were already working at the cutting edge of e-business projects and because they were working successfully within the environment of a managed team they assumed there was nothing wrong with it.

The reality, however, is that the frenzied rush of so many businesses to get a web presence had been so great that all rational thinking had been cast aside. E-business solutions were proposed and readily accepted, based upon the business thinking prevailing in the conventional world of bricks and mortar. Projects based upon careful plans and put into operation by well-managed teams was the way things had always been done. Why should it be any different for e-business?

Very few could foresee the limitations of a managed team and, like a crowd of lemmings, everyone was following the example of everyone else – the blind leading the blind – structuring their e-business solutions around the the inappropriate concept of a managed team.

It seemed to most that managed teams were highly successful in the newly emerging world of e-business. The team-based organizations were in high demand and making lots of money. Investors and most core business executives, who didn't fully understand the technology, were quite happy to see their solutions being handled by what appeared to be competent teams of experts working in conventional, time-honoured ways.

The reality, however, was that most of these teams were not truly focused upon coming up with competitive e-business strategies based upon core business considerations. They were simply competing with each other to explore different imaginative ways to use the latest technological advances.

The bottom line for these team-based solution providers was not the profitability of the underlying business, but the profit they were getting from creating websites and back-end solutions. They just had to build them. It was almost irrevelant as to whether or not the results of their work actually provided a competitive solution in the world of commerce. This resulted in thousands of e-businesses being painted into expensive corners, while the real game had moved goal posts and was being played in a new field. (Note: an apt, industry expression used to describe this situation is: 'The wheel is turning but the hamster is dead.')

Because of this universal disregard for the real purposes of business enterprise, there was the illusion that vast numbers of businesses, based upon managed teams, were succeeding. They were all making a profit – even though it was based upon the ignorance of funding authorities and clients. In such a situation, there seemed no logic in going against the flow to try out unconventional strategies. It was only when vast sums of money had been invested in e-business ventures that showed no signs of real-world success that people stopped to think about how they should really be approaching the problems.

team management
Let's stop to think for a moment. Let's consider the implications for a managed team approach in light of 18 of the initial 24 assumptions described in the introduction.

ASSUMPTION 2 Nobody knows all the answers.

ASSUMPTION 3 The environment of the internet and the world wide web is beyond your or anyone else's ability to be able to understand it completely.

ASSUMPTION 4 Everyone is occasionally unreliable.

ASSUMPTION 7 Whatever you know, there are many more important things that you ought to know but don't.

ASSUMPTION 8 Nobody is going to cooperate with you unless they see there is something worthwhile in it for them.

ASSUMPTION 9 Whatever you know, somebody knows it better.

ASSUMPTION 12 Whatever you do, there are thousands of others trying to do the same thing at the same time.

ASSUMPTION 13 Sudden and dramatic changes will occur constantly.

ASSUMPTION 14 Whatever you do will be rapidly outdated by new technological developments.

ASSUMPTION 15 Whatever you do or say will quickly be known to everyone else.

ASSUMPTION 16 Whatever you do will be copied or bettered by your competitors.

ASSUMPTION 17 All services and products will get progressively cheaper as increased competition, reduced costs and increased efficiency bring prices and profits down to a minimum.

ASSUMPTION 18 Whatever you are offering, there will be a plethora of similar alternatives in the marketplace already.

ASSUMPTION 19 Nobody can have more than one area of real expertise.

ASSUMPTION 20 The solution you have to come up with is beyond your, or anyone else's, imagination.

ASSUMPTION 21 Whatever technology, programs, tools, methods and techniques you use will rapidly become unsuitable or irrelevant.

ASSUMPTION 22 Any final solution you come up with will have to be abandoned or radically altered within a very short period of time.

ASSUMPTION 23 Everyone is going to distrust you until you have built up a relationship of trust with them.

If these assumptions are taken seriously – as they should be – how will they affect the efficiency of a team approach to e-business strategy?

Fundamental to the concept of a team are the roles of management and leadership. Although these functions are complementary – good managers can be good leaders and good leaders can be good managers – they are distinctly different. It is better then to consider each function separately. Let's start by looking at the function of management to see how this would be affected by the uncertainties implicit in the list of assumptions.

'Manage' comes from the Latin word meaning 'hand' in the context of handling something. Management usually implies the handling or carrying out of policies and plans laid down by someone else (one's own self, if management and leadership is through the same person). It is more of a science than an art, where procedure and protocol are all-important and satisfactory fulfilment of the management role is highly reliant upon calculation, statistics, methods, timetables and routines.

The role of the manager is therefore one of stewardship: necessitating qualities of good administration, abilities to make efficient and effective use of resources. Managers like and tend to preserve the steady state. They don't like anything that rocks the boat. They should be capable of handling crises, but it is expected that they should have enough forethought to be able to avoid them.

Looking at the list of the 18 initial assumptions one should make before creating an e-business, it is not hard to see how the conditions in the environment of e-commerce would be a manager's worst nightmare. Procedures and protocols would be constantly changing; calculation and statistics unreliable; methods and plans would always be temporary and in a state of flux; timetables and routines in continuous disarray.

Clearly, the role of management is severely compromised in an e-business environment, yet it is often rigidly retained even though the whole concept of managing in a rapidly changing e-business environment is totally inappropriate. The way it is retained is by using the equally inappropriate technique of specifications. Where work is done in house, funding is usually allocated against a formal plan of action. This is designed with targets, budgets, cash flows, monitoring procedures and controls. This turns a project into a form that has to be handled by a

> THE ROLE OF MANAGEMENT IS SEVERELY COMPROMISED IN AN E-BUSINESS ENVIRONMENT

manager. Unfortunately, from a management perspective, such plans are unworkable if they are based upon false assumptions or predictions that do not materialize.

This state of affairs is most apparent when technical work is outsourced to specialist contractors. For their own protection, contractors try to tie down requirements to as detailed a form as possible. Contractors in e-business projects usually have much experience of projects needing constant change and they have to make sure that these changes are the responsibility of the client so that they can get paid for making them. This common practice, designed to protect the contractor, has the unfortunate effect of turning a project into a planned form that is suitable for management, but unfortunately is not an efficient way to create or operate an e-business venture in a highly volatile environment.

It is probable that this need to pass on the responsibility for decision making and ongoing costs keeps the idea of management alive and is the reason why so many people think that the role of management is still appropriate in an e-business environment.

NOTE the role of management discussed here is applicable only to the side of a business involving digital communication and its associated technologies. The conventional, bricks and mortar parts of any e-business, which are often the established core of a business, would see the traditional role of management relatively unaffected.

team leadership

With conventional cooperative teams, managers may be necessary, but team leaders are essential. So, if managers are not appropriate in the world of digital communication, what about leaders? Surely, leaders can't be redundant? There would be no visionary, no driving force, nobody to take responsibility or to change the plans if things start to go wrong.

What about the role of the project leader or the entrepreneur? What is the best paradigm with which to view their functions? And the businessman in Chapter 3 – with his range of indefinite options, who is actively interacting with others in the listserves, waiting for a business opportunity to emerge – how will he be able to exploit and exercise control over the situation when the right combination of factors come together? To answer all of these questions, let's look at the conventional idea of leadership and leaders, to see how this stacks up against the realities of the communication environment.

'Leader' is a word originating from the ancient word for a 'path' or 'road' – its original meaning is one who guides you on a journey. It implies the path setter, the one who knows the destination and the route to that destination and can arrange for an orderly and efficient passage. Translated into business speak, this means one who has a clear idea of the objective. One who has a plan to reach that objective and can show others how to cooperate together to achieve a common goal.

A good team leader should have clear realistic goals, a sense of purpose and effective communication skills. He or she should be able to gain mutual trust and support, be effective at resolving conflicts, able to use resources wisely, able to create an atmosphere of openness, learn from mistakes, build on experience and ride out storms. Leadership is about personality and vision. It is an art.

For a team to achieve a task, it will need: a defined purpose – planning – briefing (explaining purpose and aims) – controls and monitoring – evaluation (review, evaluate, feedback) – group standards (invisible rules, discipline, subordination). These are the functional duties of a leader.

> LEADERSHIP IS THE SENSITIVE USE OF POWER

Leaders are responsible for the task of building a team; developing the individuals within the team so that they can give of their best. Leaders will have authority and command respect, set the standards, create the purpose, provide example and inspiration. They must have an ability to influence others, to elicit enthusiasm and have a sense of conscientiousness. They should be able to earn people's trust; exhibit qualities of warmth and fairness, yet be firm and positive.

Leaders should be able to respond to individuals yet show no special favours. They should be able to settle disputes and misunderstandings, resolve conflicts amongst team members. They should be constantly vigilant for signs of inefficiencies, slackness or non-cooperation. They will thwart attempts at personal empire building, reprimand the holding back of information. They will recognize when individuals become frustrated or underused. They will be on the alert for incompetence and under-motivation because this dilutes efficiency.

Leadership is the sensitive use of power. The leader who wields this power is not only responsible for the efficient goal-seeking functions of a team but also the less tangible needs of the individual team members.

Each individual within a team will need support, coaching and direction. They will each need to experience growth, personal development and a sense of accomplishment. They will need security, protection, a sense of belonging, social interaction and even affection. They will be looking for self-respect, status, recognition. The fulfilment of all these needs is the responsibility of the leader.

Leaders must be able to analyse the needs of a group to achieve the tasks at hand. They must have an awareness of individual skills and have the knowledge to leverage those skills to maximum advantage. They must be able to capitalize on team strengths and be able to make due allowance for weaknesses. Above all, leaders must create a sense of unity; provide a unified framework of communication so that team members can work efficiently and in harmony with each other.

Does that sound about right for a description of an ideal leader? Now let's see how such an ideal leader might fare in the uncertain and constantly changing environment of e-business where nobody can know all that is needed to be known – even the leader.

problems for a leader
The idea of a group of people combining their skills and knowledge, acting together in cooperative activity under sound management and with a strong leadership, is a powerful paradigm. It seems hardly worth even contemplating that there could be a more suitable alternative. However, there are several weaknesses with this kind of organizational structure when it is ported across to the world of the internet – because it is suited only to relatively stable business environments.

Look again at the list of 18 initial assumptions above. Think about how they might affect a leader's duties and responsibilities. Ask yourself the following questions in light of the volatile nature of e-business:

1   How can a leader have a clear and unambiguous vision of the task that is required of a team?

2   How can a leader provide a team with a concise plan, with targets, specific goals and standards for the team members to achieve?

In other words, in e-business situations, leaders will have to lead by the seat of their pants where they will be using strategies of adaptation and reaction rather than predictive planning. Without a fully detailed plan in place, a leader cannot lead a team according to the accepted definition of an ideal leader.

The leader is not going to know all the technical and strategic options available to the team and is quite likely to make many errors of judgement. The team leader is also unlikely to be able to keep up with all the possible strategies of competitors, especially if they are taking advantage of new technological developments that the leader is either not familiar with or not aware of. These realities of the digital communication environment will greatly compromise the ability of a leader to be able to exercise firm judgement and provide clear direction.

In the world of e-business, with super-fast communication and mass connectivity, competition responds instantly to take advantage of any inefficiencies. Any weaknesses in a managed team will soon show up as an inefficiency and allow the competition to get in. Consider the effect the following will have on the efficiency by which the team leader can function:

1   Rapidly changing technology and varying forms of competition are likely to cause continuously recurring mismatches between the knowledge and skills available within a team and the requirements of the competitive marketplace.

2   Teams as well as individuals can have severe knowledge and skill gaps of which neither the team leader nor the members of the team will be aware.

3   Teams tend to design solutions that suit their own skill and knowledge sets rather than design for optimum efficiency.

4   The ease with which team members can change employment in the environment of the internet severely compromises the stability of any managed team.

These four realities of the e-business environment will make life very difficult for any leader trying to create a permanent stable team of contented members. With the nature of solutions continuously changing, it will be difficult to separate out inefficiencies, slackness or non-cooperation. The team leader will have to adopt a flexible strategy, so it would be impossible to avoid periods when certain team members are overworked while others are underused. It will be easy for team members to corner technical niches and create personal power bases. Such conditions can cause all kinds of problems, conflicts and frustrations within a team.

The vast variety of knowledge and skills that will be called upon will make it impractical for the leader to provide adequate coaching or lead by example. With a constant need to take new directions, concentrate on new priorities, react swiftly to new technology and competitive moves, how can a leader provide team members with a sense of security when the leader is probably even doubting his or her own?

Unless the leader picks a team who are not using the internet to enhance their knowledge and skills (a fatal mistake), the individual members of the team will have much greater knowledge in some areas than the leader. This ability of team members to gain knowledge and experience so easily by way of the internet can create considerable imbalances in a team. A conscientious team member can very quickly become highly proficient in a specific area and see himself as being specially valuable to the group for which he will need some form of recognition or compensation.

As discussed in a previous chapter, exceptional expertise in one area often sees specialists assuming they have exceptional capabilities in other areas and this can easily lead to them challenging each other's views if a direction is not clear; perhaps even challenging the views and authority of the leader.

A leader faced with conflicting views from specialists in different areas where he or she has limited knowledge is not in an enviable situation.

Decisions have to be made and if team members feel their expert views are being ignored they can become disgruntled. Teams can easily break up into factions if the team leader cannot assert authority, but because a team leader is certain to have knowledge gaps, such authority cannot be strictly enforced without causing animosity.

It may well be that a team leader, seeking to build a cooperative team in the conventional way, might have to make a choice between a team of people that lack personal drive to use the internet for self-improvement or try to create a team of high achievers that are actively using the web and risk creating a team of prima donnas.

A very eligible bachelor I knew was once asked why he seemed always to be attracted by unattractive-looking females. His answer: 'They don't get stolen off of me as frequently as the attractive ones.' This neatly sums up the problem that many team builders face: the more capable and expert their team members, the more likelihood of them being poached by another team. Worsening this situation: any lack of appreciation – real or imagined – detected by a team member can easily bring about a defection.

It does seem, therefore, that the environment of the internet with its massive connectivity could be a team leader's worst nightmare – even though he or she may be a perfect team leader in the conventional sense.

cooperation or collaboration?

The viability of a conventional team structure in an internet environment has to be called into question. It's not that people working together is wrong – because the variety of different kinds of knowledge and skills that will need to be brought together for any e-business solution will make it imperative that the efforts of many different people are combined. The problem is finding the way to do this most efficiently.

This is where we can look to Dr Panitz's work on learning for some guidance. By making a distinction between cooperation and collaboration, he showed that people can interact to share and combine their knowledge in two radically different ways.

With foundation knowledge, that is, knowledge that has common acceptance and a degree of permanence, it was found that cooperative group structures worked best. These groups had a leader and the learning process was based upon establishing rules and protocols that formalized the interactions so that the groups could reach goals collectively. This corresponds very well with the functioning of managed teams in conventional business environments.

He then showed that the cooperative group method of learning didn't work so well when it involved problems that included uncertainty and ambiguity, the reasoning being that nobody, not even the teacher, had any credible authority to decide absolute solutions. Everyone had the same entitlement to their own considered opinion.

The collaborative learning process encouraged each student – and the teacher – to come up with individual solutions through creating their own cognitive structures for understanding. This they did by interacting with each other to test and refine their individual, internal mental models. In this way, the students didn't necessarily have the same thought processes to come up with solutions, neither did they necessarily have to come up with the same answers. But between them, they could come up with a range of possibilities that took into consideration a wide range of different viewpoints to cover many different contingencies.

The essence of this method of learning is that there is no necessity to agree upon a single solution. There can be many solutions and by interacting with each other, each can be aware that solutions exist other than their own and if their own solutions don't work, there are other approaches to be tried.

Clearly, this collaborative approach maps across to an e-business environment more appropriately than a cooperative approach. A situation where people can collaborate to reach individual conclusions is far more suitable than trying to get everyone into common agreement when solutions contain many unknowns and uncertainties.

On first thoughts, such an approach to creating an optimum e-business solution seems ludicrous. How can people cooperate if they are not in agreement? But the resolution of this paradox requires a sharp paradigm shift – which we shall deal with in the next chapter.

8

THE ENIGMATIC NATURE OF CREATIVITY AND SUCCESS

how do you make collaboration work? Immediately the last chapter went out to the review readers in the virtual café, posts started to come in indicating that people were identifying with the problems that teams and team managements were having in the information environment. This post by Al Stanley was the first of these:

After reading this chapter, I am at last beginning to appreciate what Peter is writing about. What Peter is saying here about managers, leaders and cooperative projects is something I've lived with all my working life. For the most part, those structures have served their purpose well. But of late (the past eighteen months or so), I have gradually seen a disintegration in our working environment, particularly in the working relationships between managers, leaders and peers. The start of this period coincided with our company's migration from traditional products to intranet/internet related ones.

I got that 'eureka' feeling while reading Chapter 7. Suddenly I could see why our teams are not functioning efficiently; why our nerves are on edge; why people who've worked happily together for years are snapping at each other.

ing. Yet no individual person is to blame. It is the
structure.

So now I understand Peter's point of view about collaboration. But
unfortunately, it would be an impossible sell at my place of work; so I won't
even try. But it's something I have gained.

Al Stanley's post, like many other similar posts commenting on the last
chapter, accepted that there was a problem but could see no practical
solution. This presents us with the dilemma: 'How do we apply the
technique of collaboration to e-business?'

Before proceeding any further, it is worth re-emphasizing the key reason
for preferring collaborative rather than cooperative techniques. As was
explained in Chapter 6, it is preferable in situations where there cannot
be any definitive answers. It is preferable where there is a large amount
of uncertainty, or where there are knowledge gaps. Just like game theory,
it is a technique used where rational thinking and logic cannot be relied
upon to come up with the right answers.

an industry founded upon collaboration

As was noted
earlier, it is not practical to move gradually from one paradigm to another.
There are no in-between steps. The change from one perspective to
another is a quantum jump, a leap from one way of thinking to another.
This is why it is so difficult to envisage a collaborative way of working
from within a cooperative framework. To make the necessary paradigm
shift, we need some kind of example to show how it works in practice. If
we can find such an example, we can think from inside that framework to
apply the principles to e-business.

In fact, it is not difficult to find examples of successful collaboration at
work; there is a whole industry based upon collaboration: the movie
industry. Although there are some very important differences (which we

NOTE the descriptions of
the movie industry that are
used in this book are not
meant to apply universally.
Like any complex industry
there will be many
different ways things are
done. The descriptions are
selective, to extract only
the particular aspects of
the film industry that are
comparable to situations
in the world of e-business.

shall deal with later), there are also many parallels with the current world of e-business.

Movie making, like e-business, covers a very wide range of different subject areas and includes huge variations in scale: movies vary from the multi-million dollar blockbusters to small technical documentaries. Despite these variations in subject matter and scale, there is a similarity in the way all movies are created and produced. This is not to say that all movies are made the same way, or that there is a common set of rules; the common factor is that they can all be produced through collaboration rather than cooperation. It is this aspect that we are interested in here.

The key to understanding the organizational structure of movie making is to realize that the success of any movie cannot be predicted in advance. Having star actors or actresses does not guarantee success, neither is success inevitable if there is a great script, an expert camera crew, brilliant sets or extraordinary graphics and special effects. Not even millions of dollars of finance can ensure a movie will be successful and even the most talented directors and world-famous producers can have their failures.

The movie business is about handling risk and uncertainty. It is about intense competition and pleasing customers. In this sense the movie business is very similar to e-business so it can be expected that there is much that e-business entrepreneurs can learn from the techniques that have evolved during a century of movie-making experience.

in the beginning

Like the world wide web, the movie industry was an instant success and grew rapidly (at least, by twentieth-century standards). From being a fairground novelty in the first years of the century, the first main street cinema – a nickelodeon, as they were called at the time – opened in 1905. By 1910, there were 10,000 of them.

The first movies were bought outright by these nickelodeons as permanent exhibitions. Very soon, it was realized that to survive, they would have to be constantly changing their shows. This is when middlemen – distributors – appeared on the scene, who leased or bought movies from the movie makers and rented them out to the nickelodeons. This established a three-tier system, which has remained a permanent structuring of the industry ever since – content maker; middleman/distributor; customer interface.

As with e-business, major companies came into the game almost immediately with a view to monopolizing the industry. They used copyrights to drive all the smaller producers out of business, culminating in Thomas Edison forming the Motion Picture Patents Company (MPPC), which combined the nine most powerful copyright holders under one umbrella. These nine then pooled their patents and used their combined power to take full control of the industry, not allowing any independents to make, buy or lease any movies.

The independents fought back by uniting to form the Motion Picture Distributing and Sales Company which successfully sued the MPPC under government antitrust laws. The MPPC responded by employing strong-arm tactics, using gangs to break equipment and intimidate casts and crews. Despite this, the independents won out and by 1917 most of the MPPC companies had folded, with the organization becoming outlawed by the courts.

We see many similarities to the beginning of the movie business in the beginnings of e-business on the web. There is a frantic struggle for control through the use of patents. It is not clear how this battle will play itself out but it is almost certain that the millions of players in the world of e-business are not going to stand idly by while a handful of big-time players try to monopolize every aspect of e-business technology. It may not result in physical violence this time but it could easily see the system of patents falling into disrepute.

Although the independents won out in the patents battle, the movie industry was still dominated by the giant corporations for several decades because the showing of movies needed expensive and prominent locations and these, although large in number, could easily be controlled by exclusivity coupled to distribution. This allowed production, distribution and presentation to become dominated by a relatively small number of giant studios (corporations), who ran the industry in a classical, twentieth-century industrial management style: involving teams of cooperative employees, producing movies on a production-line basis.

It was only when the movie industry was challenged by the rise of television that the small independent movie makers could once again get back into the game in any significant way. With the need for vast amounts of content involving a huge variety of subject matter, even the large companies couldn't cope with the demand. This is when the independents came into their own. Using techniques of collaboration, rather than cooperation, they were far more efficient than the large studios and eventually took over the industry – driving many of the mammoth companies that had previously dominated the industry to the wall.

It is interesting now to take a more detailed look at the contemporary movie industry to see why the evolved methods of collaboration became so much more successful than the cooperative team efforts of the corporate giants. This may yield the clues we are looking for in determining a suitable strategic approach to creating e-business solutions.

the process of creation

For a movie to come into existence, somebody has to initiate the process. Whoever that person is, we can liken them to the businessman in Chapter 3 who is waiting for the right set of circumstances to emerge that will trigger the start of an e-business venture.

For the purpose of this comparison, it may be convenient to use the theory of film making known as auteurism, which sees one prime mover – the auteur – as being in charge of the overall process. This is not a universal model of the way in which films are made, but it provides a convenient framework with which to compare the nature of movie making to that of creating an e-business.

The term auteurism was first brought into widespread use by Andrew Sarris, who in 1962 wrote an influential paper entitled 'Notes on Auteur

Theory'. This theory evolved from an essay written in 1950 by François Truffaut entitled 'Une certaine tendance du cinéma français' (published in a French film enthusiasts' journal called *Cahiers du Cinéma*). Truffaut was writing at a time when French film makers had recently become aware of the progress American films had made during the period when the French were prohibited from seeing them under the Nazi occupation.

Writers in the journal *Cahiers du Cinéma* had observed that although most American films had been made under the studio system – where a director was appointed as a manager and given a script, a crew and a cast – the films often carried a characteristic stamp, identified exclusively with the work of the director. This stamp nearly always carried through to other movies to which the director was assigned.

Recognizing the importance of a director's contribution to the making of a film, *Cahiers du Cinéma* started focusing on the style of directors rather than the content. This elevated the role of the director from that of a mere employee of the studio, carrying out a managerial role, to that of the creative engine behind the film. At a time when the movie industry was dominated by the all-powerful studios, who effectively employed everyone involved in the production of a film, this was a radical viewpoint. Movies at that time were produced along similar lines to automobiles, where individuality was subservient to the system of production.

Isolating the creative input of the director was thus seen as pretentious eccentricity by the main movie makers – and the journal was regarded as a maverick voice. That is until Truffaut's essay attacked the traditional French film makers for sticking rigidly to literal translations of plays and literature. He proposed that the whole approach to film making be changed: to use 'shooting scripts' written specifically to take full advantage of the expanding techniques of cinematographic technology and working with locations rather than studio sets.

His paradigm saw films as being the creation of a special kind of author who could use the technology of cinematography to interpret literary subject matter in new and exciting ways. He described this kind of film making as 'a cinema of auteurs' (a cinema of authors); thus auteur – the

French word for author – entered into the vocabulary of film makers (via Andrew Sarris's influential paper, 'Notes on a Theory of Auteurism').

At the time, this theory was seen as a radical paradigm shift, which Sarris defended by pointing out that auteurism had always been a principal method of classification in the arts. He explained that artists are compared, rather than individual works of art: composers are compared rather than musical compositions; writers rather than individual books; etc. Looking back at creative work done in the past, it seems perfectly natural to judge an auteur or creator by a range of works. It doesn't make sense to compare individual pieces or different artists.

If there are similarities between movie making and e-business solutions, it would make sense to try to identify the auteurs of the e-business world and examine their techniques and strategies. However, there is a problem with this. It is not easy to spot creators or creative work at the time of creation. In judging contemporary creativity, it is far easier to judge and compare individual pieces. A good example of this is pop music. This is judged on the basis of immediate impressions of a single piece in isolation. Pop charts reflect this kind of comparison.

This kind of classification can be seen to change when pop groups, who have had a number of hits, build up an expectancy for their next creation to be a hit. The passage of time can give greater or lesser credence to the creative efforts of creators, as can be evidenced by the way in which some pop musicians have become legends, i.e. Lennon and McCartney, Bob Marley, Elvis Presley, etc. Only in retrospect have their works proved to have some lasting impact in their field. As strange as it may seem to us today, it was not obvious at the time of their first records that they had any more chance than many other pop stars of achieving lasting fame.

Similarly, the passage of time can raise the notoriety of any creator above the level of their creations in a variety of different creative arts, such as literature, art, jazz, classical music, etc. There are two reasons for this:

1   At the time of creation, there is much other work being created. This acts as noise, which can mask out true innovation and brilliance.

2   Creativity is not a continuous and constantly successful process. A

true artist is recognized only over a range of work, which may include several failures.

If we now look at the work of innovators in the field of information technology, we find something similar. There are so many innovations and new directions happening all around us that it is difficult to spot the winners from the losers. Who can really judge at this moment in time who will emerge as the successful auteurs of the Information Age?

the enigmatic nature of an auteur's contribution

If we are to assume that there is a correspondence – between a director as the auteur of a movie and an initiator or organizer of an e-business venture – we ought to take a closer look at the way in which a film director works. We need to know exactly what are the similarities and what are the differences.

Firstly, it isn't obvious that the role of a film director is that of a creative auteur. Film directors are not creators of tangible work, such as a pieces of text or sheets of music: they are adapters, arrangers and interpreters of the creative works of others. This makes their type of creativity and innovation more subtle and less easy to identify.

The most obvious parallel is with the role of the conductor of an orchestra. Concerts are not judged by the musical composition, or by the playing skills of the individual musicians. A concert is judged according to the perceived skill of the conductor in bringing out some enigmatic quality that differentiates one rendition of a musical piece from another.

This interpretation of creative works can be seen in other kinds of performing arts. It is common to talk about a particular actor's portrayal of a Shakespearian character, or the interpretation of a classical ballet by a particular dancer. Even the compositions of Lennon and McCartney have had better interpretations of their musical compositions than those performed by the Beatles.

Such adaptations and interpretations are not so easily defined and described as the original creative work that the auteurs deal with. In a similar fashion, it is not easy to describe the way in which successful entrepreneurs use the innovations of digital technology to create successful e-business solutions. This problem of identifying the input of the auteur is even more difficult in collaborative environments, where the results depend upon the input of many others. How, for instance, do you untangle the mixed inputs of entrepreneurs, media creators and programmers when they collaborate together in an evolving e-business enterprise?

Ascertaining the contributions towards the success of a particular venture is even further complicated by the fact that success itself is difficult to discern. Success can be temporary; it can be no more than a transitional phase before competition or a new technological development snuffs it out. Successful techniques and strategies may not even be recognizable in the present; they may be drowned out by the noise of so many other attempts to succeed. This makes it probable that only in retrospect can we really know what are successes and what are failures.

On first thoughts, the enigmatic nature of the success of e-business auteurs, together with the difficulties inherent in recognizing what causes success, would appear to make it impossible to define and emulate strategies for success. However, this really only applies to the tangible actions and decisions of auteurs; what we really need to find is the abstractions upon which the auteur's actions and decisions are based.

In other words, we need to discover the successful auteur's mindset, the paradigms that allow auteurs to succeed in spite of uncertainties and competition. We need to find the essence that gives rise to the distinctive influence that e-business auteurs can bring to a venture to raise the results of their contributions above those of others.

when you run history at fast forward

In the next chapter we shall be seeing how and why the film-making business uses a collaborative rather than a cooperative organizational framework. But before going there, we might bear in mind that there are substantial differences between making films and creating e-businesses.

First and foremost, film making is based upon a set plan. This plan is the story and script of the film. This is more or less finalized before shooting starts and forms a definitive organizational framework around which all other activities are based: determining what kind and what number of collaborators are needed in a production.

The content, or basic story, is used to create a shooting script. From this shooting script a production schedule will be planned. This production plan is known as the sub-plot of the film, where scenes are filmed out of sequence for better efficiency. An example might be where the film story involves returning to a particular scene several times during a film. To save reassembling cast and crew a number of different times, all the scenes involving a particular set or location will be shot together, but out of sequence with how they will appear in the final editing.

For similar reasons, out of sequence scenes will be shot to make the most efficient use of actors and actresses. Their time might be very expensive and it will obviously be preferable to shoot the scenes they are in all together, so that they are involved for the least possible time. Similar considerations are made for the participation and involvement of all the collaborators in a film-making project, to ensure that the money being spent on these services is minimized as much as possible.

In this sense, film making is fundamentally different from the creation of an e-business because the existence of the plan – the script – allows managerial skills to be brought into play to optimize the efficiency of the film-making procedures. This allows the work of the film director to be divided into two quite distinct categories: creative and managerial.

Because the management side of film production can be described and defined, managerial functions are best handled by a professional film production manager who will have been schooled and trained in all aspects of film production. This will leave the director free to concentrate on the more enigmatic features of film making – allowing him or her to be more of an auteur than a manager.

last-minute good ideas
This arrangement works extremely well in the film-making industry, but it can easily be disrupted by what is

known as LMGIs (last-minute good ideas). This is where the director arrives in the production office just before filming a scene saying, 'Last night I had this wonderful idea to improve the film.' Both directors and production managers are primed to avoid this kind of situation like the plague because it can disrupt production in all kinds of unexpected ways. Ideas have to be properly evaluated, budgeted and scheduled in order to fit into the planned production of the film. Trying to fit new ideas in at the last minute can play havoc with costs and schedules.

In the creation of an e-business, the rapidly changing technology and competition will produce effects very similar to LMGIs. It's not that a director will come up with a new idea, it's that new ideas, which were not available in the planning stage, suddenly impinge themselves on the production because of a new technological advance or an unanticipated competitor's strategy.

In the film-making business, it is possible to outlaw the use of LMGIs because of the relatively slow rate of change. The technology and film-making techniques wouldn't be expected to change dramatically and unexpectedly over the course of the time in which the film is being made, and certainly not anything major that would be unpredictable to an experienced and knowledgeable director and production management team.

The situation in the creation of an e-business solutions is considerably different. This can be appreciated if the same rate of change being experienced in the e-business environment could be imagined to have happened in the film industry. Consider how the film industry might have evolved if all the changes and developments in film making during the twentieth century had been speeded up so that every change and development that occurred over a hundred-year time span happened over the course of just five years: from one-reelers to multi-reelers in months; within a year sound introduced; within two years films become coloured.

Imagine starting the production of a film with a one-reeler and by the time it was distributed the cinemas were demanding multi-reelers. Imagine choosing a cast of actors and actors skilled at mime and then finding that the market needed to hear them speak as well. Imagine starting a film in black and white, then discovering that the target audience will only go to films made in colour. Imagine planning and preparing to make a musical with a cast of thousands only to find that they've gone out of fashion before you'd finished shooting.

Film making is about producing entertainment that people want to experience. People will want change and novelty; this will be subject to changing fashions. In the twentieth century, the rate of such change in demands and fashion could to some degree be anticipated, so that a director could be reasonably sure that the kind of film planned at its inception would be in fashion at the time of showing. In a fast-forward scenario where the time elapsing between unpredictable fashion changes is less than production times, a director could never be sure that an initial idea would still be viable at the time of the premiere. This is the state of affairs in the world of e-business.

Putting the history of film making into fast-forward mode, to imagine everything that happened in a century of film making happening in about five years, gives a pretty good approximation of the rate at which the world of e-business is changing today. If the film industry had changed at that rate, what kind of strategy would an auteur have had to have? More interesting to most, what strategy should the actors, actresses, crew, technicians, screen writers and all the other kinds of collaborators have to employ? They would be just as vulnerable in a rapidly changing, volatile environment as any auteur director.

NOTE the various kinds of auxiliary collaborators involved in any collaborative project will be far more numerous than the auteurs initiating and directing e-business projects. So, it is likely that the reader might not be able to self-identify with the role of an auteur or an entrepreneur. But, as we shall see later, the optimum strategies for success used by different kinds of collaborators have many more similarities than is readily apparent and will be far more aligned than would be supposed.

9

A COLLABORATIVE
ENVIRONMENT

getting business ideas into perspective With so many differences between the world of film making and the world of e-business, it would seem that very few lessons can be learned from the former that would apply to the latter. To get the problem into perspective though, we are not concerned at the moment with the eventual running of a successful e-business: we are more concerned with its initial creation and a strategy that will enable it to survive. In this sense, the creation of an e-business solution has more in common with the pre-production activities of the movie makers than the more mechanical details of the production process itself.

Pre-production of movies (and television programmes) is an enigmatic area of activity that defies logical description. It concerns the finding and selection of the subject matter. It is about assembling together the right mix of key collaborators that will provide a reasonable degree of confidence that the project might become a reality. It is about constructing a rough framework for production and providing a convincing strategy that will attract funding in what is basically a high-risk venture.

This is the way to look at the creation of an e-business solution. It isn't simply about having good ideas: ideas are only of any use if there is a suitable environment in place to nourish them. Ideas are like seeds; plants produce thousands of them based upon an evolved strategy that takes into account that only a few of them will ever find their way to just the right set of conditions that will allow them to grow.

Just as seeds are useless without a growing environment, so are ideas useless without an infrastructure in place to make them realizable. Thus, power and initiative lie not with the people who have the ideas but with the people who have the contacts and control the infrastructure that can put the ideas into practice.

It is always the mark of the inexperienced novice, when they place undue emphasis upon the value of initial ideas in the creation of a business. Referring back to Chapter 3, business ideas are the seeds upon which businesses are grown and developed, but until ideas are brought to fruition their value has to be heavily discounted to allow for any uncertainties and unrevealed problems.

This lumps good and bad ideas together, because which are good and which are bad is only truly discernible after they are put into practice. In the uncertain environment of e-business, this usually means that the process of selection between competing ideas is more a matter of chance than rational judgement.

Many people feel frustrated when they consider they have what seems to be a great idea for a business but lack the necessary resources to be able to put the idea into practice. If they could have emotions, this is probably how millions of seeds would feel when scattered to the wind. Every seed has the potential to turn into a great living plant, but unless they land in just the right place at just the right time, they will not be one of the lucky ones that succeed.

You might cast your mind back here to Chapter 3. It may have struck you as being utterly bizarre to venture into the world of e-business without a sound business idea. But if you have only a great idea, with no contacts or strategy to be able to put that idea into operation, then you might as

" POWER AND INITIATIVE LIE NOT WITH THE PEOPLE WHO HAVE THE IDEAS BUT WITH THE PEOPLE WHO HAVE THE CONTACTS AND CONTROL THE INFRA-STRUCTURE "

well consider it in the same light as the genetic content of a newly released seed from a plant. Unless the idea can be introduced into a suitable environment, it is useless. For this reason, establishing contacts and creating the right environment in which to introduce an idea must have a higher order of priority than the idea itself. Common sense tells you that it is a waste of time dreaming up brilliant ideas unless you have this side sorted out first.

To be practical and realistic, ideas should only be conceived within the context of an infrastructure that is either in place already or easy to assemble using established contacts. To be in this position involves establishing sufficient credibility to be able to communicate effectively to obtain the confidence of suitable collaborators. It is an exercise that relies upon techniques and skills more usually associated with entrepreneurs – the ability to inspire trust and confidence. Ultimately, it is about communication strategies.

the emergence of a system of collaboration

If we are to approach the creation of an e-business from the aspect of the infrastructure rather than the business idea, we have to know what we are looking for. This is difficult to formulate in the rapidly changing, noisy environment of the internet, so it is best that we return to the environment of film and television programme making, to see how infrastructures evolve there.

The role of the auteur kind of film director did not come into its own until the competitive pressures of television imposed too much of a burden on the large movie-making studios. Just like those early nickelodeons, television demanded a continuous change in content. Television, however, devours content at a vastly greater rate. It isn't sufficient to change television programmes once a week, or even once a day: programmes have to be changed continuously throughout every day, requiring a huge variety of different kinds of content.

The large studio system could probably have handled the volume, but it was completely out of its depth when it came to supplying the variety.

Competition between many different television channels exacerbated the problem, creating a demand for volume and variety that was totally beyond the capabilities of the big studios to provide efficiently.

This demand was recognized by many entrepreneurs who saw the opportunities for combining ideas, talent and specialist skills with sources of finance to create novel productions. As with the auteurs, the skills of an entrepreneur are hard to specify or formulate. Somehow, out of nothing, they have to create an environment where many complementary functions come together in a collaborative association to create a product. By its very nature, the making of a film or a television programme is fraught with risks and uncertainties, yet the entrepreneur must create an atmosphere of confidence that enables a production to take place.

If we can capture the essence of the way in which these entrepreneurs work, we may be able to work out an appropriate strategy for establishing a personal niche in the somewhat similar environment of the world of e-business – where similar opportunities are available for any entrepreneur who can combine inspiration with technology and get it supported with suitable funding.

The fact that entrepreneurial activity was successful in answering the gargantuan needs of television is self-evident. A myriad of different production companies came into existence, specializing in a huge variety of television content. The many common needs of these production companies created openings for speciality niche services to make their appearance. Dedicated companies were set up in every possible aspect of film and programme making, whose services could be called upon by any production company that didn't have the resources to set up their own speciality departments. In the space of a few years, any entrepreneurial auteur could plan and make a film using a range of expertise and facilities previously available only to the film directors employed by large studios.

As more and more film and programme productions came on stream, the demand for niche specialist services increased. This created duplication of services, which in turn led to competition between the niche specialists. Specialists were in competition with each other to get work and acquire reputations. This competitive pressure had the effect of making these speciality services far more competent than the same services available in house to the big studios, where the employees did not have any 'live or die' pressures to excel at their work and keep up with the latest developments.

This splitting up of all the specialities involved in film and programme making into independent services greatly increased production efficiencies. There was no longer any need for an organizational level to integrate the production of many films to ensure all departments had consistent workloads. Speciality services could be hired as needed, hired only for the time needed for them to complete their functions.

This fragmentation of the film and programme production into components spreads the responsibility for efficiency and progress throughout the various service organizations involved, each niche speciality group being responsible for its own efficiency and direction of specialization and learning.

This situation has many similarities with that of a collaborative learning environment. Taking each niche group as a single unit (because it will be expected that the individual members in a group will have a common mindset through being organized around a cooperative team structure), it can be seen how each unit will act and think differently and independently of any other. The niche groups will not have to have a common goal because they will be focusing only on their limited area of speciality as it is needed by the auteur. This means that although different units might be collaborating in the process of making a production, they have no need to cooperate with each other, except perhaps at a basic logistical level.

From a creative director's viewpoint, this system of film and programme making is far superior to the organizational framework of a large studio. The director's scope for innovation and novel interpretations is not handicapped by the restraints of a system designed to optimize the workload of a fixed number of permanent employees. The director does not have to work with allocated teams who may have questionable knowledge or technical abilities. The director is free to select particular expert technologists and specialists on demand – and be reasonably confident that any particular aspect of a production will be competently handled. In other words, the director is freed to work at a higher level of organization – the creative level – in the production of the film or programme.

Film making thus changed, from being the sole province of the large studios with their managed teams of cooperative employees, to a system that involved the bringing together of a number of different specialist individuals and groups to collaborate on a production under the direction of a principal auteur.

This is more similar to the situation we now have in the world of e-business, where a collaboration between independent specialists is more effective and efficient than teams of cooperative employees, organized and managed in house.

It is seeing e-business solutions as systems, assembled by entrepreneurs and made up of independent specialists collaborating under the direction of auteurs, that can provide the appropriate mindset for thinking about creating a personal niche in the world of e-business.

an autocratic system

For most of the last century, it was possible for competent film directors to have a pretty good grasp of all the main technological aspects of film making and to know where the frontiers of the industry were. This allowed them to work with most technicians at their own level of expertise and be able to direct them in their functional activities and take an active part in any innovations or breakthroughs.

This is not the case with e-business solutions today, where even the best auteurs and entrepreneurs are unlikely to have any clear idea as to where the frontiers of e-business lie or be able to become involved at the specialist level of many of the technological niches of the creations for which they are responsible.

The inference that collaboration rather than cooperation might provide a solution to this problem points to a method of working where there is no authoritative leader, or, even worse, a situation where there may be several leaders. This presents a paradox because any e-business solution has to have some kind of leadership to provide guidance and direction.

> " SEEING E-BUSINESS SOLUTIONS AS SYSTEMS [...] CAN PROVIDE THE APPROPRIATE MINDSET FOR THINKING ABOUT CREATING A PERSONAL NICHE IN THE WORLD OF E-BUSINESS "

Yet, as we have seen, the role of the type of leader favoured in the corporate world will be greatly compromised in the fast-changing, technological environment of e-businesses.

From the paradigm of a cooperative project, the idea of a group without a leader and everyone with a different perspective seems a sure recipe for anarchy. How can you get everyone to agree on a course of action when everyone has a different viewpoint and there is no leader to unify the thinking? But this is where a paradigm shift is needed – away from the perspective of a cooperational environment and into one of collaboration – because with collaboration, agreement is not necessary, and neither is a common understanding.

soliloquies as an e-business strategy

The paradigm shift from cooperation to collaboration is not easy. It came to me by accident, when my 11-year-old son asked me to help him with his homework. He had been given a piece from Shakespeare's *Romeo and Juliet* where Juliet was thinking aloud while she was contemplating the possible consequences of drinking the potion that would put her into a death-like trance to save her having to marry the man she did not love. My son's homework was to read through the passage and list the doubts and fears Juliet was expressing to herself.

The heading of this exercise was 'Soliloquies'. It struck me that this was a very sophisticated word for an 11-year-old, so I asked him if he understood what this word meant. 'Yes,' he replied, 'My teacher told me it means people talking to themselves out loud.'

A little bell rang in my head. Isn't this what people do in a collaborative learning environment? Don't they talk out loud to themselves, but with a view that others might hear? I then imagined a play consisting of all the actors engaged in speaking in soliloquies rather than dialogue. At first this idea seems bizarre and eccentric, but upon reflection it's not as ridiculous as it seems. Why shouldn't an audience be entertained by actors speaking aloud their innermost thoughts? There isn't really any necessity to have interactive dialogue. An audience can learn from, be interested in and enjoy a performance consisting of soliloquies focused around a particular theme just as easily as if the actors were all contributing to a common discussion through verbal interaction.

Of course, such a performance might be somewhat odd if each actor were soliloquizing on a totally different topic, but if each actor were soliloquizing on a common situation or subject matter, the audience would have the benefit of many different independent viewpoints. There would be no scripted interaction that forced the views into common alignment. There would be no coercion or influence that caused any viewpoint to change.

Each different personal perspective on the common theme would be available to every member of the audience for them each to make their own deductions and decide for themselves which of the various viewpoints they preferred. They could even select parts from the different viewpoints – to arrive at a unique viewpoint of their own. Isn't this the essence of collaborative learning?

This mental model did it for me. I could see how a conventional play is fixed by the thinking of the original script writer at the time of its conception. There was little scope for change if the audience didn't like it. With a production based upon an evolving selection of soliloquies, a performance could be changed at every new performance – simply by replacing one or more soliloquies. In this way, a performance could be made to develop, to adapt and respond to theatre-goers' changing needs, allowing a performance to continuously improve and have an indefinite life.

If we abstract the essence of this hypothetical performance of soliloquies, we find that it consists of many independent units contributing to a common theme. They do not interact with each other; the only interactions are between them and the members of the audience. The role of the auteur is to judge the audience's reactions to the performance as a whole and change the soliloquies as he or she sees fit.

This provides a suitable way to consider the structure of an e-business solution. It isn't about having a fixed and stable structure. It is about having a modular arrangement where the modules can easily be changed to adapt to clients' or customers' changing needs. This may not seem a sensible approach if an audience's (or a customer's or client's) needs and expectations are known or can be predicted, but this is very seldom the case in e-business. There is too much uncertainty, too much change, too many unknowns and the actions of competitors can be totally unpredictable when technology is changing so fast.

Not having a fixed plan to work with, an entrepreneur can be guided by the reactions of customers. Just like the arranger of a performance of soliloquies, the need for change can only be derived from audience reactions. If the arranger knows what the audience is responding to and where their interests are changing, the components of the performance can be altered accordingly.

the role of the auteur
In imagining the above hypothetical production of evolving collections of soliloquies, it is hard to rationalize the exact role an auteur plays. On the face of it, the performance is created by the person who selects which of the soliloquies are used and which are to be replaced. Is this the work of a true auteur, or the mechanical reactions to feedback from the audience (or customer in the case of an e-business solution)?

> IF THE ARRANGER KNOWS WHAT THE AUDIENCE IS RESPONDING TO AND WHERE THEIR INTERESTS ARE CHANGING, THE COMPONENTS OF THE PERFORMANCE CAN BE ALTERED ACCORDINGLY

This is not such a mechanical selection process as it might appear because there has to be a judgement made, and the making of such judgements is creative: and that is the function of the auteur. The selecting auteur will have to have an awareness of what is likely to be most interesting or entertaining for an audience. It necessitates being aware of what audiences like and applying the right combination of ideas and innovations to produce an appropriate mix. This is best explained by looking again at the role of the auteur in film making.

When Andrew Sarris wrote his article on the theory of auteurism in film making in 1992, there were many critics of this theory. Chief amongst these critics was Pauline Kael who accused Sarris of a crude sort of Platonism: espousing theory that could not be applied in practice. She claimed that Sarris was trying to establish fixed concepts and objective standards for a medium that was inherently ephemeral. Each film, she said, was an art form that could only be judged on a personal subjective level, involving taste and intellectual competence. As these were not scientifically definable, she said it made a nonsense of having standards whereby one film could be measured against another. She claimed that judgement on films could only be made on the basis of experience and emotional reaction and there was no place for any rationalization of the elements that determined the quality of a film.

The weakness of Pauline Kael's argument is that there is no logical relationship between what a person says about a film and their competence to comment. In other words, her view is lacking some form of criteria in judging which judgements are valid. This takes us back to Chapter 5 where the work of Kruger and Dunning showed that incompetent people are likely to have totally erroneous views which they are quite positive about because they are unaware of their own lack of knowledge and capability of making judgements. Pauline Kael's arguments would make such views equally valid as those of people who were competent and appropriately experienced to make judgements.

Pauline Kael was against using the qualities of the director as a basis for judging films because, as she argued, the input of a director wasn't necessarily the critical factor in determining the success of a film. She argued that if universality did not apply then the theory of a director as an auteur was not viable.

In 1971, she wrote a controversial essay entitled 'Raising Kane' (http://www.cinemazine.com/engels/archief/kael/eng1.html), about Orson Welles' masterpiece film *Citizen Kane*. In this essay she argued that the auteurism was not the work of Orson Welles but was a result of collective achievement. She claimed that rather than being an original work of genius, the ideas were already developing in Hollywood at that time and the important contributions to the film by the scenarist Herman J. Mankiewicz and the cameraman Gregg Toland were being ignored.

To Pauline Kael, Welles was not a creative auteur at all, but simply somebody who was good at bringing out the best in the people he worked with. Such a view fits in with the twentieth-century concepts of production, which would see Orson Welles as a good manager and leader, rather than being the inspired creator.

This highlights the paradigm shift between a cooperative and a collaborative viewpoint. From Pauline Kael's viewpoint, Orson Welles was the leader of a cooperative association of exceptionally skilled technicians, who together brought about the creation of an exceptional film. From Sarris's viewpoint, Orson Welles was the source of the exceptional creative activity that produced *Citizen Kane*, in collaboration with the appropriate technologists whom he used to bring his vision to life.

There can be justification for both of these viewpoints, but they are both found wanting in a situation of continuous change, where the results are neither planned nor visualized but continuously evolve in response to changing audience expectations.

10

DIFFERENT INTERPRETATIONS
OF COLLABORATION

the main players in the game At this point, we can begin to
see how the paradigm necessary for creating solutions in the fast-
changing world of e-business is going to be radically different from that
used in the creation of businesses in the Industrial age.

The engine that will drive innovative developments is not going to come
from highly structured organizations, but from small cores of main
players. In the film-making industry this core might consist of:

1   the original story writer;

2   the auteur, or director, who adapts this story to the screen;

3   the producer who arranges the financing;

4   the entrepreneur who brings the first three together to make it
    happen.

Although these roles are separated out, there is no reason why a single
person shouldn't be able to perform all of these roles in a small production. In fact, any of these roles could be combined, so that the main
players in the game could consist of one, two, three or four people.

The paradigm shift is to see the initial creation of an e-business as the creative work of a very small group who have no need to permanently hire all the functioning components of the production. This initiating group would then be seen to consist of:

1 the originator of an idea;

2 the adapter of the idea who can bring it into reality;

3 the funding organizer;

4 the entrepreneur who can make it all happen.

As with the production of a film, all of these roles can reside in a single person or be split between two, three or four.

There is one very big difference, though. The uncertainties involved in the rapidly changing environment of e-business mean that ideas are uncertain to work. Adapters are unlikely to know the best way to bring the idea into reality. The funding organizer has no tangible product with which to attract investment. This leaves the most difficult part to the entrepreneur who has to find a way of coping with this uncertainty to make it all happen.

Making the entrepreneur's task even more difficult is the probability that the original idea may quickly become a bad idea; an adaptation may turn out to be less than suitable and the funding can quickly evaporate before a credible result has been achieved.

Clearly, this is not a job for careful preparation or planning: it's a job for game theory.

the collaborator's viewpoint

In a cooperative situation, all cooperators will be made aware of the main goal and be given details of the plan to reach this goal. But in a collaborative situation, where collaboration is preferred because of the unknowns and uncertainties involved, this cannot happen. The principal initiators will not know any certain way to reach the goal, and will have to be directed by customer or client feedback during the process of reaching the goal. How does a collaborator respond to such uncertain leadership?

This situation would seem to be totally ambiguous. A leader who doesn't know what direction to take? To appreciate the position of a collaborator, it may be useful here to use another metaphor. Metaphors are very useful when dealing with novel or unfamiliar situations – they allow you to create abstractions that cut out irrelevant detail to enable you to focus on the critical elements of a problem.

In a gold-rush scenario, there might be a mountain full of gold but nobody knows where the gold is. Many miners might converge on this mountain seeking their fortune, but none of them can be certain of success. They will need tools and supplies. Fairly soon the miners are joined by suppliers who have no interest in taking a risk by spending their time looking for the gold themselves. They will be able to get more reliable money by supplying the miners with what they need. These suppliers then become collaborators in the miners' attempts to make a fortune but they are not involved in the same way as cooperators might be (i.e. as a miner's partner or employee).

When some of the miners make a strike, their needs will increase in order to develop and expand their operations. These new needs will attract new suppliers. The lucky miners will have money to spend on entertainment and pleasures. They'll need banks and other kinds of services. They'll need to employ labour, which will attract new people into the area. In no time at all, a boom town comes into existence – and in this boom town it will be the suppliers and providers that will be making more money than most of the miners.

Mapping the essence of this scenario – the abstraction – back to the film-making business, doesn't Hollywood consist of more than just the people involved in film making? Isn't everyone there just as much a collaborator in the making of movies as any of those involved on the shooting sets?

Seeing movies as just events that occur within a complex community can provide a totally different perspective on the roles of the various kinds of collaborators. Then, the question to ask yourself is, 'Do I want to be a speculative prime mover or one of the specialist collaborators?' Now map this across to an e-business environment. What kind of role do you want to play? Do you want to be one of the entrepreneurial speculators, or one of the collaborators who makes a living from the money of the speculators? This is a critical decision when contemplating a possible niche in the world of e-commerce.

how collaboration emerges

Time for another paradigm shift. As a collaborator – as opposed to a cooperator who is aligned with a common goal – you don't have to make an exclusive choice. You can have your fingers in more than one pie. Just as a store owner in a gold-rush boom town can take a day off now and again to to search the hills for gold, so a specialist can dabble with a personal e-commerce project of their own. Just as a gold miner can go broke and spend some time working for others to build up enough capital for another start, so a specialist can spend time collaborating in projects to build up capital for their own venture. In the e-business environment it is possible to combine all of these alternatives rather than to be locked into a single one.

This is a common occurrence in e-business start-ups where collaborators might be offered equity in a project in lieu of payment for services. Media might take equity in lieu of payment for advertising. Many e-businesses are based upon creating strategic alliances, partnerships or affiliations. This allows niche specialists to have a number of options whereby they can earn conventional fees, build up a portfolio of shares in other ventures and even experiment with their own start-ups on the side.

In the film industry, the switching of roles is common. There are plenty of examples of producers taking on the role of director and effectively becoming the auteur instead of the funding specialist – and vice versa. Actors and actresses often become directors or producers, as do cinematographers, production managers and script writers.

Billy Wilder, who produced, directed and wrote his own movies, started off in the business as a script writer at a time when script writers weren't

NOTE this is something different from employee equity schemes where payment for full-time employment is supplemented with equity. This is usually on the basis of a cooperative association rather than one of collaboration. In such cases the equity beneficiary does not have the (official) option of participating in multiple ventures.

even allowed on the set while a movie was being made. When asked one time how he got into directing, he explained that it had happened over his insistence that he had some control over the way his scripts were being interpreted. To placate him, the studio gave him a small film to direct, thinking that this would be such a trying experience he'd happily return to script writing and leave directing to a professional director. Happily for the film industry, Wilder had the flair and the aptitude for being an auteur – as was evidenced by his successful career as a combined script writer, director and producer.

Wilder, in an interview with Bernard Dick, once explained how the advent of television made it so much easier for niche specialists to transfer to directing. He explained how they could be involved as a specialist in many small productions and learn about the functions of other specialist collaborators on the set. This allowed them to get to know and form associations with a full complement of other specialists, sufficient to bring together a production of their own.

This, then, is the mindset needed to see how collaboration can emerge from a group of specialists. They are not brought together to decide how to make a production. One, or a small group of them, can take the initiative to bring others in to collaborate on a particular film project.

how nature finds solutions

A strategy that ensures people retain individual ideas that do not converge into common agreement may seem bizarre until you stop to think how nature handles uncertainty, competition and the unexpected. It arranges for each individual in a species to have a unique combination of genes. Then, at each generation, a vast number of different solutions are thrown at the problems of survival and production in the form of individual variation. Nature doesn't know what the future holds, but there is an inbuilt strategy that makes sure that all contingencies are covered and even in the event of catastrophic change somewhere there will be some combination of genes that will be able to cope.

It is this conceptual model that should form the basis of a strategy in the

STRUCTURES THAT CAN ADAPT ARE MADE UP OF INTERCHANGEABLE PLUG-IN MODULES To resolve this paradox, it is best to think of mindsets or cognitive models as being made up of components that come together to be applied to a current situation: a collection of many small conceptual models, similar to the way a Lego construction is made up from many different component parts. Lego have an interesting sales strategy. Most of the Lego components are not sold as kits but as small made-up models. When my two sons had a Lego building craze, they would buy these models not for what they were, but for the components they contained. Each new purchase was immediately disassembled and cannibalized for the novel parts it contained, which they could then add to their own creations. Soliloquies should be treated like this, not as single entities but as assemblies of components, each of the components able to be extracted separately and used in other soliloquies.

Richard Dawkins, in his book, *The Selfish Gene* (1990, Oxford University Press; ISBN 0192860925), created the concept of a meme. This is a mini-concept that can be thought of as a component of an idea in the same way that a gene is a component of a genome (the genetic material that provides the building instructions for an organism). Just as genes vary from one organism to another to create different species or as gene variations create individual characteristics and traits, so memes can be varied to create different ideas or variations of ideas.

The breakthrough that Dawkins' meme concept brought about was to allow ideas to be seen as capable of evolving through an evolutionary process similar to the way in which biological organisms evolve: through the evolution of the changing genes on the genome. This means that ideas do not necessarily have to change dramatically, but can change in small increments according to the addition or subtraction of individual memes.

As is evidenced by the observations of evolutionary biologists, changes caused by altering genes are not necessarily linear. A newly acquired gene may make hardly any difference but on occasions the new gene can totally change the nature of the organism in a significant way. This is the way it is with memes and ideas. Just as a newly acquired Lego component can sometimes inspire a completely new design for a Lego construction, so a new meme, insignificant in itself, can bring about a sudden and dramatic new line of thinking or reasoning. Such unpredictable dramatic change also describes the phenomenon of paradigm shifts that we covered earlier.

It is in this way that we should interpret the idea of soliloquies or individual mindsets. They are not static, permanent viewpoints, but flexible assemblies of mini-ideas that are a current snapshot of an evolving cognitive model. Collaborative learning can then be seen as a form of mating, where expressing viewpoints is a way of exchanging memes. After the exchange, new memes may or may not be incorporated into the ongoing conceptual model of any individual receiving them.

It is in this light that the reader should be reading this book. Maybe you are familiar with most of the memes it contains. Maybe you disagree with many of them. Maybe the conclusions are not entirely acceptable. But the value of the book is not in its entirety, but as a receptacle for holding many memes – any of which the reader can use as appropriate, taking them out of context if necessary, to add to his own conceptual understanding of the world of information.

uncertain environment of e-business. The more simultaneous options being explored, the greater chance there will be for survival and success.

It's not the rate of change, but the changing rate of change that is the problem

John Farrell also made another point:

I think Peter should make a caveat up front, and that is regarding the rigid conservatism behind the movie-making enterprise. While the collaboration involved in the making of film is clear, it's also clear to most people that film makers do not consider what Peter calls 'the suitability of the subject matter ... perceived changing trends in audience interests.' This is the last thing on most movie producers' minds. Given the money needed to produce a film, producers and investors are petrified of losses and confine themselves (and sadly the audiences) again and again to re-creating only what they know was a hit before.

This illustrates the problem of using metaphors. The way in which people collaborate in the movie business has many useful parallels in the world of e-business, but these apply only up to a point. In movie making, there is constant change in fashion and technology, but this change (as it was in the twentieth century anyway) is reasonably steady and the extent of any change can be predicted with sufficient accuracy to make a reasonable assessment of downside risks.

In e-business, there is no way of assessing the risk because the production cannot take the form of a set plan where there can be a fixed budget and a specified time for completion. Certainly attempts can be planned and given a time scale, but such attempts cannot be guaranteed to produce a satisfactory result or at least a result that is appropriate for any length of time.

Realistically, e-business solutions have to be designed as open-ended projects with no fixed costs or completion dates. Solutions have to be developed on the basis of many short steps with reappraisals and redirectioning at every step. This is likely to involve more than just a few changes in direction: occasionally it may necessitate the scrapping of everything that has gone before to make a completely new start with new ideas and even new people.

In this sense, the similarities between movie making and e-business creation break down. In e-business, there is no equivalent of the planned shooting stage. There is no planned production as such. The whole process of creating e-business solutions is more like one continuous pre-production phase. Thus the usefulness of the film-making industry metaphor stops short of the actual production.

Differing also from the metaphor of the movie is the need for e-business strategies to administer several alternative solutions at the same time. This would be like a film director starting out by making several different movies at the same time and abandoning those that seemed not to be working out too well. This requires a unique way of thinking that only makes sense in the context of game theory.

more than one solution

There was a very mixed reaction to the interpretation I'd used in Chapter 9 for applying collaboration. It seemed to mean different things to different people. Stephen Townsend, a student from Australia, recognized that it can take different forms when he wrote:

I thought I already understood the collaborative learning thing, but this chapter delves into a whole new level.

I've participated in a few 'collaborative learning' programs, and I can separate these programs that I've participated in into two types: one is a system where the (learning) outcomes are already defined, and everything is all very structured. This was in the case of our 'Business Week'. It was a week of team-based collaborative learning focused on business – we all split up into teams and each team was a company. It was all very structured – no matter what our responses were, there was a set program that was acted out step by step. Since none of us knew anything about business, each 'company' was given a mentor. They were discouraged from telling us exactly what to do, but at the end of the day – they knew all the answers and we didn't.

The other type of program I participated in was developing a multimedia kiosk with two other students. We didn't know any programming languages, and hadn't done anything like it before. We were given the task and our computing teacher suggested we try using the multimedia authoring application 'Director'. However, he didn't know how to use it any better than us, so we were forced to teach ourselves and share what we learnt.

The goal set for us was to develop this multimedia information kiosk for the school, and we were given free rein over all the other hundreds of decisions that had to be made. From start to finish it took us three months to complete the project (outside of class hours). This type of collaborative task has no structure – there was no way to predict what the end product would look like, both the function and the interface changed from week to week as we learnt more and more about lingo. There was no leader – each of us settled on our own area of 'expertise', and developed it.

In terms of which type of program was most effective (the aim was to give us new skills and knowledge), the flexible approach wins hands down. However, even the structured collaborative approach beat the pants off the standard teacher/classroom experience. So if this is paralleled in any way in the business environment, I can see why collaborative strategies are so powerful. I really liked this chapter.

For me, the most surprising reaction to the last chapter came from Dr Ted Panitz. As I'd used one of his conceptual building blocks (the distinction between cooperation and collaboration) I'd expected him to concur with what I'd written. Instead, he was of the opinion that I was misusing the principles of the collaborative learning process. He wrote:

I think the use of collaborative learning as described in Chapter 9 has gone a bridge too far. Specifically, to call for collaboration without ever asking the participants to meet face to face is a contradiction of collaborative learning paradigms. Also to focus all the decision making in one person flies directly in the face of both collaborative and cooperative learning paradigms. The intent of collaborative learning and collaborative decision making in business is to harness the power of the group, enable members to contribute their expertise to the group and receive feedback from the group.

The process is much like brainstorming and strengthens each individual in the group as well as providing many perspectives from which a consensus will arise. There is a great synergy obtained through the collaborative process where the whole becomes greater than the sum of its parts.

‹snip›

... the organizer would make the final decision as to what should be included, but I can assure table members that if the process is run properly the final decision will be very close to the group's consensus. It may take a little longer for a conclusion to be reached and things like conflict resolution and personnel agendas need to be dealt with, but the consensus response will be much better than an individual decision. The idea of consensus decision making is the real paradigm shift.

I see another contradiction in the approach Peter suggests, where one person makes all the decisions by pulling together information provided by individual experts. Peter provided an excellent analysis of how technical experts manage to hold companies hostage by the way they share their information and how they complicate systems which they then must deal with. How is the proposal in Chapter 9 any different?

If the entrepreneur building an e-business calls upon experts only as needed then he/she will fall into the same trap or worse because there will be no sharing of ideas or critiques of ideas from outside observers. Also, these experts are very cunning in their attempts to make businesses dependent upon them for their expertise (I hope we all are for that matter). I doubt they would be inclined to come into a project, solve all your problems and simply leave, even if their compensation was substantial. Some consultants do work this way by providing turnkey operations, but even they calculate their fees based upon a one-time effort and often expand the time frame to meet their budgets.

‹snip›

Even in the industrial model when companies use teams they are following a cooperative model not a collaborative one because the charge of the team or problem the team is dealing with is controlled by the bureaucracy and the participant interaction processes are supplied by a facilitator. In a collaborative process the members share power equally and contribute equally in the decision making. This is indeed a major contradiction to our current system and hard to accept unless one has experienced the incredible results which come from a collaborative group.

Dr Panitz's post illustrates perfectly the kind of problems that can occur in e-mail discussion groups. I thought I'd been using his mental model. In fact, we had totally different models in mind.

Dr Panitz sees the collaborative group as a mechanism for melding disparate ideas together, combining the views, knowledge and experience of all participants to evolve an agreeable common solution. My view is quite different from this because I see the point of collaborative discussion (as explained in terms of soliloquies) as producing not a single solution, but several solutions.

In mathematical equations where there is more than one unknown, there can be several equally correct answers. For example, the equation consisting of 'x divided by y equals two' can have an infinite number of equally valid solutions – with x able to be any value as long as it is twice the value of y. Something very similar happens when a business problem has many unknown or unknowable factors involved: there can be very many equally valid possible solutions and there is no way of knowing which of them will be correct.

Using collaboration to provide a consensus produces a single solution which might subsequently prove to be incorrect. This can easily happen in the e-business environment where technological developments and unpredictable competitors' strategies can radically alter the playing field. My idea of a collaborative environment therefore is not for the collaborators to arrive at a consensus but to arrive at as many different solutions as possible.

There was much puzzlement and protest at my starting this book off with a few lessons in probability theory, but this shows the reason why. The experiments with the roulette wheel showed that when playing in a non-zero sum game, where everyone can be winners, it pays to have many smaller gambles rather than a single big bet. The consensus opinion represents the big bet because once the consensus is arrived at, all the money and effort goes into that single solution – which may turn out to be wrong. On the other hand, the collaboration that offers many solutions is a far more efficient way to play the game even though it would at first appear to be inefficient.

Another misunderstanding that must be cleared up is the idea that an auteur or entrepreneur weighs up the various options and the opinions of others to make some kind of rational decision. In the world of e-business it cannot work this way because nobody, not even the auteur or entrepreneur, is in a position to give positive judgement on the alternatives that are available. In an environment of unknowns, uncertainty and unpredictable competition the auteur or entrepreneur doesn't make decisions: the optimum strategy is for them simply to generate as many options as possible commensurate with the circumstances.

" THE APPROPRIATE STRATEGY IN AN E-BUSINESS ENVIRONMENT IS TO BE AWARE OF ALL THE DIFFERENT POSSIBILITIES AND PLAY THEM CONCURRENTLY "

In other words, the auteur or entrepreneur will arrange for as many different paths to follow as is practical with the resources at their disposal. Like poker players, they don't play the game to win any specific hand, they play to win as an outcome of many different hands.

It is not about decision making and judgement. The appropriate strategy in an e-business environment is to be aware of all the different possibilities and play them concurrently. Solutions are eliminated as and when they are proven non-viable – not as a result of any rational decision-making process. In this way, it can then be arranged that the real decision makers are the clients or customers and the role of the auteur is to create as many different choices for them as possible.

an example from the world of bricks and mortar

The difficulty in explaining and understanding complex systems, where most analysis is in terms of abstract modelling, is that it is often hard to relate the theory to the real world. This is particularly true with e-business where the rapidly changing environment doesn't allow the use of case histories. The idea of creating an e-business solution that emerges without prior planning; running several solutions simultaneously; collaborative learning without a consensus; these are difficult concepts to visualize without any concrete, real-life examples.

Searching for suitable examples and case histories in the world of e-commerce at this time of writing is fraught with difficulties. Bearing in mind that there is a time delay of months, maybe even years, between the writing of this book and the reading of it, makes it almost impossible to find examples that are certain to remain in existence over such extended periods of time. A year or two in this rapidly evolving world of e-business is the equivalent of decades in previous eras.

For this reason, I have to go back to examples taken from the pre-internet world which, although not identical to today's situations, exhibit the same fundamental issues we are dealing with now in the new and uncertain environment of e-business.

The world of fashion is one such environment, very similar to that which exists in the world of e-commerce today. It is an environment of continuous and unpredictable change. Advanced stock planning is not an option and the whole industry is geared to watching market trends and responding rapidly to any change.

Large companies can deal with this situation more easily than small companies because they can offset misdirections by spreading risk over a larger number of different fashion styles, quickly repeating on lines that are selling and putting the slow lines into an end-of-season sale to recover some of the cost. For smaller companies, the risk is greater because there is less chance to spread the risk, but they have the advantage that they are more adaptable and can respond more quickly to radical new changes in fashion.

During the 1980s, I made the mistake of putting all my eggs in one basket. I'd had an initial success with a range of female fashions, which suddenly put me into a higher league where I could open many in-store concessions spread around the country. Filled with the rush of success, I plunged headlong into this newly discovered world of apparently unlimited wealth.

The realities of this larger and more complex business environment soon became apparent. I encountered cash flow problems, manufacturing problems, logistic problems, a new kind of customer and on top of all this – a sudden change in fashion. Like a fish out of water, I was powerless to deal with the mounting uncertainties and was knocked completely out of the game, losing the whole of my business in the process.

Starting again, poorer but wiser, I was determined to avoid getting into a similar vulnerable position. I managed to rent a large shop at the back of a run-down shopping mall in London's Oxford Street. The rent was cheap because the mall was due to close within a year or two so I knew there was no permanent position I could build up.

As this shop had two entrances, I divided it into two. In one half I sold cheap fashion clothes that I could buy from local wholesalers. The other half I retained for developing my big plan. At the same time I rented a workshop where I had a designer making up clothes which I was selling in a boutique fashion market in Kensington High Street. Although I was spread pretty thin, I had a flexible range of options that could provide a number of different directions to pursue.

My big plan had been to create a shop that sold jewellery components that people could have made up into jewellery of their own design. This was my principal interest and I was certain it would pay off big because everybody was telling me what a great idea it was. Starving all the other businesses of cash, I spent lavishly on display and decor for this exciting and revolutionary new venture. Unfortunately, it didn't take off. I tried everything I could think of to get this jewellery shop going, but the great idea just didn't work. More problematic, it was draining all the profit out of the other businesses – limiting my ability to develop them.

The mall in which my shops were located was situated at what was then the 'scruffy', unfashionable, eastern end of Oxford Street. There were always many street traders around, fly-pitching in the empty shop doorways, and it wasn't hard to see that some of them were making quite a lot of money. In my frequent walks along the street I'd often talk to them, asking them how trade was that day, the type of customers that were on the street, the state of the weather and the activities of the local police.

Although to the casual observer these fly-pitching traders were scratching together an uncertain existence, in fact some of them were quite established and had been working the street for many years. They'd found that the fines imposed by the occasional arrests for street trading were far less than what they'd have to pay in regular rents. Also, the police arrests were very infrequent because when they were arrested, their stock had to be removed and taken down to the police station with every item recorded and booked in. This was a miserable task for the arresting officers because the street traders' stock usually amounted to thousands of items. This made them very reluctant to make arrests so, as long as the street traders didn't cause any flagrant annoyance to passing pedestrians, they were usually left alone. This gave them a kind of permanence that allowed them to adapt to the unique trading conditions in this particular part of Oxford Street.

I learned a lot about trading from these street traders. I'd often have long chats with them in the local café, which most of the local traders frequented at various times of the day. During one of these chats, a wily old street trader, whom I'd got to know quite well, propositioned me to run a table outside of one of my shops selling leather wallets (purses as they are called in America). As I was despairing of the success of my custom-made jewellery business and was somewhat intrigued by his business acumen, I took up his offer.

The street trader took me to a run-down warehouse in London's East End, where we spent a few hundred pounds on a miscellaneous assortment of cheap wallets that had been made in China. The wallets were bought at a range of different prices, so I was quite surprised when the wily old trader told me we had to sell the wallets all at the same price. 'Won't we sell all the dear wallets and be stuck with the cheap ones?', I asked him. He just smiled, then tipped all the wallets out together on to an old baker's tray he'd picked up in the street somewhere and laid them out on a trestle table outside my shop.

To my amazement, the table was soon surrounded by people. They were sorting through the many different wallets and, unbelievably, the cheap wallets were selling almost as well as the dear wallets. Even more surprising, the money being taken on this table was several times the amount being taken by both my shops put together. Even before the day had finished we had to take another trip down to the wholesalers to restock.

The success of this little venture, besides saving me from bankruptcy, also taught me that the type of business that was successful in the back of a run-down shopping mall was far different from the kind of original, trendy trade I'd been planning. My great plan had been too sophisticated for the kind of customer that shopped in the unfashionable part of Oxford Street. As for the dresses in my other shop, they were in com-petition with hundreds of similar fashion shops which any potential customer would have to pass on the way to mine.

The eye-opening experience of this little venture with cheap wallets gave me a fresh perspective on trading. I had many contacts with wholesalers and retailers in and around the 'rag trade' areas of London, so I went round to them buying their end of lines, remnants and second-quality garments and piled them all into one of my shops with a big sign that read 'Everything at one price: £3.99.' It was an immediate success and lasted until the mall closed, giving me the cash flow and leeway to work on my other options.

Although this example may appear to be a million miles away from creating e-business solutions, there are some fundamental issues that are directly related to creating businesses in the fast-changing, uncertain world of e-commerce. I'd moved into what for me was a new and unfamiliar environment. I'd covered myself with a number of options and one of them, which came out of the blue, paid off. The breakthrough had come as a result of mixing in what could have been viewed as an incongruous community. Through a process of collaboration I'd discovered a crucial clue to trading in an unfamiliar environment. I'd taken the clue out of context and combined it with my familiar world of contacts to produce a viable business situation.

It isn't really a big jump to map this situation across to creating e-business solutions. For everyone, the world of e-business is just as foreign as the run-down mall was to me. Just like the street traders in Oxford Street, there are many different people dabbling around in the environment of e-business – succeeding in various little ways which pass unnoticed by those who are too absorbed with their great plans and ideas. Hanging out in listserves striking up acquaintances with seemingly irrelevant specialists can produce just the right clues to bring a number of assorted ideas and contacts together to spark off a successful e-business venture.

This kind of business trading, though, is a very big conceptual jump for executives brought up in a traditional management culture. They will assume that all decision making is a rational process. But in the non-linear, chaotic environment of e-business, reasoning and rationality have no place. It is about chance, risk and unpredictable emergence. This is why game theory is preferred to decision theory.

Later, when we get on to discussing the café as a device to be used for communication in an uncertain environment, we'll see that the idea of splitting up the collaborators into different tables is to maximize the number of possible solutions that can emerge. The worst thing that can happen is for everyone to get together to form a consensus.

If I'd put the idea – of selling cheap wallets out of an old bakery tray on a trestle table outside my shop – to the team of people working for me at that time, it would have been laughed out of existence. No rational brainstorming session could have ended up with this as a possible solution because no one would have been able to identify with the situation of selling cheap wallets in the street.

CREATING A GROUP
OF CONTACTS

PART FOUR IS ABOUT CREATING A STRATEGIC
GROUP OF CONTACTS ON THE INTERNET. THERE
IS A SAYING THAT GOES, 'IT'S NOT WHAT YOU
KNOW, BUT WHO YOU KNOW THAT IS
IMPORTANT.' THIS IS DOUBLY TRUE IN E-
BUSINESS.

CREATING A GROUP OF FRIENDS AND CONTACTS
REQUIRES A VARIETY OF LEARNED SOCIAL
SKILLS, BUT WE ARE ALSO HELPED BY MANY
NATURAL INSTINCTS THAT GIVE US MUCH
EMOTIONAL GUIDANCE.

MAKING FRIENDS AND CONTACTS ON THE
INTERNET, THOUGH, IS A TOTALLY DIFFERENT
EXPERIENCE FROM THAT IN THE WORLD OF
BRICKS AND MORTAR. ON THE INTERNET,
THERE IS A CHOICE OF MILLIONS AND NO
LEARNED BEHAVIOUR OR INSTINCTIVE
EMOTIONS CAN OFFER ANY HELP WITH THE
PROBLEM OF OVER-CHOICE. THERE IS ALSO
THE QUESTION OF TRUST. HOW IS IT POSSIBLE
TO TRUST AN E-MAIL CORRESPONDENT ON THE
INTERNET IN THE SAME WAY THAT IT IS
POSSIBLE TO TRUST SOMEBODY IN THE REAL
WORLD WHERE YOU CAN MEET THEM FACE TO
FACE?

THE UNESCAPABLE REALITY IS THAT MAKING
FRIENDS AND CONTACTS ON THE INTERNET
REQUIRES A COMPLETELY NEW SET OF
ATTITUDES AND VALUES. NOT ONLY WILL THESE
ATTITUDES AND VALUES BE DIFFERENT, THEY
WILL CONFLICT WITH CONVENTIONAL
STANDARDS OF LEARNED SOCIAL BEHAVIOUR
AND MANY NATURAL EMOTIONAL INSTINCTS.

AGAIN, GAME THEORY CAN PROVIDE A SUITABLE
FRAMEWORK TO HELP SOLVE THESE
PROBLEMS.

11

INTRODUCING THE GENETIC ALGORITHM

scary words and arcane theories This chapter might seem somewhat esoteric: at least, it will do if you have never come across genetic algorithms before. But, like most theoretical concepts, they are not complicated at all once you get into them. It's just that they are difficult to explain, so it makes them sound complicated.

If you are at a complete loss with the explanation in this chapter, you might have a quick read through Chapters 16 and 17, where the genetic algorithm is put to practical use; you'll see then how the whole thing is really not much more than common sense.

Why should you bother to learn about something as arcane as a genetic algorithm? Answer: because, for the design and implementation of any kind of e-business solution, it is essential knowledge. For any kind of involvement in e-business, it the most powerful and useful concept you'll ever find.

> " WHY SHOULD YOU BOTHER TO LEARN ABOUT SOMETHING AS ARCANE AS A GENETIC ALGORITHM? "

word of mouth and viral marketing At the time visionaries first reveal their visions there is nothing to distinguish them from hopeless dreamers. It is only in retrospect that visionaries are identified as such. This is because visionaries' visions (and hopeless dreamers' impractical ideas) are usually in the form of abstract models that are difficult to describe. Only the success of the outcome determines whether a person is a visionary or a dreamer.

It is very much like this with business ideas. When an idea crops up, it is usually in a form that only makes sense to the originator of the idea. Most times, these business ideas never pass the tests imposed by reality, but just occasionally those ideas take off – only then do they become good business ideas. Whether this is a matter of luck or judgement is hard to say, but what is true is that business ideas seldom turn into practical reality unless they are based upon a sound strategy.

Consider the phenomenon of the 'craze', the sudden, rapidly accelerating need for a product or service. Crazes are most common amongst school children, where periodically something crops up that everyone has to have. The most mystifying thing about crazes is that they are seldom created through advertising: they are usually generated by means of word of mouth which propagates rapidly through a population.

This is frustrating for advertising and marketing specialists because they'd all like to be able to start a craze, but the method by which a craze can be engineered is elusive. A craze is a kind of positive feedback, a reverberation between a product supplier and the market. Think about it for a moment. How would you go about starting a craze? How many people do you know who have started a craze? Is it something that happens spontaneously or is it something that can be arranged?

This is more than just idle curiosity because creating a 'craze' is likely to be the marketing strategy of choice in the world of e-business. The connected world of the internet is a perfect environment for creating crazes because of the ease and speed by which ideas can spread to millions of people through the modern-day equivalent of word of mouth – person-to-person e-mail.

This kind of marketing has a name; it is called 'viral marketing'. It gets this name because of the way an idea can spread though a population like a virus, multiplying and expanding outwards with a powerful and unstoppable momentum. It is the ideal marketing strategy for e-business, once the technique has been mastered.

engineering a craze
In fact, the creation of a craze isn't as enigmatic as it might seem. It can be engineered and, as proof of this, I've used the technique many times to create crazes in the world of fashion. The trick is to take your mind off the product or service and concentrate first on the strategy and the logistics. Once you have the strategy worked out you can then use a statistical method of trial and error to arrive at the exact nature of the product.

In fashion, the statistical method of picking a winner takes the form of creating many different designs that are offered to the market. Nobody can tell in advance which particular designs will work. I know this because I had a fashion design studio where each proposed design was first shown to all the designers, all the sales staff and a large assortment of customers for them to give their opinions. It never happened that a successful design could be recognized at this stage. Successes, when they came, were always unpredictable and were identified only through subsequent results on the shop floor.

It is extremely important to realize that in certain kinds of markets a successful design will seem to appear at random rather than through a process of logical reasoning. Knowing this, the optimum design strategy is to create as many possibilities as possible and have a system prepared to follow up when a demand becomes evident. Thinking in this way is quite different from the way in which most products are conceived, planned and marketed in the world of bricks and mortar. But this may well be the most appropriate strategy for the massively connected environment of the internet.

" THE TRICK IS TO TAKE YOUR MIND OFF THE PRODUCT OR SERVICE AND CONCENTRATE FIRST ON THE STRATEGY AND THE LOGISTICS "

In 1977, practically every teenager in the UK was wearing button badges. It was one of those emergent crazes that from time to time seem to come out of nowhere and spread like wildfire. This was the result of a predetermined strategy. I know, because that strategy was mine and I supplied all the button badges that fed this particular craze – millions of them.

When I first explained my idea to a group of friends in the Shakespeare's Head (a pub where we used to hang out in Carnaby Street), it was met with derision. I spoke of the power of evolutionary biology and the way those principles could be used to create businesses. At the time, this pub was a hang-out for dope dealers so it was assumed by my friends that I'd been sampling their wares. Nobody took me very seriously.

In fact I was serious. I'd just spent a miserable time recovering from a disastrous business experience that had seen me go literally from riches to rags. With absolutely no money left, there was little to do but spend my time contemplating the world, trying to think of a way to start up some kind of new business enterprise. In what was left of my possessions, I had a two-year collection of *New Scientist* magazines. I'd always had an avid interest in science and had been buying this magazine for many years.

It occurred to me that I might find a good idea for a business somewhere in these pages, so, having nothing better to do, I started to read through the magazines one by one. Without consciously realizing it, as I read sequentially through the weekly editions I became interested in the many different articles relating to evolution. Gradually, it occurred to me that this was a phenomenon that could inspire a business strategy.

> **A PROCESS OF BREEDING AND SELECTION WAS TURNING CHAOS INTO ORDER**

Having spent five years at a scientific research establishment that was developing guided weaponry, I was fairly familiar with system control theory. But evolution seemed to involve sophisticated systems of automatic control that went far beyond anything I had ever come across before. What was most surprising to me was that biological systems, in the form of organisms and nervous systems, were being designed without any theory or planning: sophisticated control mechanisms were just appearing. A process of breeding and selection was turning chaos into order. It was against reason and couldn't be explained by any kind of logic that I was aware of.

Finally it clicked. This evolutionary process was a kind of natural feedback loop that caused a system to auto-correct as it proceeded towards some form of optimum efficiency. Moreover, systems evolve towards a particular state according to what rules are used in the selection process. This I could understand. I'd spent years studying the nature of negative feedback and the way in which it can be used to give a predetermined stability to inherently unstable electronic circuitry. The idea caught my imagination. If evolution resulted in viable organisms emerging out of inert chemicals, then there was every chance that these same principles could be used to create a viable business enterprise.

Nothing specific came to mind, but several months later I saw a hippie selling button badges in the Portobello Road market. It struck me immediately that this was a neat way to earn small amounts of money to get by each day. Only a week later, I was at a trade show and saw a stand selling very cheap button badge-making machines. The technique was very simple. It needed a circular punch to cut out a picture and a special press that clamped a circular metal frame around it. Hey presto! A button badge, for just the few pennies it would cost for the components. Here was a way to eke out a living while I worked on a real plan for my next business venture. So I bought a cutter, one of the presses and a few hundred components.

It was easy to make the button badges, but I was faced with the problem of what to put on the badges. How could I know what kind of badges would sell? It was then that I thought of the way in which evolution finds successful genes: it tries a whole lot of them out and lets the results separate the winners from the losers. With this thought in mind, I used the cutter to cut out a random selection of pictures from various magazines. By putting them all on a board and observing which sold and which didn't, I could use this as a guide to making more. Those that didn't sell I could throw away.

I'd arranged with a friend of mine who had a shop in Carnaby Street to let me put a badge board outside his shop for a percentage of the takings. Pretty soon, this board was acting like an intelligent marketing device: showing me what kind of badges were selling and which were not. It was so successful that some of the other shops in Carnaby Street were asking me if I could supply them with a board and some badges. It was then I had this great idea.

In the Shakespeare's Head that evening, I explained my idea about how the principles of evolution could be used to expand my little badge board into a national business. I asked if anyone wanted to come in with me. There were no takers. They just laughed and asked me where I was getting such good dope.

But I'd seen the light. I was soon attracting the attention of many other traders who wanted to buy my badges; they'd noticed how my board was always surrounded by customers. With this wholesale trade increasing, I'd stopped using cut-outs from magazines and was using a photocopying shop around the corner to print many copies of the designs that were selling well. Soon I was employing outworkers to make up the badges for me.

It wasn't long before I had to give up running my badge board to concentrate on supplying badges to my wholesale customers. Even so, the increasing demand was exceeding my ability to supply and I was forced to look for a new manufacturing solution. It was then I noticed that in some of the shops there were a few button badges that had been around since the craze on the Beatles – some ten years previously. These were similar badges to mine except that they had obviously been mass produced.

I tracked down the supplier and found it to be a company whose main business was making ornate metal cake tins. They'd perfected a technique of printing on to enamel-coated steel sheeting and besides pressing these out into cake tins, they'd branched out in the 1960s to use the technique to make button badges for Beatle mania.

It was a solution to my problem. They had the facilities to produce any number of button badges I could possibly need. The snag was that their technique and machinery was based upon printing very large sheets of steel – which printed 340 badges on every sheet. As it was not viable to print less than 100 sheets at a time, it meant that my minimum order had to be at least 34,000 badges.

A few calculations told me that I could sell this number of badges but the problem then became which designs to choose to be printed. My evolutionary system was great for providing instantaneous customer response – printing on demand – but, as this demand was continually changing, it wouldn't be any use in helping me predetermine an advance order of many thousands.

It was then that I applied the evolutionary model again. Evolution works by putting genes into an ecosystem, letting the unsuccessful die out and the successful survive and multiply. How could I apply that principle to a button badge-making system? It then occurred to me to think of each button badge design as a gene. If I printed 340 designs on a sheet, it would be the equivalent of testing the market with 100 each of 340 genes.

As this method of manufacturing was cheaper and there was a high mark-up on the cost to sale price, I figured I could work like nature and allow for some redundancy. A back-of-the-envelope calculation told me that the business would still be viable if the manufacturing costs were doubled. This would allow me to work with a 50 per cent redundancy rate. In other words, if like nature I created a surplus and allowed for half of the badges not selling, I could still be profitable.

Effectively, this allowance for waste halved the number of badges I needed to sell. Instead of having to sell all of the 34,000 badges in a print run, I'd only need to sell 17,000. As by this time I was selling around 2,000 badges a week, it meant that within two months I would need to print more. Looking at this in terms of an evolutionary strategy, this second print run would in effect be a second generation. By copying nature's strategy, I could arrange for this second generation to repeat on the designs that had sold from the first print run and leave out the others. This equates with the strategy of nature, which increases the successful genes at each generation while reducing those that are less successful.

After the first two months of sales, it was becoming clear that some of the designs were far outselling the others. It was only common sense therefore that these designs were repeated several times in the second generation of printing. This meant that instead of 340 different designs, the second print run (generation) would contain less than 100 repeats of the designs – some of them being repeated two, three, four or even more times according to how well they seemed to be selling. At this second print run, the second generation, I also took the opportunity to add in 50 fresh designs to try out. This is exactly the way nature works: multiplying the best, reducing the worst and adding in a few new variants (mutations).

When it became time for the third print run (the next generation), I could look at the stock of badges and set the 340 designs such that it would replenish designs running low, allow for the increased sales of the best sellers, plus add in a few more variants. This ensured that I always had a regular stock of the button badges that were selling and at the same time I was continuously increasing the variation of the range. I could continue this strategy for any number of generations.

Certainly some of the designs turned out to be duds; sometimes best sellers were overestimated in some generations; but overall this method of working in generations and adjusting the designs to respond to the constantly changing demand for button badges was surprisingly efficient. There were many badges that remained unsold but these turned out to be far less than expected, such that this method of creating a 'living' and 'adapting' product resulted in only a 10 per cent increase in costs through wastage. This was easily absorbed by the profit margin.

Another advantage was that it was easily scalable. As the craze for these badges took hold and I started supplying shops all over the country, I could use exactly the same method of production but increase the print run every month. To increase the efficiency, I could divide the print runs such that print runs of three or four hundred would be used to print the best sellers, while shorter runs of 100 would be used for the slower sellers and the new experimentals.

When I'd begun to supply other traders with badges, I'd realized that I couldn't rely on magazines for designs because there would be problems of copyright. Besides hiring some designers, I also made a deal with a photographic studio who supplied pictures to magazines. He had hundreds of thousands of pictures for me to choose from, but I had no idea which would be the best ones to choose – especially as I had to pay not an inconsiderable amount for any that I did pick.

Remembering my evolutionary strategy, I explained to the owner of the studio that I had no idea which would sell and the only way I could find out was to try them out. I proposed that instead of paying for selected designs, I gave him a regular sum of money each week to be able to experiment with his photographs to find out which worked and which didn't. This arrangement was accepted, so, for a relatively small overhead, I had access to a large gene pool of button badge designs that I could regularly introduce into my evolving system.

This simple application of nature's evolutionary strategy allowed me to create a successful and efficient business that fed a runaway craze with the utmost simplicity and efficiency. That happened a quarter of a century ago. Since then, I've used variations of that evolutionary strategy in all kinds of businesses, often with spectacular results.

To me, the e-business environment offers the ideal situation for this strategy to be employed in many different ways. Particularly so, because in the time since I first used it to create the button badge business in 1976, many more secrets of the evolutionary process have been revealed. This allows the concepts of evolution, generations, genes, selection and mutation to be applied not only to designs and print runs, but to people, ideas, information and knowledge.

> THE CONCEPTS OF EVOLUTION, GENERATIONS, GENES, SELECTION AND MUTATION [CAN] BE APPLIED TO PEOPLE, IDEAS, INFORMATION AND KNOWLEDGE

For the rest of this book I shall be speculating on these possibilities and I hope the reader will not react like those friends of mine did in the Shakespeare's Head – who thought the ideas were simply those of a dreamer who had smoked too much 'funny tobacco'.

a very simple strategy for success

The easiest way to become successful is to find someone else who is successful, study how they have become successful and then emulate them. In a competitive world, this strategy can be taken further by finding somebody who is successful, studying what they do and then finding a way to do it better.

While writing this book I chanced to meet a young entrepreneur who had gone from a computer in his bedroom to a rapidly expanding business in a matter of months. Venture capitalists were falling over themselves to give him capital. He'd started off by setting up a server and offering web space and advice to local businessmen for them to be able to run their own e-businesses.

How he had succeeded so quickly was that he'd studied the services being offered locally by other hosting services. He'd arranged his system to be able to offer these same services, but then looked around to see what other services he could add to his system that could give him a competitive edge. This allowed him to sell his service because it offered more. It is a simple strategy that has been used since time immemorial.

Of course, he is vulnerable. He has played a game of leap-frog. There is no way that he can prevent his competitors playing the same game and leap-frogging over him to regain the initiative. In a multitude of different ways this is happening in all areas of the e-business environment. It is the strategy that is the driving force of change in the world of technology and electronic communications.

With the realization that in an environment of constant change a successful strategy is to keep leap-frogging, it becomes sensible to examine this process of leap-frogging more closely. After all, it is a very simple strategy and is available for anyone to play. The question then becomes: 'How can you play leap-frog better than your competitors?' This leads to the question: 'Who are the best leap-froggers?'

The answer to this question is not found in the world of e-business, or even in the world of business at all: it is found in the biological world of nature. There, vast ecologies of organisms are constantly trying to leap-frog over each other in a constant struggle for reproduction and survival. In this environment, organisms are continually keeping ahead of their competitors by adding new or improved features – through acquiring new genes.

There is another important similarity. Take a close look at any biological ecosystem. Is it possible to find any single organism that exists in isolation? Isn't every organism dependent upon others for its existence? Isn't there a variety of different food chains? A variety of complex symbiotic partnerships and associations? The more one looks, the more one finds that the existence of any organism is integrated into an enigmatic, complex whole of interacting life forms. Isn't this similar to the way humans and their organizations exist? Isn't this the way the internet is evolving?

It is in seeing the world of e-commerce as being similar to a biological ecosystem that any business enterprise can be put into perspective. Success can then be seen in terms of a competition to efficiently integrate within an ecosystem rather than to strive for individuality.

the structure of an ecosystem
Looking at a biological ecosystem, it would seem silly to ask who are the leaders and who is doing the planning. Common sense tells us that it doesn't work that way. Existence, success and survival in the biological world are about adaptation, not forward planning. This involves a strategy of species dividing up into large numbers of individuals, each with a slightly different genetic make-up. Each species maintains its existence through having a large variety of solutions to cope with unpredictable changes that may happen to, or within, the environment. There is no planning. The strategy is simply to provide enough options to cover all contingencies.

Seeing success in terms of blind moves, with chance and probability deciding the results, a biological ecosystem appears to have very little relevance to any kind of business model, let alone provide any clues for an individual who is seeking to find a suitable niche in the world of e-business. The trick though is to use another paradigm shift. Instead of focusing on the whole system, the species, or the individuals of the species, think about the ecosystem from the genetic level.

Any individual of a species can be looked at as a specific combination of genes. These genes each have a particular function and their interactions result in the manifestation of the form of the particular individual of a species. Now think of the ecosystem as a civilization. Think of each species as an industry. Think of each individual of a species as a business or a company. Where would a human fit into this metaphor?

> IT IS IN SEEING THE WORLD OF E-COMMERCE AS BEING SIMILAR TO A BIOLOGICAL ECOSYSTEM THAT ANY BUSINESS ENTERPRISE CAN BE PUT INTO PERSPECTIVE

Human activity would equate to the role of the genes, the small units whose activity creates and performs the functioning of the individual (the business). In the process of evolution, genes are *not* randomly selected from a pool. They are preferentially selected from genes that have succeeded in the past.

Does this ring a bell? Aren't most groups of people, put together for a business project or a competitive game, selected in a similar way? A selection process based upon performance in the past?

the magical algorithm

It was not until the 1980s that science realized the full subtlety of nature's evolutionary selection process. The breakthrough came when a researcher at MIT, John Holland, began to question the direction that mainstream AI (artificial intelligence) was taking and began to look at biological systems for a new solution. His insight was to realize that the creation of human intelligence hadn't been based upon any planned system of organization. It had resulted through the process of evolution: a blind process of trial and error.

This non-planning process had created millions of different organisms, whose complexity far exceeded anything that had ever been devised by human intelligence. It had also resulted in the creation of the human brain: the source of the intelligence that everyone was trying to emulate with computer systems.

The enigma John Holland faced was that the probability of objects as complex as biological organisms in general and the human brain in particular being produced by chance was astronomically large. The mathematics would seem to suggest that it would take longer than the age of the universe to produce even the simplest of organisms, let alone human beings. Yet, it had happened, so there had to be something going on, some mysterious mechanism, that had yet to be explained. John Holland spent five years finding out what that mechanism was.

After studying what was then known about evolutionary biology, he reduced the process down to an abstract form that he could model on a

computer. He created simple organisms where the genes were represented by sequences of binaries (noughts and ones). He then created a
hypothetical perfect organism (consisting of a random combination of
these noughts and ones). With his model – a computer program which he
called a genetic algorithm – he experimented to see how he could get
organisms, consisting of different randomly selected sequences of noughts
and ones, to evolve into this perfect form through a process of blind chance.

This can be likened to throwing 25 dice to create a hypothetical perfect
organism, then working out a way for that same sequence to come up
again by throwing the dice in different ways. Mathematically, it seems
impossible, but nature was doing it and John Holland was trying to see
how nature was performing this impossible trick.

John Holland designed his computer program to emulate the process of
biological evolution as closely as possible. This required working with an
expanding population that could be periodically culled to select the best
for survival and allow the worst to die. The selection process was simply
a method of choosing which of the pseudo-organisms came nearest to his
designated perfect specimen. Those selected in this way were then
arranged to breed.

The breeding process consisted of putting the selected survivors into
pairs; then making a randomly chosen division in each pair and swapping
over the genes at that division. Figure 11.1 illustrates one pair of organisms
creating two offspring by each splitting at point 5.

This division and gene swapping is repeated for each pair several times,
with a different division of the genes chosen randomly at each
recombination. This creates the new generation of organisms which will
then consist of different mixes of the gene combinations that proved
most successful in the previous generation. (Note: mysteriously, the odd
random change to one or other of the genes during the exchanges –
mutations – greatly improves the efficiency of the process.)

This pairing and swapping of strings of ones and noughts may seem
arcane, but it exactly simulates the mating of individual organisms in a
population where the most successful of a generation breed offspring for

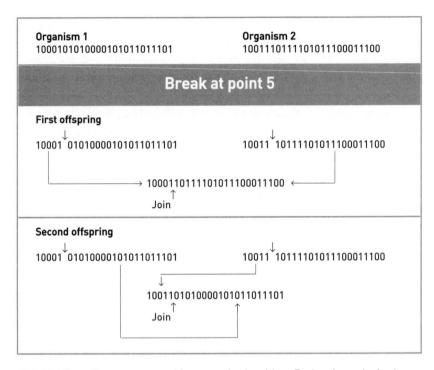

FIG 11.1 Breeding process used in a genetic algorithm. Each pair can be broken at several different places to produce different pairs of offspring. This shows two offspring being created by swapping genes at point 5

the next generation. It emulates what appears to happen in most kinds of mating, where groups of male and female genes randomly combine to create the offspring. This same process is then repeated with the offspring. These are tested for their nearness to the 'perfect organism' and the selected individuals are again paired and arranged to swap genes to produce a new generation. This can then be repeated over any number of generations.

John Holland soon found that this incredibly simple process caused the 'organisms' to evolve rapidly towards the exact combination of noughts and ones that had been chosen as the sequence for the 'perfect organism'. Magically, the impossibility – of a long random sequence rapidly turning into a specific sequence – was now not only a possibility, it was demonstrable.

This was a revelation. This computer simulation of the mating procedures used by nature was effectively providing a speedy way to find optimum combinations of large numbers of variables. More discoveries were to come. It was found that not only could a combination of independent variables be quickly and efficiently found, the process could be used where there were dependent variables (where the value of one variable would have an influence on the value of another). These genetic algorithms could even discover the rules that linked the values of dependent variables. Previously, this kind of problem solving had proved intractable, even when using the most sophisticated of mathematics.

Within a very short time of John Holland publishing his research results, his technique of optimization (the genetic algorithm) was finding applications in all kinds of technical areas, where previously the right combination of variables had proven too complex to find by rational analysis. Today, genetic algorithms are essential tools for many scientific and business applications and are even built into conventional spreadsheet programs.

NOTE the mechanism of genetic algorithms as described here is illustrated as an animated demonstration on the CD-ROM *How God Makes God* and is explained in more technical programming terms in the book *Magical A-Life Avatars*.

To summarize: the technique discovered by John Holland can solve problems where there are large numbers of unknowns. Isn't this what creating e-business solutions is all about?

applying genetic algorithms to e-business strategies

The technicalities of genetic algorithms are relatively unimportant because the underlying principle is so elegantly simple:

Periodically select winning combinations of objects or ideas and mate them to achieve a fast route to optimization.

The vital key to the efficiency of this process is that genes are transferred during the mating not singly, but in groups. Keeping certain combinations of genes together – across generations – allows interdependence and relationships to be taken into account. As this is a very abstract concept, it may best be explained in terms of a football team.

It has often been observed that when a football player is transferred from one team to another his performance undergoes a radical change. This may be because the player's ability had been enhanced (or reduced) by the particular combination of other players he'd been playing with previously. A star player might become quite ineffective at his new club with a different combination of players. In some cases this may work the other way – a player who has not appeared to be playing well in one team might prove to be a star in another team, where the play of some of the other players especially suits his particular style.

The way in which nature transfers genes across generations is not singly, the transference is in groups. This can be likened to football players never being transferred as individuals, but always together with some of the other players they have been playing with. This allows not only individual skills to be transferred, but also the indefinable associations that enhance those skills.

By arranging random breakpoints, different combinations of elements can be tried out without permanently losing the combinations that work most effectively together. In the example of the football team this is like being able to try out different combinations of players in different teams to discover which combinations work best.

Clearly, this form of optimization has important implications for collaborative business activity. Just as genes can be shuffled around in a mating process, so can collaborators. If this results in the more efficient creation of solutions, the entrepreneurs or prime movers who use this strategy may be at an appreciable advantage to those who rely on fixed teams.

If we now relate this back to the strategy of a film director, who makes a series of films, we might think of him as starting out with a randomly chosen assortment of people to fulfil all the roles that are necessary for the making of the film. It is likely that for the second film, the director will choose some of the people who worked on the first film to work on the second because they worked well together. The third film might see the director again choosing combinations of people from the second film to work on this new film, dropping those that didn't perform so well. It can easily be imagined how, over a series of films, an astute director can gradually improve the efficiency by which he can create a film by judiciously selecting the right combinations of people to collaborate with.

Directors do not always have to use their own judgement, though. It is quite common for stars or other important people involved in a film to insist on certain personnel working on the film with them. They get to know the people they can work with best, those that bring out the best in their performance. In this way, like the biological mating process, the elements are put together not only singly, but also in groups.

Now map this scenario across to an e-business solution. An e-business solution provider can work the same way as a film director, choosing collaborators from a pool of freelancers. The first attempt may not bring about the optimum mix of collaborators, but the second allows an opportunity to alter the mix to retain those who produced good work in the first attempt and replace those who didn't. As the solution provider tries more attempts at providing a solution, the team of collaborators (freelancers) is likely to get more efficient.

Just like the director of a film, the solution provider need not specify every single collaborator. Collaborators might have worked successfully with other freelance specialists on other projects and might recommend that they be brought in as well. In this way, a solution provider will work with groups of collaborators rather than individuals.

If the complex nature of an e-business environment is likened to that of a biological ecosystem, even more advantages of this system of working become apparent. Just like the strategy of a species, the approach to a solution can be arranged through a number of simultaneous approaches. Several alternative solutions can be tried out at the same time. This can be likened to a film director starting several movies simultaneously, or an entrepreneur working on several different ideas at the same time. Groups of collaborators may be used, as and when necessary. Good ones can be re-employed, bad ones dropped and the collaborators transferred between separate approaches.

Seeing collaborators as groups of genes also allows projects to be divided up into periods of time – with each period acting as a new generation – where successful groupings of genes go forward and the least successful drop out. This will enable solutions to evolve in much the same way as species or organisms evolve in the biological world – able to adapt quickly to any changing conditions. The successful approaches can be considered as living through successive generations, while the unsuccessful approaches are allowed to die off. In this way, a best solution can emerge as a survivor.

Unpromising or dead-end approaches can be killed off at period ends, but it may not be necessary to kill off all the collaborators who worked on them. They may be able to be absorbed into surviving approaches or used to embark on a new approach. In this way, an e-business solution provider can emulate the strategy of nature; retaining the best sets of genes in successive generations even when there are failures at the individual level.

For maximum efficiency, the time periods – the generations – into which projects are broken up should be as short as possible. In this way, risks would be minimized and the chances of going widely off course would be lessened. Mistakes could be quickly rectified and the effects of sudden or unpredictable changes accommodated without too much disruption. In effect, this will give any strategy the same resilience and adaptability as a biological system.

Summarizing:

In a relatively stable environment with a reasonable amount of predictability, a conventional planned approach with a managed team concentrating all effort on a single solution would be preferable.

In conditions of uncertainty and unpredictable change, many simultaneous approaches would be the best approach with periodic rearrangements of people and ideas.

the position of the collaborator or freelancer As far as

the collaborators (or freelancers) are concerned, this can make life easier for them – if they are at all competent. They have no necessity to spend their time continuously trying to find auteurs and entrepreneurs who are needing their services. They will be able to form associations and alliances with complementary collaborators where they might introduce each other into projects.

Above all, they will be able to concentrate on their own areas of speciality where their growing expertise can provide a stability that is under their own control. Groups of such specialists might evolve viable interrelationships that survive and prosper independently of solution providers and the solutions they work on. Having the opportunity to collaborate with each other over a number of different projects, there will be an element of stability introduced that exists outside of the production environments. This can be enhanced through the ability of collaborators to maintain contact with each other via e-mail discussion groups even when not working together on the same project.

In the specialist e-mail discussion forums that I belong to, this is a growing trend. Collectively, the members have a large number of contacts and the nature of the projects that crop up nearly always require several different types of speciality. Members are constantly asking for others to participate where speciality assistance is required. In this way, the speciality collaborators, as a network of contacts, create a flexible swarm of experts that can selectively configure to tackle any kind of project.

Such an approach to creating business solutions would not have been practical in the pre-internet era. Without access to a large number of possible specialists and experts, it would have been far more efficient to maintain a permanent team. With the ability to create and maintain contact with a large number of experts in any niche speciality, it is now more efficient to build up a suitable list of contacts and bring them in whenever there is a need. This facilitates strategies that use the genetic algorithm approach, where uncertainty and unknowns can be coped with by mixing and matching different combinations of people and ideas in a continuously changing and evolving system that adapts to, rather than predicts, change.

Significantly, this opens the way for collaboration between experts from all parts of the world. In the environment of the internet, an expert is an expert whether they live in Silicon Valley or the back streets of an Asian community. As long as they have a real expertise and a connection to the internet, there are no geographic separations.

12

A QUESTION OF TRUST

advantages of using a genetic algorithm strategy

The use of a multiple approach to solutions with a continuous changing around of collaborators can eliminate many of the problems inherent in a strategy that uses a cooperative team:

1   It can allow a solution to be continuously infused with fresh ideas and different perspectives.

2   It can safeguard against the project getting locked into a single solution.

3   It can correct for conflicts of personality.

4   It can allow separate approaches to a solution to run concurrently.

5   It provides a means of increasing the efficiency of the collaborators.

6   It can allow all collaborators complete independence.

7   The sudden defection of a collaborator will not be critical.

8   Destructive cliques can easily be broken up.

9   All collaborators will have an incentive to contribute valuable input regularly.

10 Several opposing viewpoints can be accommodated.

11 Specialists and experts can be brought in for short stints to assist in the more technical aspects of a solution.

12 Several different types of leaders or initiators can be accommodated.

13 Oddball characters can be included for their speciality knowledge without causing disruption.

14 Slackers, incompetents, troublemakers, disrupters and non-enthusiastic collaborators can be quickly evolved out without animosity.

15 The solution does not have to include any common agreements.

apparent problems with a genetic algorithm strategy

These are very strong incentives for using a genetic algorithm style. E-business solutions created in this way will take the form of flexible adaptive systems that constantly adapt to a changing, highly competitive and unpredictable environment. But it will require a more detached, hands-off style of leadership. There can be no fixed goals, only experimental excursions into the unknown. Each generation of a solution would need to be more in the nature of building prototypes than designing a finished project. This would appear to present many problems.

A system of collaboration must have direction. It must have feedback and a controlling influence that ensures there is no wastage of time, money or resources. There has to be a realistic and tangible element of trust between collaborators, to ensure that everyone has confidence that their time and effort will be suitably rewarded. Responsibility, guidance and trust are absolutely essential to the viability of any collaborative project, so how are these going to be achieved using a seemingly unstructured, loose strategy?

There will be three questions to be answered:

1 Who would be in a position to exercise control over such a strategy?

2   How can the all-important matter of trust be established?

3   How can a project be given stability, a goal and a direction?

On listserves and e-mail discussion forums all over the internet attempts are constantly made to organize collaborative or cooperative activity. It very seldom happens because few people take into consideration that the environment of the internet is a virtual world, where anyone can pretend to be anyone they want to be. Men can pretend to be women, women can pretend to be men. Novices can appear to be experts. The pauper can appear to be rich. A student working from a bedroom at home can create the impression of being a substantial business operation.

Although this levels the playing field for the start-ups and the disadvantaged, it also provides an ideal environment for cheaters, hucksters, confidence tricksters and pretenders. What's to stop people from reneging on promises, being unreliable, delivering shoddy products or incompetent work?

Even worse than deliberate dishonesty or misrepresentation is misunderstanding. This is the bane of internet communications. How do you safeguard against, and avoid, collaborative associations that go wrong through misunderstandings?

It is by being able to answer these questions and solve these kinds of problems that a collaborative strategy will stand or fall.

what is the role of the auteur?

The obvious objection to a collaborative approach to creating an e-business solution is that there appears to be no control over the direction that a solution takes. If nobody is taking a conventional leadership role, guiding the direction of the multiple approaches, it might seem that this can lead to confusion and much wasted effort.

The book *The Entrepreneurial Web* dealt with this problem. That book was written in the same way as this: with a virtual café of readers who commented and gave their views and objections at each chapter. The strategy for creating e-business solutions, as proposed in that book, was to evolve a solution without any pre-planning, without any pre-conceptions. This was described as a bottom-up approach where the solution emerged as a direct result of feedback.

At first, there was great concern that such a strategy would be directionless and could lead the solution into a dead end. However, when it was explained that the strategy depended upon the construction of a suitable communication framework that provided the right kind of feedback to keep the project on course, the fears were allayed.

This is the key to the success of a genetic algorithm strategy. The leader, or, auteur, of the solution is not the architect of the solution: his role is more that of a conduit, to funnel and filter all relevant information to the collaborators working on the various approaches to the solution. Primarily, the leader is a skilled communicator whose views are not self-generated but are the aggregate input of his or her sources of information. This doesn't direct the system specifically, it creates a continuous feedback that keeps projects on track in the same way that feedback will keep the direction of a guided missile on target even when the target weaves and turns.

At this stage it is important to visualize the structure of a system that is developing an e-business solution. The critical factor is that an e-business solution is being created in an environment of unknowns, unpredict-ability and an evolving knowledge base that is expanding too fast for any single person to be omniscient.

The system creating the e-business solution can be broken up into two distinct areas. For want of a better way to describe them, let's call them 'inside the box' and 'outside the box'. Inside the box will be the collaborators. This will be organized along the lines of a genetic algorithm strategy, where collaborators are mixed and matched, come and go. The collaborators will each be bringing into the box their unique set of skills or specialized knowledge.

Assuming that no collaborator is omniscient, they will each have to confine their focus of interest to a fairly narrow field: their particular area of speciality. As we saw in an earlier chapter, experts often assume they have knowledge in areas outside their own particular speciality. This is a constant source of danger inside the box, especially if a collaborator assumes a knowledge that none of the other collaborators have sufficient experience to be able to contradict.

To counteract this danger, the auteur has to provide independent influences that can prevent an e-business solution drifting off in a wrong direction. This is a problem for the auteur, because he or she is also unlikely to be omniscient. The auteur will almost certainly have large knowledge gaps just as surely as any of the collaborators. To plug all the knowledge gaps, the auteur has to look outside the box.

Outside the box is a vast confusion of conflicting knowledge and information. The auteur will have to devise a strategy to make sense of this confusion and filter out just the right information to fill the knowledge gaps of the collaborators working inside the box. This is the area of the auteur's speciality: focusing an adequate and appropriate information flow from outside the box to the inside. This is illustrated in Figure 12.1.

It is often assumed, by people who have never been in an entrepreneurial position, that an entrepreneur is a wheeler-dealer, a manipulator and an autocratic exploiter of other people's talents. This is seldom the case. The

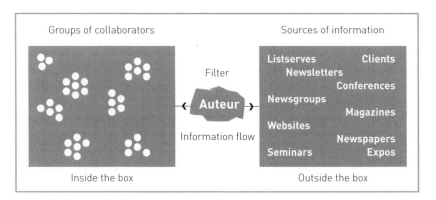

FIG. 12.1 The role of the auteur in the creation of an e-business solution

role of the entrepreneur is more usually that of an information provider: an auteur, who works not as a decision maker but as the organizer of appropriate information for others to be able to make decisions. In this way, the entrepreneur or auteur will function in an evolving system similar to the way in which oil functions in a mechanical engine: the essential element that seems not to be doing any of the real work, but is vital to the running.

The entrepreneurial input has to create an environment of trust and confidence. Trust that collaboration will be rewarded and confidence that the whole venture will succeed. This is quite different from the role of leadership as understood by most management theories where trust and confidence may have different connotations. The difference is that an entrepreneur has to create an environment of trust and confidence that is completely independent of people – even independent of the entrepreneur that creates this trust. This is particularly important in the fast-changing, technological world of e-business, because neither the entrepreneur or any of the collaborators can be omniscient – they will all be fallible.

Mostly, an entrepreneur will rely on an honest reputation and evidence of adequate funding. This will ensure collaboration, because collaborators can feel assured that they will be rewarded according to any under-standings agreed upon at the commencement of their collaboration. However, this isn't sufficient to assure that the system of collaboration will proceed efficiently. It needs individual confidence that not only will the result of any collaboration lead to a successful conclusion, but that any collaboration will lead to more opportunities for profitable collaboration in the future.

With cooperative teams, where team members are engaged as employees on a permanent basis, the necessity to give confidence that further remunerative work will become available isn't an issue. With colla-borative work, this may be a critical issue, not only for an agreement to collaborate but also as an incentive for a collaborator to make the maximum effective effort. The ability to inspire this kind of confidence is dependent upon how successfully the entrepreneur, in the role of auteur, can find and filter information from outside the box.

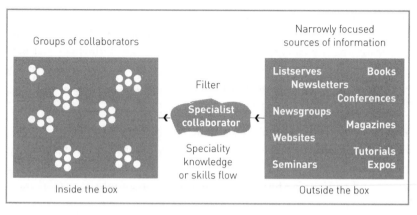

FIG. 12.2 The role of the specialist collaborator in the creation of an e-business solution. Each will have an area of special interest outside the box

In the fast-changing world of computer technology, all experts and specialists will have to focus narrowly. They will need to be not only expert in their chosen field but constantly on the alert for changes and new directions. This will require full-time concentration. Just like the auteur, they will have to be continuously linked to a plethora of different information sources to be aware of changes in their field and to know what they have to learn to keep abreast of the changes – they will also have an interest in what is happening outside the box, albeit in a limited area of knowledge. This similarity can be seen by comparing Figures 12.1 and 12.2.

Like the auteur, the specialist collaborators will have to make sense of a confusing world of uncertainty. They'll have to take risks: as to the way they spend their time; the sources of information they choose to be influenced by; which new areas of study to pursue. In almost every instance of speciality in the e-business environment, the expert will need all the time they can find, just to avoid going backwards. They will have very little time to spare to become more than casually acquainted with what is going on elsewhere.

For this reason, a collaborator will be looking for more than just fair payment for the work they do. They will be looking at the effect the participation is going to have on their progression in their chosen speciality profession. They will be looking to collaborate on projects that can bring them into contact with new people, new influences and new directions. They will want to be able to enhance their reputations so they will want to be associated with successful projects, especially if they involve innovations or cutting-edge technology.

It is down to the communication skills of the auteur to make sure that the collaborators are made aware of the latest advances in technology, made aware of the progress of competitors, made aware of possible dead ends and pitfalls. This needs dedicated and full-time work and concentration by the auteur, so he or she will have very little time available to mollycoddle people and cater for their moods swings or changes in temperament.

Certainly it won't be the cosy atmosphere that would be the hallmark of a cooperative team. It will be an association of professionals who are enjoying the freedom to do their work well, improving their reputations, making new contacts: all in the heady atmosphere of a project in which everyone has confidence that it is heading in the right direction. It's not about loyalty and altruism, it's about being part of a universal revolution that is applying digital technology to improve the way in which everyone can lead their lives.

dealing with the problem of trust

During the writing of the past few chapters, the reviewer comments have repeatedly brought up the question of trust. This was felt to be the most crucial element in the success of any e-business venture. This is absolutely true, but, in the world of the internet, where there is often no face-to-face communication and deception is so easy, it is necessary to use rules and standards that are completely foreign to the conventional world of business and management.

Trust in the communication environment of the internet has to be totally disassociated from the conception of trust used in the world of bricks and mortar. Subjective judgements have no place. Reputations and promises have little credibility. Friendships are uncertain, advice is always suspect, reliability is always questionable. Allegiances are subject to reversals. Defection is always a possibility. It is easy for people to renege on a deal if they get a better offer.

Conventional thinking would see this as a state of affairs where it would be impossible for anybody to be able to cooperate or collaborate with anyone else. However, this is no more than conditions of uncertainty and is easily accommodated within the framework of game theory.

The trick is to dispense with the notion of trust and in its place substitute the notion of risk. At a stroke, this simple expedient removes all the problems associated with trust. Instead of considering how much you trust somebody, you estimate the risk factors involved and use those in a strategy for collaborative associations. To explain this, two models might be useful: a game of Solo Whist and a game of Tit-for-Tat.

In the game of Solo Whist, all the cards are dealt out to four players at a table such that they each have thirteen cards. At each trick (round of play), every player plays a card of their choice and the winner of the trick is the player who has played the highest card. In this way it is very similar to bridge, with players working out a strategy to win as many tricks as they can with the cards at their disposal.

> THE TRICK IS TO DISPENSE WITH THE NOTION OF TRUST AND IN ITS PLACE SUBSTITUTE THE NOTION OF RISK

The game starts with each player proposing how many tricks they will win. The one who proposes to win the most is the one who plays to win (or lose) the points associated with that call. The highest proposal is of course the player who proposes to win every one of the 13 tricks in the hand. Surprisingly, the second-highest call is not to win 12 cards, but to win no cards at all. This is a special call named 'Spread Misere': the word 'Spread' indicates that the caller must lay down his cards at the start of play so that all the other players can see the hand they are playing against.

It is this element of playing with open cards that is an important element of any business strategy on the internet. In fact, it is a good strategy in any business situation for anyone who seeks to create a relationship of trust.

Without entrepreneurial experience, the idea of playing a competitive game with all your options exposed may seem to be a foolish strategy. People can always anticipate your next move. They can know how you are playing the game. But, if you stop to think about this for a moment, whom would you rather collaborate with: somebody whom you can anticipate, or someone who might pull an unexpected trick out of the bag?

When a player calls 'Spread Misere', they will know that every card that they are able to play will be obvious to everyone else. They will then have to feel certain that whatever way the others play they will not be able to defeat the call. They can therefore only have confidence in the call if they have anticipated all the possible ways in which the other players can combine to defeat them. Such a strategy would be disastrous in a zero sum game where winners win what losers lose, but, in a non-zero sum game where everyone can be winners, this is likely to be the optimum strategy.

In a game of cards, such as the game of Solo Whist, the term 'trust' is out of place. For example, if you see somebody play a card from their open hand after they have called 'Spread Misere' you wouldn't say that you trusted them to make that play: you'd say you expected them to make that play because that was the sensible card to play. It is this concept of 'the sensible way to play the game' that replaces the concept of trust and it is this same concept that replaces the element of trust in dealing with people on the internet.

For this replacement for trust to be effective, an auteur, or entrepreneur, hasn't got to convince people that he is trustworthy; instead he has to convince people that he is skilled at playing the game of risk. To do this, he has to make all the other players aware of the options open so that all can see that they choose the most sensible options and are therefore skilled in playing the game. In this way a collaborator can be 'trusted' to do what is expected of them.

To fully understand why such a strategy works, it is necessary to understand another game: the game of Tit-for-Tat. This was a strategy that evolved out of a competition set by the political scientist Robert Axelrod who, in the 1970s, invited a number of universities to take part in a competition to see who could devise the best computer program to play 'The Prisoner's Dilemma'. This is the classic game theory scenario where two criminals are arrested for a crime and are taken to separate cells to be questioned.

Each criminal has a choice of blaming the other and getting off scot free, or pleading not guilty and being charged with a lesser offence that carries a small penalty. Without knowing what the other criminal may say, it would seem that the best strategy for each of the criminals is to blame the other. However, if they both blame each other they will both get the maximum sentence. The optimum strategy is for each to plead not guilty and trust that the other will have the sense to do the same.

In the computer version of the game, the options open to each computer program are to cooperate or defect. This is described more fully in *The Entrepreneurial Web* but, in essence, when two programs compete against each other there are four possible outcomes:

1 A program wins 3 points if it decides to cooperate and the other program also decides to cooperate.

2 A program wins 1 point if it cooperates but the other defects.

3 If the program decides to defect it will get 5 points if the other program decides to cooperate.

4 If the program decides to defect and the other program also decides to defect it will get 1 point.

To two competing programs, the option to defect seems to be the optimum choice, but if they both defect then they would have lesser rewards than if they had both decided to take the seemingly less favourable option of cooperating.

The tournament was played on a round robin basis with each of the programs playing against each other many times. Despite the sophistication of some of the programs that took part, the winner was the simplest program of all: a program named Tit-for-Tat. This program would play a cooperation when it first encountered another program, but at every subsequent meeting it copied whatever choice the other program had made in the previous encounter.

Although this Tit-for-Tat program was an algorithm, it was effectively looking to establish unbroken sequences of mutual cooperation. If other programs could detect its pattern of play, they could establish a strategy of mutual cooperation which would enable them to gain more points. In other words, it was looking for other programs to play the game sensibly, which could be trusted to choose the option that would be most beneficial to them both in the long run.

This simple strategy was only ever beaten at subsequent tournaments by a program that was similar, but allowed the occasional exception where it played a cooperation when the other program had previously played a defection. This would be the equivalent of occasionally forgiving another program for making a mistake, enabling a fresh start to be made to perhaps establish a new relationship of mutual cooperation.

Robert Axelrod used these results to describe similar activity that occurred with humans in the real world. He showed how mutual cooperation emerges spontaneously through a similar strategy used in all kinds of business, social and political scenarios.

His empirical observations revealed a highly critical factor: mutual cooperation would be more likely to take place if there was a chance of further cooperative encounters – such that the anticipated accumulative rewards from future encounters would have the expectation of providing more gain than an immediate defection.

> SENSIBLE PLAY WOULD ENTAIL COLLABORATORS BEING SKILLED ENOUGH TO SET UP SEQUENCES OF MUTUALLY PROFITABLE ASSOCIATIONS THAT BUILD UP SLOWLY TOWARDS A POSITION OF JUSTIFIABLE CONFIDENCE

sensible game play

If the model of 'Spread Misere' is combined with that of Tit-for-Tat, it may be possible to provide a viable alternative to trust for establishing collaborative associations on the internet. Sensible play would entail collaborators being skilled enough to set up sequences of mutually profitable associations that build up slowly towards a position of justifiable confidence.

If it is understood by collaborators that the rules don't include any notion of loyalty, friendship, commitment, altruism, allegiance or obligation, then decisions about agreeing to collaborate would have to be based upon a more tangible value system. This would mean making sure that defections from collaborative associations are always seen as having negative values. In other words, anyone in a collaborative association will have the responsibility of making sure that their associate collaborators have a credible expectation of further benefits at a future time – after the time of any current or proposed collaboration – at least sufficient to ensure that it would be unwise for them to defect.

This can be arranged in practice by starting off collaborative associations with activities that involve small risks and small rewards, then gradually increasing the value of the collaborations as confidence is built up that the other person knows how to play the game and is unlikely to defect. In such a strategy, much effort would have to go into establishing confidence in the beginning – for little or no real benefits. This foreplay would involve a substantial amount of time and effort, which would be wasted in the event of a defection. This loss of build-up effort is often sufficient in itself to make defections less likely – especially by players who understand how to play the game sensibly.

The small risks at the start of a series of collaborative associations will also allow collaborative associations to be built up from nothing, even between complete strangers, because it insures against too much being lost by collaborating with somebody who doesn't know how to play the game – and defects at an early stage.

This is not a radical strategy: it is the way collaborative associations are normally built up in the non-internet world of bricks and mortar. The difference is that in the non-internet world, relationships are forced to proceed at a slow pace; whereas in the world of the internet there is often the mistaken impression that relationships can be established as easily and instantaneously as one can communicate with people. Such a misconception is a serious strategic mistake, because there is every reason to believe that reliable relationships for dependable collaboration via the internet will take much the same length of time to become established as in the non-internet world.

Sensible game play should make suitable allowance for collaborative associations to build up slowly, with risks at each progression being suitably counterbalanced by adequate penalties for any defection by one or other of the collaborators.

The idea of taking little steps towards building up a mutually beneficial series of cooperative associations is accommodated neatly within the framework of a genetic algorithm strategy. The separation of any collaborative project into many generations will offer the opportunity for all collaborators to cooperate or defect. Just as in the game of Tit-for-Tat, collaboration could be seen as a series of plays that are used to establish a relationship that can blossom into a long-standing series of mutually profitable subsequent associations.

Just as a genetic algorithm strategy can cope with many simultaneous ideas or approaches at various stages of development, so it can cope with collaborative associations. A few, already established, profitable collaborative partnerships can provide a reliable income while, at the same time, new relationships are being developed for future projects. In this way, sensible play would see a collaborator's list of contacts evolving: becoming increasingly more extensive and reliable as time goes by. There is no shortcut to this process.

the importance of credibility

As a strategist, in a world where anyone might defect if it is profitable to do so, the sensible play is to make sure that every collaborative deal is very much biased in favour of cooperation rather than defection. This is not as straightforward as it sounds because it requires being able to anticipate the thinking of others. This can be illustrated by another of the dialogues from *How God Makes God*, where an experienced businessman is advising a novice how to arrange a collaborative partnership:

To make money you will need to be able to persuade and influence. To do this effectively you'll need to have a good reputation. Every promise you make in any negotiations is going to be discounted according to your credibility.

Credibility?

That's much the same as track record. Credibility is a measure of how much truth or believability there appears to be in whatever you have to say to anyone.

Give me an example.

If you were to offer me a 50 per cent share in a proposition which you see as certain to make a profit of $100,000, and I turn you down to do something with an old business pal that will make me only $10,000, you probably wouldn't understand why.

You are right. I wouldn't.

As I know you have no experience of making money, I would not have a great deal of confidence that your plan would work out. Therefore, I might well think that I would be better off earning a reasonably certain $10,000 with my friend, whose judgement I know I can rely on, rather than take a long shot chance with you to gain $50,000.

Thank you very much.

The point I am trying to make is that when you make an offer, an inducement, or a promise to anyone, it is utterly useless to assume that the other person is going to see it as being as valuable as you might see it yourself. Most people new to business get really upset because they never allow for this and think people are trying to cheat them all the time.

How would I know the perceived value that other people place upon my promises or inducements?

Common sense, I suppose. You always have to put yourself in the other person's place. See things as they might see them and remember that this discounting works both ways.

Both ways?

Why, yes. The other person might be seeing a greater value in what they have to offer than you can recognize. You will be discounting the risks and uncertainties from your point of view – which they might not be able to appreciate.

You make it seem impossible for people ever to be able to believe in each other enough to begin collaborating.

It is difficult, I agree, but this is why it is so essential to develop continuous relationships in business, where you can become familiar with each other's abilities and values. This is a far better strategy than making quick, one-off deals – where values always have to be heavily discounted.

I had a bitter experience that emphasizes this point. It happened after I'd built up a very successful retail jewellery boutique in the trendy 'Hyper-Hyper' fashion market in London's Kensington High Street.

As a direct result of the success of this unit, I'd been offered concessions in all the stores of a national fashion multiple: some 30 units spread throughout the UK. I was hesitant to take up this offer, even though I knew it could lead to a huge expansion of my business, because I knew I'd have difficulty in obtaining sufficient designer jewellery to meet the potential demand.

Then one day a lady came into my Kensington boutique offering me some of the best pieces of costume jewellery I'd ever seen. They were of a style that I recognized as Art Deco – the style characteristic of the 1930s. They were very reasonably priced and I bought every piece she showed me. I asked her if she could get any more and she said she could get plenty because her husband had just bought the contents of a old jewellery factory that had just closed down in France. I was extremely excited and arranged to go to France to meet her husband to buy more of this jewellery.

When I arrived, I was driven way out into the French countryside where I was taken to a picturesque old building. Inside were the remnants of what had once been a highly productive costume jewellery factory. There were presses and various kinds of ancient belt-driven machinery and strewn around the floor were countless numbers of jewellery components. The walls were covered with shelves, stacked with dies and moulds for jewellery manufacture. Looking through them, it was clear to me that this was the production facilities of decades of jewellery making.

I immediately thought of these production facilities being put to work again, to supply a string of jewellery units in the chain of national outlets. Excitedly, I explained how we could collaborate together to create a great business. He had access to this manufacturing capability and I had the

contacts and the organization to set up the retail side. I suggested that
we set up a partnership.

He said it was a great idea, but told me he had yet to complete the
payment for all this stock. I asked how much more he had to pay and he
told me he would need £25,000 straight away to complete the deal. It
was a lot of money and would take all the money I had, but it seemed
such a great opportunity I agreed on the spot. No formal agreement, I
just gave him the money. Well, he seemed such a genuine guy.

The reason why I could agree so quickly was because I knew that just the
components lying around on the floor would probably return most of the
money because the arcade where I had been running the '£3.99' shop was
shortly due to close and I could use this shop to sell this stock off cheap.

When the rubbish stuff from the floor was shipped over from France, I
was surprised to see that it was accompanied by an invoice. All the items
had been given an excessive price and the invoice total came to exactly
£25,000. I'd been had. He'd reneged on the deal and ripped me off for the
money. All I'd got was a lot of rubbish jewellery components which were
hardly worth a tenth of the money I'd given him. I found out later that
this guy was in fact a confidence trickster, who had cheated many people
in the past. And once he'd worked this scam with me, he worked it on
several other people as well.

The pity was that the situation could probably have resulted in a very
profitable business and he'd have made much more money playing it
straight. But how was he to know? He'd had no experience of creating a
business based upon having units in a retail chain of stores, so my idea
was to him just pie in the sky and it made perfect sense to him to defect.

Of course, it would be easy to say that I should have gone to a lawyer
and had everything put into a watertight contract. Would that really
have saved my money? He'd have probably found a way to cheat me
anyway and it would have cost me a lot more in the long run – plus used
up a large part of my time. At least I discovered he was a crook very fast
and I was quickly free to start building up again, without dragging the
thing out for perhaps many months or even years of anguish.

In the world of e-business, a similar scenario is happening time and time again. Investors are investing money, time or effort into dreams that not everyone shares. The problem is that it is not just confidence tricksters that are catching people out. Genuine people, with ideas they honestly believe in, put up seemingly realistic business plans that subsequently fail. This has exactly the same result to the investors as if the instigators had deliberately tricked them out of their money.

A developer on one of the technical e-mail discussion forums I belong to mentioned that he'd had a couple of unfortunate experiences with collaborative associations. He told me that the first was where he'd paid his team of workers to develop software for a company on the basis that he'd get a percentage of the business. He wasn't cheated out of his share, it was just that the idea hadn't worked out the way they all thought it might and the lack of profits caused the business to fold. Different circumstances but the end result was no different from what had happened to me when I was cheated out of my money.

He told me of another experience, where he and another programmer had formed a business association with a very good salesman with a wealth of experience and contacts. Halfway through the project, the salesman had been offered a better opportunity and he just cut away from the business and left them on their own. Without any salesman to sell their product, they had no choice other than to close the business down. Again, he wasn't cheated, but he'd been so convinced that the techno-logical solution he was designing would lead to a profitable business that he hadn't even considered the possibility of the salesman walking away from it. But, to the salesman, the technical details were so beyond his comprehension that he wasn't able to assess the value. A more tangible opportunity presented itself and it seemed rational to the salesman to defect.

Again, it might be considered that this was just a question of being either unlucky or stupid enough to choose a collaborator who had no scruples, but this is not the way to look at it in the world of e-business. The deal should have been set up with the expectancy that a collaborator would defect if it was to his advantage to do so. This is the way it would be looked at in game theory and because of this, a collaborative arrangement would have been structured quite differently. It would have been arranged that instead of big risks, the whole deal was arranged as a series of small risks, which always ensured that defection at each stage became progressively less attractive for the collaborators involved.

This is where an evolutionary strategy provides a solution. Instead of collaborating in one major plan that is fully defined and structured, it is better to develop an idea or a business as a series of small steps or generations. Each step should have a short-term goal and the decision as to the next step should be taken only when the results are known. This will allow a business to build upon experience and knowledge and at every step the risks and rewards can be freshly assessed.

planning or strategy?

After the developer had told me about his unfortunate experiences with collaborative associations, I asked him if these had changed his attitude towards creating e-business solutions. 'Definitely,' he replied. 'For me it is now Planning, Planning and Planning.' This response intrigued me because I would have thought that his experiences with the defections would have convinced him that you couldn't rely on planning.

I knew he was responsible for some very large projects with major companies, so I asked him how many people he employed. 'None,' he replied. 'There is only myself and a partner. We have found it to be too inefficient to employ people on a permanent basis, so we outsource everything to subcontractors and freelancers.' He then went on to explain that besides the massive overheads involved in maintaining a permanent technical staff, employees working at the cutting edge of technology are prone to leave at the most critical times and if they didn't leave they were subject to burn-out.

I asked him what he meant by burn-out and he told me that the most talented employees seemed mainly to work in bursts of energy and enthusiasm. They'd be brilliant for a few weeks, working all hours of the day and night, but would then suddenly seem to lose their enthusiasm and find it difficult to concentrate. He added that besides exhaustion, this was often because they hated anything repetitive, so their interests quickly moved off into other areas.

'So if you subcontract all the work, you can't actually supervise what they are doing?,' I asked him. 'Good heavens, no,' he replied. 'I specify what they have to do and give them a strict deadline for completion. If they don't perform well, they are out and I get somebody else to do the job.'

It was then that I realized that we were thinking along similar lines, except he was describing it as planning and I was describing it as strategy. Our differences were only semantic. He was in fact breaking up his 'plan' into steps and reassessing the situation at the end of each step.

I asked him how many projects he had going on at that present time. 'Nine,' he told me. 'My partner and I handle nine separate assignments and they are all perfectly controlled and we always come in on budget. It may not seem efficient to work this way because we often make mistakes, but it is far better than working with a large managed staff. It's not that this is a good way to work, it's just that any other way is vastly inferior.'

It is interesting to note that this developer was working in the role of an auteur as opposed to an entrepreneur. He was not responsible for the overall strategy of the core businesses, only for the implementation of the interfaces to the connected world of the internet. In this way he was using his knowledge, experience and contacts to find solutions for companies who wanted to explore the potential of the internet to enhance their businesses.

The developer in question had built up a relationship with his customers over a number of years. He was in a position of trust whereby they could rely on him to create a suitable strategy to handle their e-business solutions efficiently.

It struck me that even though he might work efficiently, by his own admission he made mistakes. I wondered if his clients relied only on him, or whether they used a more complex strategy and were using several different people, each providing separate solutions that could be measured against each another. That would seem to be the most appropriate way to work, but it seemed that all of his clients had chosen him as the single solution provider – and hoped that he'd get it right.

various kinds of cooperators

Soon after the discussions with this developer, I visited the annual Internet World trade show being held at Olympia in London. I was wandering around, looking at the various companies exhibiting their products and services, when my eye caught a stand that was offering the services of expert programmers from India. I spoke to the Indian director of this company who was in London for a short visit and asked him how they operated.

He told me that they worked exclusively through a company in the UK, who got contracts for them. Apparently, there were a team of 50 programmers and graphic designers in India who were working for a tenth of the salaries that were being paid to their counterparts in the UK. He was at great pains to stress that all of the employees were highly skilled and took great trouble to make sure the work they carried out was exactly to specification and tested exhaustively.

I asked if they could work flexibly with a very loose specification that was incomplete and could be constantly changed and updated. He looked at me as if I was mad. 'No,' he explained patiently, 'We have to have an exact and detailed specification otherwise we can't handle it.'

Immediately, the flaw in what would seem to be an ideal solution for cost reduction was exposed. These expert workers may be working cheaply, but they were confined to working within a predetermined structural plan. Any form of genetic algorithm approach to create an evolving solution would be impractical.

Comparing in my mind the flexible strategy employed by the developer I'd been speaking to and the services being offered by the firm of low-cost employees in India, I wondered if there was a way in which these could be combined and brought within the framework of a genetic algorithm approach where solutions evolved. It seemed to be a suitable problem for game theory to solve.

As I visited the various stands at the Internet World show, I was amazed at the multitude and diversity of the approaches and solutions to e-business and the exploitation of the e-business environment. Every stand I visited had some novel twist, a different kind of solution, a fulfilment of a speciality niche. Some were offering exciting but unproven products and services, others were offering solutions that had already passed their sell-by date. I wondered how many of them would still be in business by the time the show came around again in the following year.

The thought struck me that this was very similar to a rapidly evolving ecosystem. But ecosystem evolution is driven by chance and probabilities. Did the survival of all these companies depend upon probability? It seemed as if it might, because many of the solutions being offered were mutually exclusive. Some of them had to fail, yet all thought they could succeed. As nobody could be in a position to know which would be the eventual winners, it did seem as if chance and probability would be major factors in determining who would still be in existence in the following year.

Then I looked at it from a lower level of organization. The companies and the solutions might be subject to intense evolutionary pressures, but most of the people, the ideas and the components of the companies were likely to survive to be there again in the following year. Maybe in different forms, in different mixes and combinations, but they wouldn't be so easily evolved out of the ecosystem. They were the genes from the gene pool and the memes from the meme pool. Their evolutionary survival, to the next generation of technological progress in the following year, would be quite separate from that of the organizational structures with which they were associated.

Thinking in this way, it became obvious that the most important strategies would be the strategies of the individuals who made up these companies. In the same way that the actors and actresses, writers, technicians and crew members were not out of the game if a film doesn't succeed, most of the people at this trade show would survive even if they were working with new companies or on different solutions.

I thought of the entrepreneurs; the auteur solution providers; the experts and the specialists; the niche service providers; the executives of the core bricks and mortar businesses that were looking for solutions. Fundamentally, these were all individuals and they were each using individual personal strategies that they were relying on to get them through to the next stages of this rapidly evolving world.

13

CREATING A COMMUNITY TRUST

a disorienting chapter Some of the readers of the first draft of this chapter commented that it confused them. They felt as if they'd lost the plot because it seemed to conflict with the mental models that had been building up in their minds over the course of the previous chapters. The reason why this chapter confused in this way is because the chapter is not about a personal mental model, but a model for a whole community.

To illustrate the idea of a game theory strategy with heuristic rules, I use as an example a community of people who have evolved a set of rules that have worked extremely well for thousands of years. Although these rules apply to individual behaviour, they are designed to make the whole community efficient: not any particular individual. This can be confusing.

The best way to read this chapter is to suspend the mental model you are building for yourself and look at this chapter simply as an example of another kind of strategy. Then, at the end of the chapter, you can think about how you might apply the essence of this kind of strategy, used by a community, for your own personal use. It needs a conceptual jump.

what is e-business really about?

In a world of continuous improvement, where business systems are frantically competing and looking for ways to leap-frog over each other, millions of people are applying their minds, knowledge and experience to finding new ways to improve efficiencies. Most of them will now have their eye on the internet to see how this new environment can be used. Undoubtedly, it is an exciting world of change and opportunity, where there is certain to be rich rewards for those who can succeed. The trick is to find a suitable strategy to be one of the individuals who actually benefits.

The problem is that, as individuals, we are not able to take a macro view of this world of opportunity. It is too vast and too complex. By the time we have studied even a small part of this world, it has moved on and the new knowledge becomes redundant. Prediction and anticipation are of little use either; each of us has to create on the fly, steering by the seat of our pants. We cannot control what is happening, we can only respond to the macro environment as it throws up short windows of opportunity – before closing them again, just as swiftly as they opened.

This macro environment consists of fluctuating and metamorphosing structures that are beyond our comprehension to imagine or understand, yet they are made up of components that we are familiar with: people. At the level of people (the level of the genes of the systems), it is a different game entirely. Here it is a competition between millions of individuals, each striving to be successful in their own characteristic way. Fortunately, this competition has two positive things going for it:

1 Everybody has a different idea of what they consider to be success.

2 It is a non-zero sum game where all competitors can be winners.

These two important elements of the game mean that unlike zero sum games where everyone has the same goal and winners win at the expense of the losers, there are a multitude of different ways of succeeding. Everyone can win because the environment as a whole is naturally evolving towards a state of increased efficiency. It is as if wealth is manifesting spontaneously within the environment and everyone is able to have a share of it. There needn't be a mad scramble to get the biggest share because the wealth being created takes on so many different forms.

In such a situation, the game is not about beating others to the spoils: it is about helping each other to maximize the benefits obtainable from this fountain of spontaneously generated wealth. It is a game of competition for cooperation and collaboration rather than a game of winning against others.

Most intriguing of all, this game, when it is played at the individual level, is open for anyone to take part as long as they have a connection to the internet. It doesn't matter whether they are an investor, an entrepreneur, an auteur, an expert, a specialist, a collaborator or a cooperator – everyone in their own different way will be able to join in the game to assist each other in reaping the rewards that intelligent use of the internet can bring.

Even the people who cooperate within the more conventional structures of managed teams can benefit from this game because, by learning to play the game expertly, they can tap into the environment of the internet to greatly enhance their individual performance and be of greater value to their teams.

The idea of an environment where everyone helps each other and everyone can win would seem to be an unrealistic Utopian dream – but it only seems unobtainable if you give no value to any process that converts raw information into knowledge or actionable information. Information, in itself, is valueless; it only becomes valuable if it can be used. Stop to think about this for a moment: information acquires value when it becomes actionable. This pinpoints the exact area where value is being created.

Click! *The transformation of raw information into actionable information invokes some form of wealth creation.* This is what the Internet and e-business is all about: it is about discovering the added values that manifest when raw information is filtered and processed to turn it into an actionable form. Isn't this what gold miners do when they are prospecting? They use intelligent strategies to sift through tons of worthless rock in attempts to unearth nuggets of gold.

The key to creating a strategy that will unlock the nuggets of gold in the environment of the internet is to realize that it cannot be done by technology alone. Computers are great for sorting and processing. They can be programmed in all manner of useful ways, but they haven't yet reached the stage where they can compete with the human brain.

The electronic environment allows four types of information transfer:

1 Human to human

2 Computer to computer

3 Human to computer

4 Computer to human

All these modes of communication are possible on the internet. Not only singly: they can be present in all kinds of combinations to form a multitude of system configurations. The trick is to appreciate that the intelligent nodes in such systems are not the computers but the humans. Success isn't about replacing humans with computers, but using computers to enhance human ability to communicate and collaborate.

With this paradigm shift, it can be seen that the creation of a successful strategy to tap into the wealth creation potential of the internet isn't about starting with the technology and seeing how to use it, but starting with human-to-human interaction and seeing how technology can be adapted to make it more efficient.

From this viewpoint, the best strategies for getting individual benefits from the environment of the internet are quite independent of either individual goals or the particular roles people have in real life. The game is totally about securing human cooperation and collaboration: not necessarily in the physical sense – but in the intelligent exchange of actionable information and knowledge.

> THE KEY TO CREATING A STRATEGY THAT WILL UNLOCK THE NUGGETS OF GOLD IN THE ENVIRONMENT OF THE INTERNET IS TO REALIZE THAT IT CANNOT BE DONE BY TECHNOLOGY ALONE

difference between a plan and a strategy

In previous chapters, we dealt at length with the distinction between cooperation

NOTE now is the time to suspend the building of your own cognitive model and think about a model that applies to a community.

and collaboration. It took up much time because it was apparent, from the reactions of the review readers of this book, that the idea of people collaborating together without having to be in agreement or having a common goal is not intuitive and therefore a difficult proposition to accept.

It seems that ingrained into our culture is an opposition to individuals having independence. This makes it difficult for many people fully to come to terms with any system that does not tie people together through some form of rules – whether those rules are explicit or tacitly rely upon some form of ethical standards. This presents a problem for the application of game theory because this doesn't recognize any universal rules, particularly if they are artificially imposed. That is not to say that game theory opposes such rules, it's just that game theory does not necessarily take them into account.

In a stable and predictable environment, game theory strategies seldom conflict with established rules and procedures because rules and procedures are generally arrived at as a consequence of previous practical experience. As game theory is also based upon building from previous experience, it is not surprising that there is little conflict.

The difficulty arises in new and unfamiliar environments where conventional rules and procedures start to break down. Then, a game theory strategy might have considerable divergence from the accepted way things are normally done. This is particularly noticeable when it comes to the concept of planning. Just as there is a reluctance to accept that collaborative activity can allow independence, so there is a reluctance to abandon the long-proven practice of careful planning.

Plans and planning, as understood in the conventional world of business management, are a subset of strategies. They are a particular type of strategy that can be used in reasonably predictable environments. In game theory, these would be called algorithms rather than strategies. Both strategies and plans (algorithms) are sets of rules or lists of instructions. They guide actions in order to achieve goals or objectives.

An algorithm or plan is used where the route to a goal can be specified as a sequence of logical steps; it is where a full path to the goal can be written down as a list of instructions or detailed in a contractual document. The simplest algorithms might be a set of instructions to use a piece of electronic equipment, or the assembly instructions for its construction. Such algorithms are used when all information necessary for reaching a goal is available.

The perfect example of an algorithm is a computer program. This consists of hundreds, perhaps thousands or even millions of instructions that cover all contingencies that will enable a computer program to perform its intended purpose. It will use conditionals (i.e. if this, do that … or do something else) as a switching mechanism to allow alternative possibilities to be built into the program. It will use logic gates (i.e. if this is true and that is true do this; if that is false and that is true do this) for decision making – using tests for true or false to determine alternative sequences of instructions to carry out. It will use repeat loops to keep repeating a sequence of operations until some criterion is met. This is the basis of all computer programming and the fundamental structure of all algorithms and structured plans.

Business plans also fall into this same category. They are a set of specific procedures that will contain conditionals, logic gates and repeat loops. They will be able to deal with predictable forms of uncertainty by providing alternatives and contingency plans. This allows estimates and predicted events to be included in the algorithms.

The main characteristic of algorithmic plans is that one way or another there is a specified goal and a specified route to reach that goal, however tortuous or complex. Specific instructions can be written down, progress monitored and checked. Everyone involved can be given a fixed role and a specific task to carry out. The efficiency with which people do their job, or the way in which the algorithm performs, can be assessed and measured.

Most conventional businesses will prefer algorithmic plans because they are based upon tangible specifications that bring some form of order and control to a project or enterprise in a form that everyone involved can understand and agree upon. For the purposes of this book we shall refer to all algorithmic-type strategies as plans – procedural plans, that are worked out in advance based upon anticipated or predicted events and circumstances. These are the type of strategies that are fully covered by all conventional management books.

Unfortunately, algorithmic-type planning is not appropriate for the fast-changing, uncertain world of e-business. There is too much uncertainty and too many unknowns for any preconceived plan to have any reasonable degree of reliability. Contrary to the view that any plan is better than no plan at all, structured planning in the world of e-business can often be a handicap. Thus, in place of conventional planning, we have to use the game theory concept of heuristic strategies.

heuristic strategies

The difference between an algorithmic strategy (a structured, forward-looking plan) and a heuristic strategy can be visualized by thinking of moving between two cities in two vastly different countries. For example, if it was intended to travel directly between San Francisco and New York without going by air, the route could be planned from start to finish simply by consulting a road map. This would then be an algorithmic plan because each step of the way could be described and written down as a list of instructions.

> CONTRARY TO THE VIEW THAT ANY PLAN IS BETTER THAN NO PLAN AT ALL, STRUCTURED PLANNING IN THE WORLD OF E-BUSINESS CAN OFTEN BE A HANDICAP

Now imagine making a surface journey in South America, having to travel from Bogota in Columbia to Salvador in Brazil by way of the uncharted tropical rain forests. Such a journey couldn't be planned. Once in the rain forest, it would be impossible to know the most appropriate paths to take until you are actually there. The terrain may force you to take all kinds of different unpredictable directions as you make your way through. However, it would be possible to navigate the journey by using a few simple rules relating to the position of the sun or stars and the setting of a compass.

The journey through the rain forest would consist of many short journeys, punctuated by stops to assess the approximate position reached. At each of these stops, the next directional heading would be ascertained by using the rules involving the compass setting and the positions of the celestial bodies. Such a strategy could be described as:

short steps to explore the way forward, then after each step the application of heuristic rules to ensure that overall progress is relentlessly heading towards the destination – much like a guided missile, constantly monitoring the position of a moving target and adjusting its flight path accordingly. This is a heuristic strategy, with the rules being known as heuristic rules.

This is similar to the strategy of evolution, which moves forward in short stages (generations) and then, at the end of each stage, makes corrections by selectively rearranging the genes for the next stage. This strategy allows a directional progress, even though unpredictable events and circumstances might arise. Any business or personal strategy for advancement can also be arranged to proceed in a similar way.

Being in the fast-changing, unpredictable environment of the expanding world of telecommunications and computer technology is very much like being in an uncharted rain forest or a newly evolving biological ecosystem. Algorithmic strategies – forward planning – are totally useless. The only possible way to make progress, reach a goal or destination, is to use an heuristic strategy. The trick is to devise the correct heuristic rules – because they will be the sole determinants of what goal or destination is reached.

Heuristic rules are often only vague and approximate. They take the form of generalizations, rules of thumb that do not work every single time but give the best results over a period of time. Success is achieved by being right more times than being wrong, rather than being right every time.

The best examples of heuristic strategies are the tenets or rules of religions. This is a fascinating area of study for game theory strategists because the rules have evolved over many thousands of years of civilization. Throughout the history of mankind, religions have provided the main guiding strategies for human behaviour. These strategies can be thought of as consisting of components where the components are rules, which act in the same way as genes in an organism or memes in a train of thought – they are replaceable and subject to evolutionary pressures. In the case of religious rules, the rules are instructions for suitable behaviour patterns that act as a strategy for individual and group survival in a highly competitive world.

As we saw in Chapter 11, the evolutionary effect of the genetic algorithm enables successful genes and combinations of genes to go through to future generations. This is exactly the same mechanism that acts on the rules of religions. Ever since religions first came into being, new religions and variations of religions have continuously been coming into existence, with the main differences between the religions and their variations being the differences in their rules or tenets.

Like all evolutionary processes, the best survive to multiply and the worst get discarded. In this way, religions that have adopted the best rules have survived and increased their following, while those with inferior rules have passed into oblivion. This has resulted in the most widespread and successful of the religions in the world today having extremely efficient rules.

a perfect example of a heuristic strategy In thinking about
the strategy of a religion, it is necessary to be aware that most religions have a common ancestry. In much the same way as humans and apes have evolved from some common ancestor in the past, so many religions have evolved from some common ancient culture.

Most Western religions have evolved from a very ancient civilization, long since disappeared, that first formed in the Middle East thousands of years ago. The tenets, or codes of law, of that ancient civilization were passed on by the Hebrews to the Israelites. Expressed in the Jewish religion, they take the form of *mitsvot* – commandments – that appear in their teaching (Talmud). The best known of the mitzvot is a group of ten commandments known as the Decalogue (in English they are commonly referred to as the Ten Commandments). This Decalogue is such a perfect example of a successful heuristic strategy that it appears, in slightly modified forms, in all major Western religions.

Most religious accounts describe the Ten Commandments as being given to Moses (by God) during 40 days and 40 nights that he spent on Mount Sinai contemplating how he might lead his people – the Israelites – after they left Egypt. Although they were in the form of commandments or specific instructions, in fact they consisted mainly of broad principles of conduct.

To see the Ten Commandments in perspective, it is necessary to understand their original purpose. They were a strategy for survival. Moses had to lead his people – a large nomadic tribe of some one million people – through a land of hostile communities to find a place to settle (a promised land). When Moses returned from Mount Sinai, he had with him a set of stone tablets that contained ten instructions that he said were the Ten Commandments of God.

Here is a dialogue taken from the CD-ROM *How God Makes God* which explains the logic of those Ten Commandments:

But what if there is no God? Moses would have had to have written those instructions himself.

Whether they were the work of God or the considered thoughts of Moses, they were a brilliant piece of work: a simple list of ten easily remembered instructions that provided an optimally efficient strategy for survival.

You mean you see the Ten Commandments as a survival strategy?

Of course, that is exactly what the Ten Commandments were. They were designed to ensure that every individual's behaviour was optimal for the survival of the community.

But I thought the Ten Commandments applied only to individual behaviour?

What you have to remember is that Moses would have been more concerned with the survival of his whole nation than with the survival of the individual. Imagine, if you can, Moses up there alone on Mount Sinai. He would have realized that it would be difficult for his nation to survive as a disorganized rabble. There needed to be some sort of internal order. It would be necessary for people to work together and cooperate with each other in order to meet the difculties of surviving in a hostile world.

How did the Ten Commandments help him do this?

For people to work together there had to be the right atmosphere, where people could have a mutual feeling of trust for each other. Moses would have realized how easy it would be for these harsh conditions to breed dog-eat-dog attitudes. He would have realized that it would be hopelessly inefficient if everybody distrusted their neighbours and if there were constant quarrelling and fighting between the people.

The Ten Commandments could prevent this?

This would have been Moses' main aim. He had to get people to act in such a way that they could trust one another and help each other to prosper and survive. The Ten Commandments were Moses' heuristic strategy to accomplish this.

Why would he have told the people that these commandments were the word of God?

He would have had the problem of credibility. By claiming that these were the instructions of a supernatural power, who had infinite wisdom, he could avoid the possibility of others doubting his judgement and suggesting alternative strategies, or perhaps ignoring his instructions altogether.

In those primitive times, there were no printing presses; communication was by word of mouth, so Moses would have had to work on his ideas to get them into a suitable form to be easily explained. The instructions would have to be short and simple so that they could be remembered easily.

Having pared down the list of important rules to include only the most essential items, he then offered these up to the people as the laws of God, for which there were the most terrible penalties for anyone breaking them. With plenty of propaganda about the wrath of God, the delights of heaven and the miseries of hell, it would have been a very brave man who chose to ignore these laws.

So, the Ten Commandments are a contrived set of rules that were designed by man to help a nation survive and prosper?

Designed by God or man, they make a lot of sense.

If the Ten Commandments are taken out of the context of religion, they can be seen in a new light that shows them to be a surprisingly complete and efficient survival strategy for a large group of people finding themselves in a foreign and potentially hostile environment. This is explained in another of the dialogues from *How God Makes God*:

Can you explain how the Ten Commandments comprise a strategy for survival?

Take the first three Commandments: Have no other God. Do not make graven images. Do not take the name of God in vain. These three rules establish the fact that there is only one authority and this authority has to be treated with great respect. They make it quite clear that this God (and His Word) is the only one to be taken notice of.

The fourth commandment?

Keep the Sabbath holy and don't do anything at all on this day except go to church. This makes sure there is a special day set aside to be used exclusively for going to church and receiving messages from the appointed servants of the religion.

The fifth commandment?

Honour your mother and your father. Remember there were no pension schemes or social services in Moses' time. This arranges for the elderly to be cared for by the family. The commandment would also have the beneficial effect of encouraging older people to keep their wealth and capital within family enterprises – rather than locking it away as a safeguard against old age and infirmity.

The sixth commandment?

Do not commit murder. This commandment would ensure that the community is a safe place for people to move around freely, greatly enhancing the opportunities for people to be able to collaborate and cooperate with each other.

The seventh commandment?

Do not commit adultery. This preserves the most efficient basic unit of organization: the family. It would also greatly reduce the possibility of situations for conflict and mistrust arising – which again would be helpful in promoting alliances and cooperation.

The eighth commandment?

Do not steal. This would save people vast amounts of time and effort in having to protect possessions and safeguard their dealings with each other. If people could feel confident that others in the community wouldn't steal from them, they would be more inclined to work with them in collaborative and cooperative associations.

The ninth commandment?

Do not bear false witness against your neighbour. This commandment outlaws deceit and lying. Lies or fabrications of any kind reduce the efficiency of communication. If people could be confident that others always told the truth, cooperation could take place with far greater speed and efficiency.

The tenth commandment?

Do not covet your neighbour's possessions. Meaning: don't be envious of others. Envy is an insidious emotion that can create havoc in cooperative situations.

The Ten Commandments are an elegantly simple strategy for improving the conditions for the prosperity and survival of a community of people in a hostile and competitive environment. It works on three levels: the individual level; the community level; the world level.

At the individual level, holding such beliefs and abiding by these commandments will be a great advantage because individuals will be trusted by others and not represent any kind of threat – an ideal position for anyone wanting to cooperate or collaborate with others. At the community level, the whole community is more efficient and productive because of the improved conditions for communication and cooperation. At the world level, the near presence of a community of people, all known to be obeying these commandments, will not be threatening in any way. This will reduce the likelihood of hostilities and increase the chances of inter-community trade.

The Ten Commandments are typical of the kind of strategies that come out of game theory; they are not intuitive or obvious. Just like the prisoner's dilemma, the individual's best play is not the obvious one. It may seem to be advantageous for an individual to murder, lie, cheat or steal when a suitable opportunity for personal gain arises and where detection or reciprocation is unlikely. But if everyone did this everyone would be much worse off.

What makes heuristic strategies particularly effective is that they are not dependent upon rational decision making. Rules are followed scrupulously and blindly, whatever the circumstances. People do not have to decide to be honest and trustworthy; it is part of a belief system that says in the short term it may seem okay to disregard the rules, but in the long term it works out best if you always obey them.

Significantly, it is constantly stressed in most religions that God and the Word of God are synonymous: God is the Word and the Word is God. Stressed also is the importance of having faith: faith in God, which implies having faith in the Word. In other words, religions stress the importance of having faith in the particular heuristic strategy adopted by the religion.

Because these commandments create conditions within a community that are excellent for the creation of wealth, and because wealth can take so many forms, the Ten Commandments can help a nation not only to survive and prosper but also to grow rich and powerful. The strategy is so far-sighted it would seem beyond the ingenuity of a mere mortal. It is a work of perfection. But the end products of most evolutionary processes often result in perfection of one form or another.

the most important of the commandments

If asked which of the Ten Commandments is the most important, few would choose the fourth. This is the seemingly innocuous instruction: 'Remember the Sabbath to keep it holy.' Ask anyone what this signifies and most people will tell you it is there to make sure everyone gets at least one day of rest a week. In the Jewish religion it is held to be a day of rest and spiritual refreshment, a time to acknowledge that God is the creator of the universe.

Think about this for a moment. The Ten Commandments make up an optimally efficient list of instructions that has been deliberately pared down to be as short as possible – such that it contains only the most important directives. If this fourth commandment were there to instruct people to take a day of rest it would be an anomaly – because, although periodic rests are a necessity, it shouldn't be necessary to issue a specific command to make people do so, and certainly not in an optimum list that should contain only those instructions that were the most strategically vital.

Another strange thing about this fourth commandment is that it didn't appear in the very earliest of Hebrew texts. Also, its meaning is ambiguously explained in many different ways by different religions.

Resolving this anomaly, to uncover the real reason for this fourth commandment, provides clear evidence that the Ten Commandments have been set up for the express purpose of organizing and ordering the behaviour of a large community of people.

Supposing there really had been such a person as Moses, imagine the predicament he would have been in. He would have had to lead about a million people with all of their belongings and their herds of livestock across a desert. How would he exercise this leadership?

The biggest problem would have been communication. One million people, no telephones or radios. How would Moses communicate with them all? How could he give even the simplest of instructions, such as 'turn left at the next oasis'? People would be going in all directions, finding camp sites, making sure their flocks had enough food and water. It would have been a nightmare to keep in touch with everybody.

The idea of a structured religion would have been an inspired solution to this problem. According to the religious histories, Moses appointed the largest group amongst the people, the Levis, to be the servants of the religion. This allowed Moses to use these servants to communicate his leadership decisions: sending them out amongst the people to give them his instructions. Moses need only make the people aware that these servants carried the word of God to ensure that his instructions were obeyed and treated with great respect.

Even with this communication set up though, with all the servants spread around the community to communicate his directives, Moses would still have had quite a problem contacting all the people because they would be spread over a large area, tending their herds and the like.

Would it not have been logical if the reason for this fourth commandment had been to improve the efficiency of the delivery of these communications?

Every form of activity was banned by the fourth commandment, except for one. That one exception was local religious meetings – presided over by Moses' message couriers – where people could hear the word of God: as proclaimed by Moses.

If these meetings were the only thing happening on that particular day, they could be sure of having a reasonably good attendance. In this way Moses could ensure that instead of his servants spending time trying to chase everyone around to give them instructions, everyone would go to these meetings once a week on the Sabbath and get the instructions there. It was a simple but extremely effective way to communicate to a large group of nomadic people.

Not only could he issue instructions, but the meetings could additionally provide feedback from the people. His servants could gather intelligence and information as to the state of the community and the conditions of the terrain and surrounding areas. From a macro viewpoint, the effect of this fourth commandment would have been to turn a disorganized rabble into a highly coordinated body of people, complete with a system of intelligent feedback. It is not at all surprising that the Roman Empire became converted to Christianity.

> " LOOKING THROUGH [THE] TEN COMMANDMENTS THERE IS NOT ONE OF THEM THAT APPLIES IN THE ENVIRONMENT OF THE INTERNET "

nomadic tribes and the internet

The current internet environment can be compared to the state of the nomadic community before Moses introduced the Ten Commandments and organized a communication system based upon a religion. There is no recognized authority and there are no compelling reasons for everyone to play the 'sensible game' that will be conducive to cooperation and collaboration.

Looking through those Ten Commandments – which have proven over time to be optimal for bringing order and sensible behaviour to a community – there is not one of them that applies in the environment of the internet. Although many people will have a belief in a God and make an effort to obey the laws of their religions, there is no way of knowing who those people are. This eliminates this as a basis for trust and credibility: at least, sufficient enough to establish a reasonably high expectation of reliable, fair and honest dealings from people.

Even more serious is the lack of overall organization and control of the e-business environment. There is no universally recognized leadership, able to communicate guidance to everyone connected to the internet. Various organizations and government bodies have tried, and are continually trying, to impose rules and regulations, but without any notable successes. They are unlikely to succeed because unlike the system created by a religious organization, there is no framework of communication in place to feed back all the various views of the whole community to a centralized body.

This was the great advantage of Moses' system: the network of agents (the Levis), which, besides passing on instructions and guidance, returned information the other way – feeding back the views and combined knowledge of the whole community to the central source. It was only the feedback of this combined intelligence that gave the central decision-making unit its wisdom to be able to provide appropriate guidance and instructions to the whole community.

Here is the problem to be solved. How can the vast numbers of people connected to the internet be induced to act sensibly and to put the efficient long-term functioning of the whole environment in front of their personal opportunities for short-term gains?

The short answer is that they cannot. People will act only in their own best interests, so, with this realization it is totally impractical to base any strategy on the assumption that people will, by their own volition, play the game sensibly.

back to a personal cognitive model
Here is where the conceptual jump needs to take place. The internet hasn't got a universal

set of rules. Everyone has to adopt their own. Each person has to create their own set of rules that applies to their own behaviour and also to the behaviour of their particular community of friends and acquaintances. The conceptual trick is not to think of imposing those rules on your friends and contacts, but to devise a strategy that chooses only the friends and contacts who seem to be abiding by the same set of rules as yourself.

an alternative strategy

Without the incentive of rewards in an afterlife, it seems unlikely that everyone connected to the internet will suddenly start to act altruistically and enter into the spirit of trusting collaboration. Yet, we know millions of people would like the internet environment to be this way. What can be done to trigger it off?

Here is where we need to stop thinking about the macro environment and start thinking locally. It may be impossible to get everyone on the internet to play the game sensibly, but it must be possible for this to happen within small groups of people who have got to know each other well and are bound together through some common interest. The trick is to find these groups of people you can trust – and, more importantly, who will trust you.

> INSTEAD OF THINKING ABOUT JOINING A GROUP OF PEOPLE WHOM YOU CAN TRUST AND RESPECT, WHY NOT FORM A GROUP OF YOUR OWN?

This needs another paradigm shift. Instead of thinking about joining a group of people whom you can trust and respect, why not form a group of your own? In this way you can ensure that every person in that group is somebody you can rely on and trust and have these feelings reciprocated.

At first thought, the idea that you can form a group of this kind seems wildly fanciful, that is, until you realize that this is what you have been doing all of your life already. Everyone does it. Everyone forms a personal group of friends and long-established contacts and colleagues, whom they know they can trust and rely on and who trust and rely on them in return.

Consider how these groups of trusted friends and colleagues are formed. They don't just manifest out of the blue. Each friend or colleague is painstakingly cultivated through a strategy not dissimilar to the strategy of tit-for-tat. Starting slowly and cautiously at first, these friendships and associations gradually build up to a point where firm bonds are established. Not every acquaintanceship will blossom into a lasting relationship, in fact most won't, but, by a process of trial and selection, a group can be formed. Isn't this the way biological organisms evolve: trial and selection? A circle of close acquaintances can be grown in much the same way as organic structures grow: through a process of evolution.

In biological systems, populations in an evolving ecosystem are limited by space and a supply of nutrients or food. In a similar way, a circle of close acquaintanceships is limited by the amount of time needed to maintain the relationships. With this limitation, a circle of trusted contacts and colleagues has a practical upper limit. As soon as that limit is reached, new associations can only be acquired by losing (or neglecting) others. This is a typical evolutionary situation. A person's circle of associates is effectively an evolving interface for interacting with the world.

Seeing a circle of contacts and colleagues as an evolving interface, it is understandable that this should change when a person changes their circumstances or takes up a new interest or occupation. The circle of associates has to change in order to adapt more efficiently to the new environment.

Seen in this light, the full potential of the internet is revealed. It is not about mass communication at all: it is about an environment that is ideal for forming appropriate personal interfaces to the world of communication. It's not practical to communicate with everybody, but it is practical to build up a personal group of trusted contacts.

Using the organizing facilities of a computer and having the ability to create many simultaneous relationships at the same time, a very much larger group of trusted contacts and associates can be acquired in the environment of the internet than would be possible in the conventional world of bricks and mortar. Internet communication makes it easy to continuously engage in tit-for-tat explorations for new associations. A genetic algorithm approach can be used to ensure that the circle of contacts are optimally efficient for personal needs and enable it to adapt to any changes of interest.

Once the paradigm shift is made from the global to the local, it can be seen how everyone can benefit by cultivating their own circle of contacts and associates. Investors, entrepreneurs, auteurs, specialists and experts are able to create their own personal interfaces to suit their own particular needs in the world of information and knowledge.

In the conventional world of bricks and mortar, building up a circle of associates, although requiring skill, is relatively straightforward. The limitation of available time and opportunity is a restriction on choice. Our brains have evolved a capacity to deal with this limited choice and it presents no serious problems. However, in the environment of the internet, where choice is virtually unlimited and opportunities abound, our ability to acquire a suitable circle of acquaintances is handicapped by our brain's ability to deal with such complexity.

This is why we need a game theory approach: to provide a conceptual framework to compensate for our brain's deficiencies. We can then use the search strategy of the genetic algorithm and choose an appropriate set of heuristic rules to provide the selection criteria.

COMMUNICATION
STRATEGIES

THE FIRST FOUR PARTS OF THE BOOK WERE
ABOUT THINKING AND THEORY. THEY PROVIDED
ESSENTIAL BACKGROUND FOR ACTION, BUT
NOT THE ACTION ITSELF. IN PART 5, ATTENTION
IS SWITCHED TO FINDING A WAY TO APPLY THIS
KNOWLEDGE TO PRACTICAL PURPOSES IN THE
REAL WORLD.

IN THE FIRST OF THESE TWO CHAPTERS, THE
INTERNET IS TRANSFORMED FROM AN
APPARENT SEA OF RANDOM NOISE INTO A
VALUABLE INFORMATION NETWORK. THE
SECOND CHAPTER SETS ABOUT DEVISING
STRATEGIES TO MAKE EFFICIENT USE OF THIS
VALUABLE RESOURCE.

WHILE READING THROUGH THESE TWO
CHAPTERS, THE FOREMOST THOUGHT IN THE
MIND OF THE READER SHOULD BE 'HOW CAN I
GET PEOPLE TO HELP ME SOLVE THE PROBLEMS
ASSOCIATED WITH MY CHOSEN NICHE IN THE
WORLD OF E-BUSINESS?'

14

THE INFORMATION ECOSYSTEM

whole world versus local world We now have to make a jump, from the kind of organization that applies at a global level to the organization that affects us personally when trying to establish a niche in the world of e-business.

Political social organization is structured logically, by reasoning and decision making. It produces man-made, definitive laws that are backed up by threat of direct and immediate punishment if they are broken. Such laws are effectively algorithmic instructions, which, as discussed previously, are not suitable for fast responses and automatic adaptability in a fast-changing environment. This is evidenced by the many failed attempts, by a variety of governments, to satisfactorily regulate the internet. For this reason, it is more appropriate to look at systems controlled by heuristics rather than algorithms.

This is why, in the last chapter, a religious rather than a political social organization was chosen as the example, because this kind of organization evolves and adapts naturally using heuristic rules and a heuristic strategy. The trick is to extract the essence of that global heuristic strategy and apply it to our own, individual surroundings.

Some of the review readers of the last chapter pointed out that even the heuristic organization of religions had little relevance to the internet because there was no way any universal standards of behaviour could be implemented. However, that is not the point. The reason for exampling a macro organization was not to try to copy or reproduce it, but to be able to isolate the important elements that give rise to the benefits of organization. These were: an atmosphere of mutual trust and an efficient framework of communication.

With the realization that mutual trust and an efficient framework of communication cannot be organized on a global scale within the environment of the internet – by either religious or political forms of organization – we have to see how this can be achieved on a local scale. In other words, if the whole world cannot be efficiently organized, how can we find a small part of it that is?

egocentric pockets of organization

Again, we need a paradigm shift. We have to stop looking at the internet as a whole and consider only a part of it: the part that we personally interact with. If this part is an environment of mutual trust, with an efficient framework of communication, then we don't have to worry about what happens elsewhere.

> " WE HAVE TO STOP LOOKING AT THE INTERNET AS A WHOLE AND CONSIDER ONLY A PART OF IT: THE PART THAT WE PERSONALLY INTERACT WITH "

This may seem to be an egocentric viewpoint, but this is the way all complex systems are known to naturally self-organize. Natural organization doesn't evolve top down, it evolves bottom up. This has been proved time and again with all biological systems. Small, localized pockets of organization emerge. These small pockets start to interact with each other to form a higher level of organization of several pockets working together. These groups of pockets then interact to form larger groups: groups of pockets interacting together. In this way organization emanates from the bottom up, spreading through a chaotic and dis-organized system to gradually bring universal order.

In the environment of the internet and e-business, we are only at the beginning stages of a naturally evolving organization. Small pockets of organization are developing. We have the choice of either joining in one of these pockets or creating one for ourselves. By joining in a pocket we leave others to create a niche for us, but in this book we are concerned with creating our own niche. This means we have to create our own personal pocket: i.e. create organization at a local level, centred upon ourselves.

Organization at a personal level involves establishing a group of contacts who can be trusted and who will be trustful in return. It also requires that this group of contacts be contained within a suitable framework of efficient communication. As this is an egocentric organization, the trust and the communication framework must be centred upon the individual setting up the pocket of organization. In effect, we each have to create our own small world where we are not simply at the focal point but are the focal point.

In this kind of organization the individual is like the hub at the centre of a wheel. All trust and communication radiate only along the spokes connecting each contact to the individual organizer. There is no necessity for this individual organizer to sponsor or create any bonds of trust between the spokes (i.e. get contacts to trust each other), or to even establish communication links between them. Organization is specific to and centred around the organizing individual.

This is totally different from the kind of organization usually associated with the setting up of cooperative groups in conventional business organizations, where an atmosphere of trust and a framework of communication are designed to be common to all members of a group. Cooperative groups, though, can only be formed within a structured, top-down organization, where higher-order organization is already in place with absolute control coming from a higher hierarchical level.

To appreciate why it is preferable to form egocentric groups rather than cooperative groups it is necessary to be aware of the particular uniqueness of the environment of the internet. It has a property that has never before been available to any previous society. This is not generally realized, which accounts for much wrong thinking about e-business strategies.

Many commentators enthuse about the potential of the internet, proclaiming that it will revolutionize the way we do business and the way we lead our lives, but few give any plausible explanations as to why this should be. This is because the world of the internet contains a surprise that is counter-intuitive: the phenomena of small-world clusters. To understand this serendipitous property of the connected world, let's look at another game: the Kevin Bacon game.

the Kevin Bacon game

Imagining a community of film makers is relatively easy. More difficult is the trick of abstracting the essence of the communication infrastructure that links all the various people in this community together. Fortunately though, there is a simple model we can use that comes from the film community itself: the Kevin Bacon game.

This game originated as a play (and film) written by John Guare in 1993 called *Six Degrees of Separation*. The intriguing hypothesis put forward by John Guare in this play was that everyone in the world is separated from each other by no more than six communication links.

In a state of inebriation, three students, Craig Fass, Brian Turtle and Mike Ginelli, from Albright College, came up with the idea that every actor, living or dead, could be linked through their appearances in films to an actor called Kevin Bacon – and by no more than six films. This idea quickly spread through college campuses, via the internet, resulting in Fass, Turtle and Ginelli appearing on a television show and then writing a book about the game, which was entitled *Six Degrees of Kevin Bacon* (1994, Plume; ISBN 0452278449).

The idea captured the imagination of thousands of different people. It became a popular game at Hollywood parties, where actors and actresses would work out their personal Bacon numbers based upon the number of connection links they had to Kevin Bacon through their own appearances in films. It wasn't long before the Internet Movie Database (http: //us.imdb.com) was being used to work out Bacon numbers. The University of Virginia set up a website (http://www.cs.virginia.edu/oracle/), known as 'The Oracle', where anyone could enter any actor's or actress's name to find their Bacon number. An example of this is the links between Alfred Hitchcock and Kevin Bacon coming out with a Bacon Number of 3:

Alfred Hitchcock was in *Show Business at War* (1943) with Orson Welles, and Orson Welles was in *A Safe Place* (1971) with Jack Nicholson, and Jack Nicholson was in *A Few Good Men* (1992) with Kevin Bacon!

Bacon numbers higher than 4 are very rare and the game soon become one of trying to find little-known actors or actresses with the highest Bacon number.

The University of Virginia also provides many interesting variations and statistics on this Kevin Bacon game. Their site allows you to enter any two actors' or actresses' names and see how many links there are between them. It also speculates on who might be at the centre of gravity of the film world: the actor or actress whose average links to all others is the smallest number. Most interesting of all these statistics is the number of actors and actresses who have the same Bacon number. See Figure 14.1.

Bacon number	
0	1
1	1,458
2	101,196
3	226,727
4	49,823
5	2,922
6	250
7	54
8	2

Total number of linkable actors: 382,433
Average Bacon number: 2.876

FIG 14.1 Number of actors and actresses with the same Bacon number

The figures shown in Figure 14.1 are significantly illuminating. Despite there being nearly 400,000 actors and actresses, working on thousands of different films over nearly a century of film making, their average separation is only about three links – with a maximum separation of eight.

It is easy to see how the phrase 'a friend of a friend of mine' can refer to thousands of possible people. These links are calculated for actors and actresses working on the same films. A similar set of figures might be obtained by linking them through the parties they have attended, the restaurants they have visited or the clubs they frequent.

Mapping this across to the internet, it can be realized how everyone connected to the internet can be linked in a similar way: particularly if the linking is confined to people who use listserves and Usernet discussion forums. It's a spooky feeling to realize that people who frequent these internet forums are mostly only two or three links away from each other.

What does this tell you about word of mouth on the internet? How do you rate viral marketing in the light of this revelation? What does this suggest in the context of internet communication strategies?

> IT'S A SPOOKY FEELING TO REALIZE THAT PEOPLE WHO FREQUENT THESE INTERNET FORUMS ARE MOSTLY ONLY TWO OR THREE LINKS AWAY FROM EACH OTHER

small-world clusters

The significance of the Kevin Bacon game wasn't truly appreciated until Duncan Watts and Steven Strogatz, at Cornell University in Ithaca, New York, worked on a project to analyse complex networks. This work was written up and published in the eminent journal *Nature* under the title 'Collective dynamics of "small-world" networks' (volume 393, pp. 440–442, 4 June 1998). This paper attracted considerable worldwide attention.

At that time, networks were considered to act in two possible ways.

1 as a network of local connections

This involves a system of nodes where every node is connected directly to a relatively small number of neighbouring nodes. Communications can then take any route through the network of nodes – travelling from one node to the next.

This can be likened to a large hall full of people. The people in the hall are not allowed to shout and there is no broadcasting or telephone system: they can only speak to the people who are immediately next to them. Information and messages can then only pass between people in different parts of the hall by means of a series of intermediate links with one person telling a person near to them, who then tells another person near to them, who tells yet another person near to them, and so on until a message passes from one person to another via all the links between the original sender and a destination receiver.

As each person is surrounded by several others, they have many alternative choices as to which of the people next to them they pass a message on to. Indeed, the message can be simultaneously passed to several people standing next to them, allowing many copies of the same message to take different routes through the people in the hall to reach an intended recipient.

Conversely, the recipient of any message coming from somebody in another part of the hall can receive the message from any of the people standing near to them, depending upon which route the message took as it passed from person to person on its way from the original sender. It is in this way that many people think of information spreading by word of mouth – the spreading of rumours in a community of people might be a good example.

The problem with this type of network is that it can easily become saturated with messages unless the messages are accompanied by a specific address. It is only truly efficient if the route from one person to another is specified beforehand and sent with the message.

Figure 14.2 illustrates a typical normal network. This network is such that every node is connected to eight other nodes. As you can see by tracing paths through the network of connections, a message can be sent to any other node by a variety of different routes. This diagram might represent a town full of people where each person is restricted to talking to only eight of their immediate nearest neighbours; it can readily be seen how information (and gossip) can spread around this community in an extremely large number of different ways.

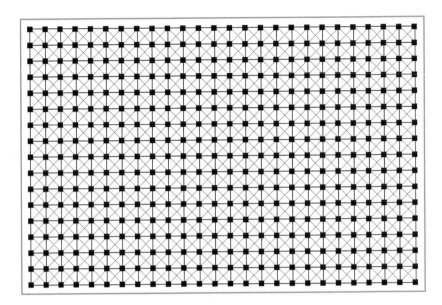

FIG 14.2 A normal network, showing each node connecting to eight neighbours. Messages can flow from one node to any other node in the network via multiple different pathways

The disadvantage of a normally connected network is that it can take a large number of steps, or links, to get from one part of the network to another. For this reason a network of random connections is often preferred.

2 as a network of random connections This is a system of network connections whereby each node is connected to a relatively small number of other nodes that are randomly distributed around a network. The efficiency of the network is determined by the least number of nodes the communication has to pass through between any starting node and finishing node.

This can be imagined by a country full of people at home with a telephone. Each of them is given a small list of telephone numbers of people randomly distributed around the country. Figure 14.3 illustrates three such people, each of whom has eight random connections to other people who can be located anywhere in an environment.

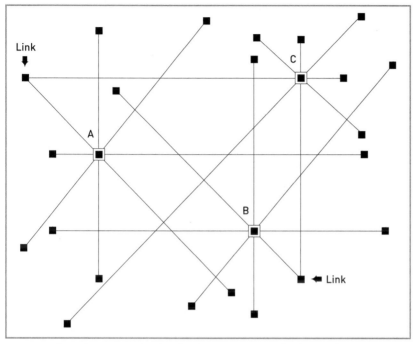

FIG 14.3 A random network, showing just three people (A, B and C) who are each connected randomly to eight others around the country. Notice how they can share people – link nodes – which has a dramatic effect on the number of steps it takes to transfer information from any part of the network to another. In this case, there is a maximum of four steps from any one node to another

Because every person is connected to several others, each can be considered to be within a small cluster of people in the same way that an actor or actress can be considered to be within a small cluster of actors and actresses when he or she makes a film. Just as Bacon numbers are calculated by looking for the least number of links between actors and actresses across films, so the efficiency of a randomly connected network is calculated by calculating the least number of links it takes to pass a message from one node (person on a telephone) to another.

In Figure 14.3, it can be seen how just a couple of common nodes between clusters can effectively connect people together in a short number of steps. This is why Bacon numbers can be so small, even when actors and actresses may not even have been working in the same decade as each other. All it takes is for one common actor or actress to span a decade, to create a link for thousands of others.

The advantage of a random network over a normal network is that, as long as there are at least a few common links, the number of links between nodes is very small. This is true however many nodes there are in the network. This is why the average number of links between actors and actresses in all films made can be as low as three, even though there are hundreds of thousands of actors and actresses.

the surprise

Duncan Watts and Steven Strogatz's discovery came about when they simulated various kinds of networks between the extremes of a locally connected network and a randomly connected network. This can be explained in terms of all the people in the hall as previously described, but a few of them have mobile telephones that enable them to pass a message to somebody in a distant part of the hall. This is illustrated in Figure 14.4, where small local clusters contain at least one node that has a random connection to a distant node.

Effectively, the kind of computer simulations Watts and Strogatz analysed on their computer helped to see how the average minimum number of links needed to transfer messages between any pair of people was affected by the proportion of people who had mobile phones. If nobody had a mobile phone, the system would represent a locally connected network. If they all had mobile phones, the system would represent a randomly connected network. Watts and Strogatz wanted to find out how the efficiency (minimum number of links between sender and target recipient) varied between these two extremes.

Computer simulations showed that randomly connected networks needed far fewer links to connect to nodes than locally connected networks. The surprise came when they started adding random links to the locally connected network. Instead of the network slowly becoming more efficient, as more and more links were changed from local to random, they found the efficiency jumped up to near the efficiency of a

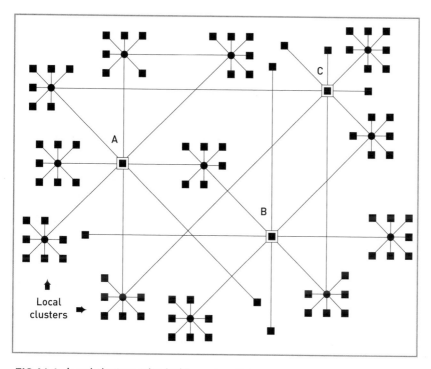

FIG 14.4 Local clusters mixed with random links

randomly connected network as soon as only a very small number of nodes were randomly connected.

These simulations can be visualized by again imagining the hall full of people. Then, a probability number is used to decide whether or not each person gets to have a mobile phone (complete with a small list of the telephone numbers of other people randomly distributed around the hall). A probability of 1 will give everyone a mobile phone, a probability of 0 will give nobody a mobile phone. Applying a probability of 0.1 to each person (one chance in ten) will give about one in ten of them a phone and a probability of 0.8 will give about 80 per cent of them a phone.

The simulations start with a very small probability (say, 0.01 – where only one in a hundred gets a mobile phone and a small list of numbers) and calculate the average number of links needed to transfer messages between different pairs of people. Then this calculation is repeated again and again as the probability is slowly increased (and more people have phones). They then plot a graph to show how the efficiency (minimum number of links to transfer messages between people) changes with the change in the number of people who have mobile phones.

The results showed that if only a few random links are placed into the network (just a few people with mobile phones) the efficiency, or least number of links between nodes, is almost the same as if all the connections were random (everyone having a mobile phone).

This is like saying that message-passing between a hall full of people where only a few of them have mobile phones (each with a limited list of the numbers of other people in the hall) is almost as efficient as if everyone in the hall had a mobile phone (each with a limited list of the numbers of other people in the hall). This was an unexpected result – causing great surprise because it is counter-intuitive.

the significance of small-world clustering Looking again

at Figure 14.4, the striking feature is that although most of the nodes in local clusters are not connected directly to the wider network, they are only one step further away from a node that is. If the local clusters were thought of as conventionally managed teams, the teams that had one of its members connected to the internet would be virtually connected: i.e. every team member being just one step further away from being connected to everyone on the internet. This is illustrated in Figure 14.5.

Effectively then, any conventionally managed team, with at least one member connected to the internet, would be directly influenced by information emanating from the web and internet discussion forums. This is also likely to be true if no members of a team are connected – because any member of the team might have a friend or contact that is connected and is likely to be influenced by their views.

With a single link to the internet, a team might be highly dependent upon or influenced by that link. It represents a portal into a vast reservoir

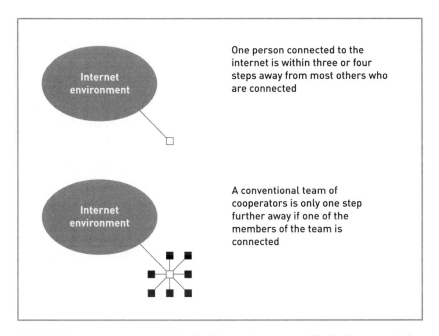

FIG 14.5 One person connected to the internet in a group effectively connects the whole group

of information and knowledge. The problem is that any human link acts not only as a conduit for the information and knowledge, but also as a filter – selectively choosing what information is filtered into the group.

This wouldn't be a problem if the human link was omniscient, able to access all information and understand all problems, but it is more likely that any single contact would have only a limited range of understanding or be able to communicate only within a limited area of knowledge. This would make it strategically necessary for a team to have a variety of links to the internet, through different people, to be able to get a more balanced information feed.

As it would be preferable for these links to have a variety of independent viewpoints – not influencing each other – the links would preferably be through isolated contacts: i.e. not directly part of the managed team. In this way the team would be less likely to be dependent upon a single source or run the danger of the information from the internet being biased or incomplete.

It would be the role of the leader of a managed team, acting in the role of an entrepreneur or auteur, to organize such a group of independent contacts, the proviso being that the leader shouldn't act as a filter themselves, but simply organize the flow of information between the team and the linking contacts to the internet. In this way, problems or requests for information can receive several different kinds of possible solutions to problems.

multiple, simultaneous meetings

The cost of having many permanent employed contacts to the internet is likely to be prohibitive. However, it would be quite viable if the contacts were temporary: used on demand and only when needed. A managed team (or an entrepreneur, or an auteur) could perhaps establish a list of appropriate contacts who would be available to provide assistance or advice whenever needed – perhaps paying them a retainer for priority treatment when the need arises. This is illustrated in Figure 14.6.

> 66 IN THE WORLD OF THE INTERNET, IT IS AS PRACTICAL FOR EXPERTS TO SERVE SEVERAL CLIENTS AS IT IS FOR CLIENTS TO HAVE SEVERAL EXPERTS 99

The 'on demand' links, or retained services, would probably involve specialists who were experts in different areas of knowledge. For them to be called upon to help or advise only on an occasional basis might appear to be somewhat disconcerting. However, this would only be a problem in the world of bricks and mortar where physical realities impose practical limitations on the number of clients a specialist can deal with at the same time.

In the world of the internet, it is as practical for experts to serve several clients as it is for clients to have several experts. This is because virtual meetings – with e-mail discussion – can take the place of real-life meetings. This can bring into play an unique feature of the internet which makes it possible to take part in several discussions at the same time.

In the bricks and mortar world, business is run mainly by physical meetings where it is impossible to be at more than a single meeting at

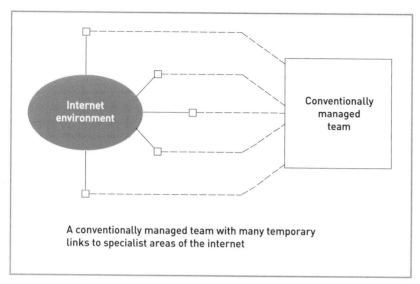

A conventionally managed team with many temporary
links to specialist areas of the internet

FIG 14.6 Conventionally managed teams can have several links to specialists
and experts linked to the internet. These need only be called into service on
demand

any one time. In the world of the internet, this is possible because the
sending and receiving of messages and information do not have to be
simultaneous. There can be gaps between when a communication is
dispatched and when it is assimilated by the intended receiver.

In face-to-face meetings, video conferencing or telephone conversations,
sender and receiver must be synchronized in time. With e-mail, they can
be out of time sync so that both sender and receiver can choose a
convenient time to either send or receive. This allows conversations to
overlap; it can allow different conversations to merge without
disharmony.

In a real-life meeting people cannot all talk at the same time, and people
cannot wait several minutes to answer someone's question while they go
across the world to get the answer from someone else. It isn't possible to
break off halfway through a meeting to join another, or ask the people in
a meeting to wait until tomorrow when you might have more time to
consider what they have been saying. Yet this is the normal way for

internet discussions to proceed. Many discussions can be interleaved without confusion. There is time for contemplation and thought before responding.

Although this method of communication can take some getting used to, it has many powerful advantages over face-to-face meetings. It is this unique feature of e-mail – not possible in the real world – that can provide opportunities for communication strategies that couldn't even be imagined in the non-internet world.

the viability of having many contacts We shall be dealing

with the mechanics of virtual meetings in a later chapter, but, for the moment, consider the advantages of having multiple online experts and multiple online clients.

In the bricks and mortar world, an entrepreneur, an auteur or a managed team might hire a consultant to provide them with expert information and assistance in solving a problem. Let's say this consultant charges $5,000 a week. In the vastly complex world of e-business, with so much changing and conflicting information, any particular consultant, however clever an expert, is unlikely to have complete knowledge. Their opinion is bound to be biased, or limited in some way. So, instead of having one consultant at a cost of $5,000 a week, wouldn't it be preferable to have five consultants at $1,000 a week each?

There would be no need to physically meet them, or any need for them to be brought together. They could be dealt with simultaneously, and in isolation, allowing five independent expert opinions to be obtained for the price of one. This is possible in the world of the internet, because the time and effort involved for both clients and experts in virtual meetings – using e-mail communication – could be used far more efficiently.

In a similar way, an expert consultant could make his services available to a number of different teams (or entrepreneurs, or auteurs) at the same time, perhaps charging $1,000 a week each to five different clients, rather than $5,000 to one – quite practical when physical meetings are mostly unnecessary. This arrangement would suit the consultant because their employment risks would be spread and they'd be in full command of their own time – enabling them to concentrate upon a narrow area of expertise where they can become truly expert.

Such 'on demand' consultants or specialists could also build up a parallel set of contacts linking them to other specialists and experts on the internet – in or relating to their area of speciality. In this way, the specialist or expert can link anyone who has hired him or her to a full range of knowledge in a particular field. This arrangement is illustrated in Figure 14.7.

Seen as a system, it becomes obvious why the environment of the internet involves collaboration rather than cooperation. It also explains how cooperative groups can work in conjunction with collaborative groups. It seems that the interface to the internet environment acts as a dividing line. Inside the internet is a world more suited for collaboration. Outside is a world more suited for cooperation.

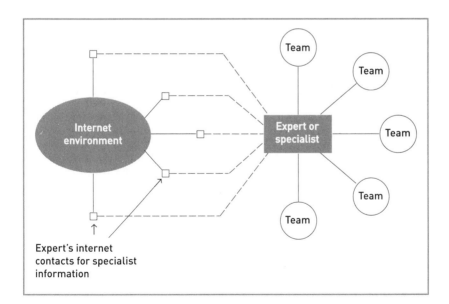

FIG 14.7 Specialists can supply information and help to a number of teams simultaneously. They can also have links to other specialists on the internet to enhance their personal expertise

Notice also from Figure 14.7 that the expert or specialist will need to establish two quite different groups of contacts:

1 for collaborating with peers, to create an on-demand knowledge base and be able to be aware of changes and new development in the chosen area of speciality;

2 a list of clients and contacts for getting work.

These are the egocentric groups that were discussed at the beginning of this chapter. The expert or specialist will be at the centre of a self-formed group of contacts, having to create a mutual feeling of trust and reliance with each contact individually, but without any need for those contacts even to be aware of each other's existence. Clearly, the relationships between an expert and the expert's contacts will be collaborative rather than cooperative. Similarly, an entrepreneur or/and an auteur can also form an egocentric group of collaborative expert contacts, who provide a suitable number of knowledge links to them (and through them their cooperative team).

Any member of a cooperative team can also form an egocentric group of their own to draw in information or assistance from the internet. This will give them indirect access to any of the millions of other people on the internet who might be able to enhance their particular function in the team.

Stepping back from the micro view of individual associations, you can get an idea of how the internet achieves a universal organization. With teams linked to a number of specialists who are each linked to other teams and at the same time linked to various other specialists, it is not difficult to see how the Kevin Bacon and small-world clustering effects can provide an efficient framework for knowledge exchange throughout the system. It is probably not a coincidence that the human brain uses a somewhat similar form of communication architecture for transferring information around its interacting network of neurons.

universal implications of small-world clusters The
results of the small-world network clustering simulations have far-

reaching implications for the whole world. What they are telling us is that the effect of the internet on the human population as a whole is going to be much the same whatever proportion of people is connected. In other words, a person who is not connected to the internet is almost as connected as someone who is connected.

It is hard to imagine that a rice planter in the paddy fields of China may be almost as connected to Bill Gates as anyone working for Microsoft, yet effectively this is what this small-world cluster theory is telling us: the rice planter may be only a few steps further away.

A friend of mine who was a chief executive of a large traditional menswear manufacturing company once told me that the internet would have no effect on his business. He explained how his company had massive factories in the UK, able to produce thousands of men's suits every week at costs far below any other manufacturer. They also had their own stores to sell the suits, with an outlet in every town in the country. He couldn't see how the internet could threaten this long-established business.

At the time, I'd just read an article about a laser machine that could quickly make a three-dimensional computer representation of any person as easily as a photograph could be taken with a camera. Furthermore, computer software was under development that could use these three-dimensional representations to create cutting patterns for clothes, to fit people exactly.

I immediately imagined the electronic details of these patterns being e-mailed to a small village in Asia where there would be a cutting machine able to use these electronic patterns to cut out the material for a made-to-measure suit. I imagined scores of local workers, coming each day to the premises where the cutting machine is located to pick up the bundles of cut cloth to make them into made-to-measure suits on their sewing machines at home. Apart from the air transport costs of sending these finished suits to the UK, all the other costs would be so minimal that I couldn't see how this large company with its mass-produced suits would be able to compete: on either price or customer satisfaction.

> A PERSON WHO IS NOT CONNECTED TO THE INTERNET IS ALMOST AS CONNECTED AS SOMEONE WHO IS CONNECTED

The company may have many retail outlets all over the country, but many small kiosks, taking orders and making three-dimensional images, could be set up very quickly and easily, involving far less overheads and management organization. I didn't see how this executive could be quite so complacent about his company's dominant position in the marketplace.

Of course, this is not a reality, only idle speculation, but it provides an example of the way in which the principle of small-world clustering could dramatically change the way in which future trade and commerce might be conducted.

effects on sales and marketing
The small-world clustering effect can influence retail buying patterns, both on- and off-line. This can be visualised by imagining a little old lady living in a cottage in a remote village in the English countryside. She never ventures outside her cottage except to go once a week to the local grocery store. A travelling salesman also stops at the store to take orders from the grocer. This salesman might have a daughter who is married to an American who works in the White House. By way of conversation the salesman might tell little anecdotes to the grocer of things that happen in the White House that he has heard from his daughter via her husband.

The grocer might repeat these anecdotes to some of his customers, including the little old lady. In this way, the little old lady in the cottage might be as much informed as to the goings on in the White House as most Americans – and would be connected directly to the President through no more than five links. She might well hear about a particular favourite dish of the President and decide to try it for herself. Perhaps, if her grocer didn't stock it, she'd ask him to buy it in for her.

In a similar way, the conclusions of a discussion about a product or service in an internet discussion forum might be passed on to somebody who doesn't own a computer. People not connected to the internet are perhaps only one or two steps further away from these discussions than anyone who actually takes part. In this way, the ideas and recommendations coming out of debates and information exchange from a multitude of different online groups spread to the population at large.

Online influences can be highly magnified because the small-world clustering effect can rapidly transfer information from one discussion forum to another. A company in the UK, by way of a promotion, once offered free theatre tickets to the first 20 people to apply at their site. They had 14,000 visitors within the first 24 hours as word quickly spread from one newsgroup to another.

The effect of small-world clustering is bound to affect advertising and marketing techniques in the Information Age. If everyone is virtually connected to the internet, even though they may not own a computer, it may be that word of mouth and viral marketing will have many advantages over mass media marketing techniques. This will undoubtedly lessen the importance of 'point of sale' as being the place to convince and influence customers: most people will already have made up their mind by the time they reach the source.

Small-world clustering effects were not appreciated by the early dot-com companies at the turn of the century, who advertised extensively to get customers – marketing costs sometimes reaching as much as $1,000 per customer. Those companies found that they could get first-time customers at a cost, but there was little incentive for the customers to stay loyal if there were better similar deals on offer elsewhere – and the internet grapevine would soon inform them if there were.

The dot-coms' mistake was to assume that customer buying patterns would be the same online as off-line. In the bricks and mortar world, a customer might be aware of a better product or a better price elsewhere but it may not be worth the time and effort to go to the place where it is available. The situation is far different when shopping online. A cheaper price or a better product is simply a few mouse clicks away. Customer loyalty is severely tested in this situation. As long as word of mouth recommendations include reliable service and better prices, there is little deterrent to customers shopping for value rather than convenience. Simply stated: a customer list is only as good as the value being offered.

The early dot-coms were very server oriented. They believed all sales could be generated at a website location. The initial clarion call was 'Content is king', because there seemed to be logic in the premise that if

> " THE EFFECT OF SMALL-WORLD CLUSTERING IS BOUND TO AFFECT ADVERTISING AND MARKETING TECHNIQUES IN THE INFORMATION AGE "

you create interesting stuff to get people coming to your website then this traffic could be used to generate a flow of revenue. Everybody was proclaiming that content was king and everyone should concentrate on content and, like lemmings, everyone charged in that direction. Billions of dollars were pumped into dot-com start-ups whose business plan was based upon this premise.

Then reality set in. The overheads and cost of generating interesting and varying content was unsustainable. Most of them ran through their capital before they had established a viable income. A new buzz expression came into regular use: 'burn rate' – the speed at which capital evaporates as a dot-com business struggles to become viable.

At the time of writing, the clarion call is for website traffic monitoring, customer analysis and content customization. It has a compelling logic. But how much of this is going to be of use when customers have already made up their mind what they want before they arrive at a site – because Jack next door has told them what and where to buy, or they've heard about it from an online discussion forum?

My gut feeling tells me that this customization for customer profiles is no more than another passing craze that's going to eat up a lot more speculative investment funding. There are now so many developers and solution providers getting into this 'new vision' that it will soon be passé. My bet is that it will be the client side that is going to be where the real influences are going to be made – and this is going to be totally dependent upon the value and the quality of the service or product being offered.

the sociogram

In the book *The Entrepreneurial Web* mention was made of the sociogram. It was explained like this:

A drug manufacturing company had been spending quite considerable sums of money mailing out expensive literature, sales packs and samples to thousands of doctors on its mailing list and was getting very disappointing results.

Using a questionnaire to try to discover what influenced doctors in their decisions to prescribe particular drugs, the drug manufacturing company discovered that by far the most influential factor was advice or recommendations from other doctors.

To investigate this clue, the drug company picked an area in the country and sent a team of investigators to call on every single doctor there. These investigators were instructed to try to find out who was speaking to whom. When these results were obtained, the marketing department took a map of the area and drew a small circle on the map to mark the geographic location of each doctor, then drew a straight line between any doctors where a communication link had been established. Such a diagram is known as a sociogram.

What they discovered, when they completed the map, was that the lines radiating out from the doctors varied immensely. Some doctors had lines connecting them with many others, some with only one or two. Looking at the overall picture, it was clear that if peer-to-peer communication was a strong influence then the influence was concentrated around a relatively small number of doctors.

Changing their marketing strategy in this particular area, the drug company found that concentrating all of the marketing effort on to only these highly communicative nodes produced far better results than if the marketing effort was spread equally over all doctors.

The computer-enhanced communication environment of the internet suggests that such a marketing strategy could be effectively and efficiently employed for all manner of products and services. Again, this is a solution involving communication between people and involves very little technological knowledge at all.

In all communities, large or small, there is always the information guru who knows where to get the best products, the best services and the best prices. Whether these are the mean types, who tell you where you've gone wrong after the event, or the type you can go to for advice before you make a purchase decision, they are always there, influencing buying patterns.

To maintain their position as the reliable information gurus, they will have to be constantly investigating and searching the marketplaces. What better field for their research and investigation than the web, the newsgroups and the listserves? In light of the small-world cluster principle, this makes sense, so what effect will in-your-face advertising and marketing have on these influential local communicators? Will they just want to regurgitate readily available information to their local group? It is more likely that they'll relay information they'd gleaned from an obscure discussion forum that none of their neighbours would know about.

It is also quite common for people who use their computers to hunt for bargains to tell their neighbours about their successes. Their neighbours then ask them to buy or look for particular bargains on their behalf. In this way a single person with a computer can act as the internet link for a whole neighbourhood of non-computer users to shop online.

It is unlikely that anyone could specifically target these local information gurus. They will be feeding off their own network of contacts and will be seeking out recommended products and services rather than looking at advertising or marketing presentations. In short, they will be relying on word of mouth rather than simply information.

It also makes you have a double think about search engines. As was covered in an earlier chapter, these are not particularly efficient and are sometimes confusing to use. Wouldn't people be more inclined to seek advice from a knowledgeable friend who frequents online discussion forums? With such a small number of links needed to connect any kind of expert to a non-expert, word of mouth by way of the small-world cluster effect is going to be a far more efficient way to get information than any kind of directory or search engine. More importantly, this word of mouth is far more likely to be driven by excellent value, reliability and efficient service than by targeted advertising.

a strategy for interfacing with the network

In light of the implications of the small-world cluster effect, it is clear that a strategy to interface with the environment of the internet is not going to be as simple as a strategy for interfacing with communities in the conventional world of bricks and mortar. Broadcasting and direct mass communication are not viable options. The only strategies that are likely to be cost-effective are word of mouth or viral marketing strategies. These can only be effective if based upon sound and competitive products because the nature of communication networks provides so many routes for information to take that any false or unreliable information will be quickly corrected by the truth.

Knowing the way in which information and knowledge propagate through networks is essential in creating an effective communication strategy for whatever purposes.

15

COMMUNICATION STRATEGY

message capacity limitations The concept of small-world clustering is a useful way of viewing the information environment. It neatly explains how information can propagate around the internet and also impinge upon the non-connected world. However, the simplicity of this model is deceiving, because it also seems to suggest that anyone can easily connect up to anyone else on the internet – making it possible to access the expert opinion of anyone in the world, simply through the process of asking a friend to ask a friend.

In practice, it isn't this easy, because humans have a limited capacity for receiving and sending messages. For example, it may seem a nice idea that you could connect up through just a few links to the President of the United States, but millions of others might have the same idea. Lines linking directly to the President would have to be drastically filtered and so too would the connecting links through several steps around him.

This same problem, in varying degrees, would apply to almost everyone connected to the internet. Straightforward connections will not always be a possibility. Everyone will represent a node with a limited bandwidth (maximum ability to deal with messages) and be forced to apply some kind of selection or filtering strategy to deal with message overloading.

This would apply particularly to people who are valuable contacts. They will have lots of people trying to get their attention and all links to them will be heavily congested and have to be highly filtered. What this means in practice is that although there is a theoretical short number of steps between people connected to the internet, bandwidth limitations restrict the number of communications that can pass through the shortest route.

Figure 15.1 illustrates the kind of electronic message flows that experts or specialists (as an example) have to deal with on a daily basis. They will have clients, important contacts, special friends and close colleagues whose communications must be given priority. Over and above this, the experts and specialists will need to be kept up to date with what is happening in

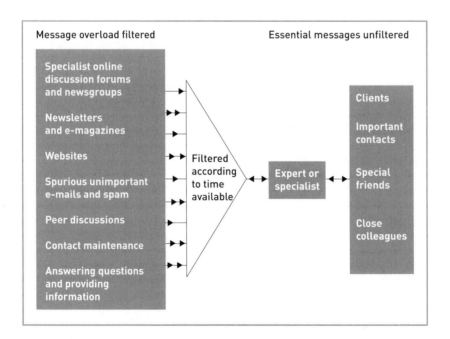

FIG 15.1 Typical electronic information load for experts and specialists who are connected to the internet

their field and be able to learn or acquire new information and knowledge. Typically, this will result in an overload of information that will have to be filtered according to available time.

Clearly, if this is the typical way in which people deal with messages, it is important to make contacts through the links listed on the right-hand side of Figure 15.1. This would need to be arranged by means of an appropriate communication strategy, as any casual communications would be subject to filtering.

the filtering process

All people using the internet will have a somewhat similar message pattern to that shown in Figure 15.1, with one group of messages deemed essential and the rest contributing to an overload that has to be filtered. Priority would be given to the most important messages, but there can be no hard and fast rules as to what to do with the others that have to be filtered. It is very likely that much of this filtering will be random.

Introducing a small element of randomness into the reading of messages can act very much like mutations in an evolutionary process: a chance piece of information may come along that can throw a new light on a problem or lead one to explore a different area of interest. It makes more sense than sticking rigidly to a communication filtering algorithm that locks you into only the sources that you are most familiar with (see Figure 15.2).

In a local network of information exchanges, such randomizing of inputs can prevent the total knowledge of a group getting into a rut. It can act like the way in which a random mutation in an individual can lead to a radical change in a biological species. In any strategies based upon genetic algorithms, occasional random inputs are essential and are often the way important breakthroughs are made in the solution to a problem.

the strategy to reach a goal

It is fairly easy to see how experts or specialists might use the internet environment to help them perform their professional functions. But they will not have to be concerned with

IT IS INTERESTING TO NOTE that researchers working in the field of neuroscience have found that the release of neurotransmitter molecules across synaptic junctions in the brain are not invariably triggered by the electrical spikes that cause them. It seems that neurotransmitter release occurs only randomly when a triggering spike arrives – sometimes averaging one time in ten, perhaps at other times one time in three. It is a random process dependent upon some variable level of probability. This is something like the uncertainty of response you get when you spill coffee on the keyboard of your computer: striking the keys doesn't always have the desired effect.

If the brain is thought to act like a conventional computer, this erratic response to signals passing through the neural networks of the brain seems totally bizarre. However, some mind scientists have suggested that the phenomenon that we call consciousness might have some control over the probabilities of the responses. By raising or lowering the probability of the transfer of molecules (information) across junctions, the brain could be consciously influenced to concentrate upon important issues and not waste time processing unimportant events.

Whether or not this is really how we consciously direct our brains to concentrate on particular issues isn't relevant here, but such a strategy makes a lot of sense in the context of processing message overloads. Rather than completely ignoring a whole batch of messages, when there isn't time to read them, we could selectively read a random few of them. In other words, provide the opportunity for a few of the surplus messages to be read, which will allow the possibility of ideas and information to arrive from unexpected sources.

It seems that many people glance through a list of unread messages before throwing them away and, if they have time, randomly open a few of them to glance at their contents. In fact, this is exactly how I picked up this information about the random response of synaptic junctions. Just before deleting several hundred e-mail messages from a variety of e-mail discussion forums, I picked out a few that seemed to have an interesting subject line. This casual process uncovered a thread where several scientists were discussing the conscious control of brain activity. Normally, I'd not have time to read through these obscure discussions, but this chance reading uncovered an interesting way of looking at dealing with message overloads.

the setting of their main goals in any assignments. This would be the responsibility and concern of a higher level of system organization represented by the client, boss or employer.

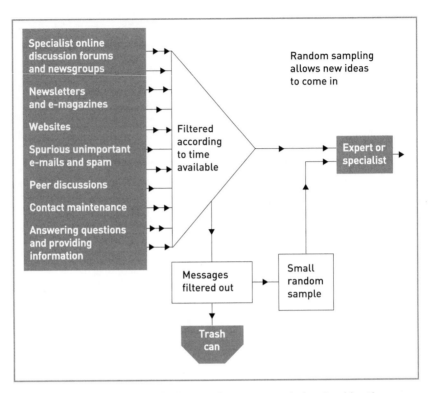

FIG 15.2 Random sampling of a few surplus messages before trashing them can introduce new ideas and directions

Game theory would describe these two different levels of organization as tactical levels and strategic levels. Unlike almost everything else in game theory, these levels are hierarchic, where tactics are specified from the higher level of the strategy. This is illustrated in Figure 15.3, where the strategist is shown as designing the strategy which defines the goal(s) and tactics. The tactics are then automatically brought into play at the right time or occasion by the rules incorporated in the strategy.

Although a game theory strategy can be flexible and adaptable, its composition is quite organized. It consists of a number of possible options and a set of rules (heuristic rules) which specify where or when these options have to be applied. These options are referred to as the

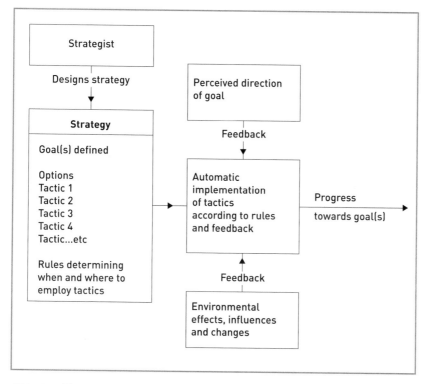

FIG 15.3 Diagram showing how a game theory strategy is implemented. Notice that the strategist designs but does not implement the strategy. The implementation is automatic according to feedback from the environment and the perceived progress of the goals(s)

tactics of the strategy. Strategists work out the strategy and tacticians take care of the tactics.

Experts and specialists, as collaborators, would be considered to be the tacticians – these are the people who would put into action the options described in the strategy. Entrepreneurs or auteurs would be the strategists – who would define the goal or goals and create the rules by which the tacticians are brought into play.

There needs to be a subtle, but very important, appreciation of the exact role a strategist plays in game theory. It is common to think of the strategist as dynamically employing a strategy to reach a goal. This is not quite the way it works. Once the strategy is designed, it is implemented automatically and the strategist then plays a more passive role – with the tacticians taking over all of the action. The only action a strategist might take is to modify the strategy according to its effectiveness and efficiency in reaching the goal(s). Note: strategists can also act as tacticians to implement their own strategies.

If you think back to the metaphor of the travellers trying to get from Bogota in Columbia to Salvador in Brazil by way of the uncharted tropical rain forest of the Amazon, there is no need for a strategist to be on this journey at all. The reading of the compass and the observation of the celestial bodies would be carried out by tacticians, who would be working to the rules defined by the strategy. A strategist would only be needed if the rules were found wanting; then the strategist would be required to modify the strategy – but not necessarily to implement it.

In stable environments, where there is little change and few unpre-dictable events, there is little work for a strategist to do once the initial strategy has been designed. In relatively stable business environments, many businesses don't even have strategists: a strategy of a successful operation can be copied by a company that is run solely by tacticians. Many large corporations are organized to run along these lines, where a common strategy is used by many different branches. A chain of multiple stores is a prime example, where practically all employees are tacticians carrying out tasks defined by a common strategy applicable to every different store.

the role of feedback

In a journey through the rain forest, there are two known facts to work with. First is the destination or goal. The second is the current location, which can be ascertained by means of measurement using a compass and the positions of celestial bodies. Progress is made by taking short excursions, stopping to take bearings and then readjusting the direction in line with the destination. This measuring process can be thought of as providing feedback – which acts to constantly modify the direction to keep progress in line with the goal.

Heat-seeking guided missiles use a similar strategy. Every few milliseconds, a guided missile will determine where a target is by searching for the location of a heat source. It will calculate its own current speed and direction and determine whether its current trajectory will coincide with that of the target. If there is a discrepancy between the two, adjustments are made to the positions of the missile's guidance fins until the trajectories are computed to converge. As the target is likely to be trying to avoid the missile, this process of target location, direction finding, computing trajectories and fin adjustments is continuously repeated as the missile homes in on the weaving and ducking target.

In the environment of the internet, the moving target would be a goal. An auteur would provide the guidance system and the role of the fins would be played by the tacticians: the experts and specialists. This is where it is necessary to think in terms of collaboration under the directions of an auteur, rather than cooperation under the management of a manager. It is only the entrepreneurs and the auteurs who will be focused on the goals of the project. Everyone else's goal will be to fulfil a tactical function as directed by the auteur's strategy.

Reverting to the metaphor of the guided missile, imagine that the target is moving so erratically that the shape of the fins limits the ability of the missile to track the target. In such a case, it would be imperative to have a more versatile system that would allow fins of particular shapes to be inserted to cope with some of the more erratic movements. This would see the missile as having not a single set of fins, but a variety of different fins that could be called into service as circumstances required.

This more complicated guidance system more accurately reflects the reality of any e-business project, where there is a constant need to make changes to keep up with changing technology and unpredictable competition. It would be essential that a wide range of expertise and specialization is available to be called upon at short notice. In game theory terminology, it would need a wide assortment of different tactics and tacticians to be included as possible options in the strategy.

A strategy that used a managed team of permanently employed cooperators would be like a missile restricted to a limited number of fins. It could adequately handle a predictable range of target weaving and ducking, but would go astray if the target weaved and ducked outside of that range. A non-permanent group of collaborators would be a more efficient solution because then it would allow a business to cover a far wider range of movement without incurring debilitating overheads.

Such a strategy would apply not only to entrepreneurs and auteurs chasing the goals of an e-business, but would also apply to the experts and technicians as they performed their roles as technicians. They would be restricted to within a narrow range of their expertise unless they had a flexible system of contacts to help and assist them by filling in their knowledge gaps and providing insights into future new directions. They would need a similar system of changeable fins to steer them towards their goals of competency and efficiency.

Seeing entrepreneurs, auteurs, experts and specialists all needing a similar strategy to achieve their goals, it is more convenient to disassociate the strategy from any particular business context and apply it only to individuals. This is illustrated in Figure 15.4, where the strategy of an individual is metaphored with the strategy of a guided missile.

the principle of the servo mechanism

The conventional corporate mind would look at Figure 15.4 and immediately identify this as a typical model of a business organization. In place of a missile's target detection function, it would see a marketing department, working out where the goal is and how much the current trajectory is off target. In place of the computer, it would see a team of specialists and experts who would work out what had to be done to keep the missile on course. In place of the fin controller it would see a team leader or manager, directing and coordinating the fin positioning.

In fact, missiles do not operate in this way. A missile's guidance system doesn't work out how the fins have to be positioned, neither does it coordinate their movements. It is far too difficult for even the most sophisticated of computers to work out what has to be done in order to

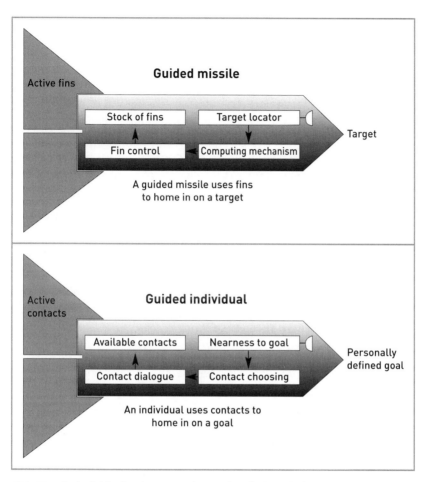

FIG 15.4 An individual trying to reach a goal or find a solution to a problem with the aid of friends and contacts is somewhat similar to a guided missile homing in on a target. This is particularly applicable if the goal or problem is continuously changing

steer the missile on a correct course to intercept the target. It uses a far simpler method of control: servo mechanisms.

Servo mechanisms are auto controls, feedback systems that steer a missile along a trajectory in much the same way as people might travel through a rain forest: a series of zigzags, where at each zig and zag there is a change of direction according to where the target is in relation to the missile.

This can be visualized if it is imagined that the fins of a missile are controlled by people: one person at each fin. Instead of a heat-seeking device, there is a spotter, looking out of a window in the missile to see where the target is. If the spotter sees that the target is diverging away from the trajectory of the missile, there wouldn't be time for the spotter to work out how everybody had to move their fins to get back on target; he'd probably shout out, 'Target is moving nine o'clock' – meaning it was moving left.

At this shout, some of the people would reposition their fins to make the missile go to the left. As the missile swung to the left it would go too far and the spotter would shout, 'Target is moving three o'clock.' At this shout, some of the people would adjust the position of their fins to make the missile go to the right. When the missile swung to the right it would again go too far and the spotter would shout, 'Target is moving nine o'clock' and once more the people would move the fins to make the missile move to the left.

This backwards and forwards movement of the fins would allow the missile to keep following the target by means of a zigzag route. It seems crude and inefficient, but it removes the need to have to work out the exact positions of the fins. This simple system of control can allow a missile to follow a target through all directions (clock positions), although of course the shouts and responses would be occurring many times a second. It is this same method that can be used by businesses where rapid change and unpredictable competition render structural plans unreliable.

It is this servo mechanism type of control that is needed in the e-business environment, where it is impossible to calculate what is the best action for all the collaborators to take and who best to take advice from. This will become clearer in the next chapter where a real-life example is described.

why should people collaborate?

The obvious question to ask is: 'Why should anyone want to be part of someone else's guidance system?' The missile will be homing in on the other person's problems and goals, not their own.

The reason would be for either reward, payment or reciprocation. When it is for payment, it's a straightforward business arrangement: paying for time and expertise. Often though, the assistance will not involve any exchange of money but be a reciprocal arrangement: 'you scratch my back and I'll scratch yours.' Most of an individual's contacts will have a similar system of contacts themselves, which they will use to home in on their own goals and problems. This is illustrated in Figure 15.5.

If an individual's contacts are treated as reciprocal collaborative associations, it can be seen how every individual can form a group of contacts

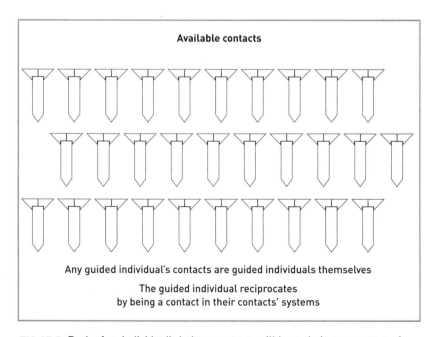

FIG 15.5 Each of an individual's helper contacts will have their own system of helper contacts. This allows individuals to make reciprocal arrangements to help each other

for themselves by means of a tit-for-tat strategy. Each contact is acquired as a result of a series of cooperative associations that start off slowly, growing stronger at each reciprocation of a favour. Because a tit-for-tat strategy provides equal benefit on both sides, each participant in a successful outcome gains the other as a trusted and reliable partner.

In this way, every person would be in complete control of their own systems which they can focus on their own goals and problems. The cost to them, of maintaining this system, would be the time they spent helping their contacts. But this is a typical non-zero sum game situation where everyone can gain. Each would help the other by imparting knowledge that they already possess so the cost to them would be very little. Yet the expert help or advice received would be of great value to the recipient. It would be a win-win situation for everyone. All it takes to put into effect is a suitable communication strategy to initiate and cultivate the relationship. This would involve negotiating the message filtering of the people in the environment of small-world clusters.

an evolving system of contacts
In a relatively stable world of little change, it is possible to establish a group of contacts and have a reasonable expectation that these associations will last indefinitely. Once a full quota of friends and business associates has been set up there is little reason to change them, or make any special efforts to add more.

In the fast-moving world of e-business, with a rapidly changing technology and continuous innovation, life is not so simple. The range of different kinds of information and speciality assistance required will be an order of magnitude greater than in the world of bricks and mortar, creating a need for a far larger and more versatile group of contacts. This would necessitate having to work continuously at establishing new contacts and relationships to cope with the changes.

This may seem straightforward enough, but the big problem is that it places immense strains on personal bandwidth limitations. It is no simple matter to go through the necessary procedures of finding and establishing new contacts that you can rely on and trust. Neither is it easy to maintain regular contact with a large group of people. Something has to give and what has to be discarded is the conventional idea of relationships.

A highly volatile, competitive environment would mean goal posts constantly on the move. As fast as one problem is solved another one will take its place. Plans and ideas are soon out of date. There will be a premium on intelligence and information to know what changes are taking place and where the future is heading. There would be a continuous need for new contacts and new sources of information and expertise.

The situation could be likened to a guided missile, trying to follow a target that is continuously getting up to newer and newer tricks of avoidance. This would necessitate designers continuously at work designing new types of fins and control systems to keep the target in sight.

Mapping this idea across to the world of e-business, it would involve strategists continuously at work to add new tactics into their strategies. As the tactics would need specialists and experts to implement them, this would generate a need for new tacticians – people – a list of associates and contacts who influence ideas and decision making. If a current list of contacts cannot cope with the changes, the list of contacts would have to be changed.

In practice, this will mean that in the pursuit of a goal, in the ever-changing environment of e-business, there would need to be pauses every now and again, to redefine the goals, and estimate how the goals were changing. Then an assessment would need to be made as to the suitability of current contacts in achieving those goals. Inevitably, this would involve changes in the contacts, dropping some and bringing in others.

In this way, a group of contacts would evolve and adapt, according to changing circumstances. This immediately calls to mind the genetic algorithm as being an appropriate strategy to use in this situation. It works in exactly this way: proceeding a step at a time and, at each step, removing the least suitable and continuing with the most suitable. This is the same, provenly successful strategy that has been employed by all biological organisms over millions of years. Organisms compete with each other to survive in the continuously changing, competitive biological world – a world not too dissimilar to that of the e-business environment.

rejection and redundancy aren't a problem
Conceptually, this strategy suffers from the same problems as the idea of discarding cooperation in favour of collaboration. It doesn't 'feel' right. It doesn't seem ethical to make friends with people and just discard them when they are no longer of any use. But this is a view that is only valid in the slow-changing world of bricks and mortar, where a loss of contact with people tends to be permanent. In the world of the internet, friendships and relationships can remain just as strong with a high proportion of discontinuity.

It has to be remembered that practically everyone who uses the internet regularly for communication has more contacts than they can comfortably handle. It suits everyone to have discontinuity because this allows them to have a greater number of contacts than their bandwidth can cope with. It is quite usual for a regular dialogue between people to suddenly cease and then resume again, as if there hadn't been a break, several months, even years, later.

IN THE WORLD OF THE INTERNET, FRIENDSHIPS AND RELATIONSHIPS CAN REMAIN JUST AS STRONG WITH A HIGH PROPORTION OF DISCONTINUITY

If you think again of the film-making industry, everyone involved in the making of a film will be highly cooperative at the time of shooting. There is no animosity when the shooting finishes. They part amicably and if they meet in the making of another film they take up their relationships again exactly where they left off. This is the spirit of many associations that are struck up on the internet.

how do you choose your contacts?
The idea of building up a circle of friends, or a list of useful contacts, in the highly communicative world of the internet seems to be fairly straightforward. It appears to be much easier to do this on the internet than in the world of bricks and mortar. The problem comes, though, if you want to be picky about the

quality of these friends or contacts. Anyone can make friends, but what use are they if they are fickle, unreliable and have judgements and opinions that cannot be relied upon?

Also, although the small-world cluster effect in theory can provide any individual with access to any person or source of knowledge on the net within a very small number of steps, it has to be remembered that these steps also act as filters. They can block out some or all of the knowledge that would be most useful.

These factors make it imperative that a suitable strategy is employed to ensure that all immediate contacts – those first links into a world of infinite information and knowledge – are chosen rather carefully. This requires a suitably efficient strategy otherwise the search could take a lifetime.

Here then is the problem: there are millions of possible people to choose from, so how do you arrange to optimally choose a relative few to be your limited number of prime contacts? Chapter 12 dealt with the problem of establishing trust and proposed a tit-for-tat strategy to establish reliable relationships. This is fine, but a tit-for-tat strategy takes a considerable amount of time and there will not be the time available to try out millions of possible alternatives. So, how do you pick the best possible out of millions?

e-mail discussion forums and newsgroups
In Chapter 4, the internet was described as a sea of random communications that contained islands of stability. These islands of stability were seen as the listserves, discussion forums and newsgroups that spontaneously form around a common area of interest. It was suggested that these would be the best places for people to go to get ideas and inspirations for e-business – and places to go to make contacts, form associations and collaborative partnerships.

The Kevin Bacon phenomenon and small-world clustering explain why these e-mail discussion forums and newsgroups are so popular.

Effectively, they are extremely large, small-world clusters and act to greatly reduce the number of steps between people connected to the internet. In theory, anyone subscribed to one of these discussion forums is connected directly – by one step – to hundreds, sometimes thousands, of others. In areas of special interest, where there are thousands of people who work within a particular field, this will result in everyone being no more than one or two steps away from each other – greatly enhancing the Kevin Bacon effect.

An e-mail discussion forum provides a powerful source of knowledge and information for all the subscribers. However, these sources of information and knowledge have to be used intelligently because of the message over-load effect. It is one thing to be one step away from thousands of people, but quite another to be able to communicate effectively with them all.

Once people discover the value of e-mail discussion groups, they tend to join several. This brings them within one or two steps of expert opinion in a number of different areas of knowledge, but it also brings an over-load of messages each day. Most lists help the subscribers to cope with this problem by giving them the option of receiving all the messages in digest form – one file a day that contains all the previous day's messages – but, however these messages arrive, there will usually be far too many for most people to read them all. Consequently, people who belong to e-mail discussion forums have to adopt a strategy of random sampling – in the same way that neurons in the brain randomly respond to activating message spikes: they read or respond only to a proportion of them.

a newspaper metaphor

As many readers will not have had the experience of taking part in an e-mail discussion forum, it may be useful to use a metaphor to illustrate the essence of this unique internet phenomenon. For this metaphor we'll use a newspaper: not a regular newspaper, but a newspaper that consists of nothing but readers' letters.

E-mail discussion forums, in their various forms, arrange for any e-mail sent in by one of the forum members – known as a subscriber – to be read by all other members on the list. For the metaphor, we might imagine that each day, instead of sending out copies of the posts by e-mail, the posts from the subscribers are printed on to large sheets of paper and a copy of these sheets sent out to everyone on the list. Effectively, this is how an e-mail discussion forum works.

Each day, the subscribers can read the letters they are interested in and, if they feel so inclined, respond to any letter by sending in one of their own. This doesn't go directly to the original letter writer but gets published in the newspaper for all subscribers to read. Some letters might be responded to by many subscribers, so the next day the newspaper might contain many letters relating to a particular topic. Subscribers reading the responses to that topic might then respond to the responses and these letters will also be printed in the newspaper that goes out the following day (note: any collection of responses, all relating to a single topic, is known as a thread).

If you imagine people sending in various kinds of letters to these hypo-thetical newspapers: asking questions; answering questions; expressing a point of view; disputing a point of view; calling attention to an interesting website; explaining some technicality; announcing a new version of software; describing an approach to a problem, etc., it isn't difficult to see how such a newspaper can provide a mine of interesting information. Not only would it provide interesting random information, it could also be used to get specific knowledge or help with a particular problem – simply by sending in a letter of request.

As each of these newspapers will be limited to a specific subject area, most people will want to subscribe to the newspapers of other groups, where they can read letters relating to other subject areas they are interested in. In this way, anyone can tap into the conversations of many people in a range of different speciality areas of knowledge – by receiving a number of different newspapers each day.

With this metaphor in mind, let's now see how these newspapers might be used.

1 as a source of random information The letters sent into these metaphorical newspapers would contain all kinds of information, some interesting and useful, others not relevant at all. Probably, there would be too many letters for you to read and you'd just skim through them, looking for interesting subject lines and reading only those that catch your eye. After a few weeks of doing this you'll begin to recognize some of the names of the people who contribute regularly and if you discover their interests are similar to your own you might start to look for their names as you look over each day's letters.

The most important criterion will be the noise to signal ratio, which is the ratio of interesting to non-interesting information. This would have to be above a certain level for it to be worth the time and effort even to skim through the letters.

Probably you'd concentrate your attention on only one or two of the newspapers, those that were most closely aligned to your current interests. The others you'd glance through briefly just to keep in touch with what is happening in other areas.

2 as a source of specific information If you required specific knowledge, or help with solving a particular problem, simply reading though letters would be of limited value. It wouldn't be the most efficient way to find out what you wanted to know because the signal to noise ratio would be too low. You'd need to send in a letter yourself – explaining your problem or asking for specific information – and hope somebody would see it and take the trouble to respond.

Whether your letter is responded to will depend upon the interest it arouses. As most people will be skimming through the paper, selecting just a small proportion of the letters to read, it would need a suitably interesting subject heading to catch the eye. It would also help if you were a regular contributor to the newspaper such that the readers skipping through the letters recognized your name.

3 as a source of making contacts All letters to these metaphorical newspapers will be accompanied by the writer's name and e-mail address. These will represent a wealth of possible contacts. Through the content of the letters, you'll know the writer's interests and can get an idea as to the extent of their knowledge and expertise. Many of them will include a website address that will allow you to see more precisely who they are, what they have done and what they may be capable of doing.

Having all this information available is very useful when deciding to make contact with someone, but it doesn't necessarily imply that that they would welcome any unexpected approaches. They would probably have too much correspondence to handle already and might be reluctant to add any more.

First approaches are best made within the context of the forum itself – so that an intended contact can see evidence of your worth before an approach is made. This might mean participating in newspaper discussions where the intended contact is taking part. It might involve supplying information or help to others in a way that demonstrates the particular values you have to offer.

The corollary of this is that if you write interesting letters to the newspaper, perhaps responding usefully to other people's letters, you might be approached yourself by valuable contacts. Looking at this possibility, it is easy to see how you'd be more likely to respond favourably to an approach from somebody you'd recognized from their published letters than you would be to approaches from a complete stranger.

The beginnings of making contact and establishing some kind of personal relationship with somebody is not easy – especially if they show evidence of being somebody who would make a valuable contact. Most likely they will have more than enough contacts already and will not be anxious to add more unless they see some exceptional benefit.

In the event that you did make direct contact with a letter writer, it is worth bearing in mind that this would be the first move in a series of tit-for-tat exchanges. It must start off with a small gift of some kind, perhaps a piece of useful information. This would give the person a chance to respond positively. A first encounter that simply asks a favour is unlikely to get a response – unless the other person saw you as being a potentially valuable contact and was themselves inviting a series of tit-for-tat exchanges to establish a relationship with you.

An initial direct approach would stand much more chance of success if it offered the possibility of future benefit, but the game theory concept of trust must be kept in mind. A tit-for-tat strategy to establish a relationship must always start with a cooperation: giving without obligation an immediate value or a promise of future value. If it is a promise of future value, this must be backed up by providing a realistic expectation that this promise will be kept.

4 as a source of ideas and inspiration Randomly sampling many different articles that appear in these hypothetical newspapers would be likely to inspire many different thoughts and ideas for: e-businesses; career advancement; new areas of speciality; interesting subjects to study or investigate. The problem would be, though, that the signal to noise ratio might be too low to make the effort worthwhile. Unless you had absolutely no idea of what you wanted to do, this is unlikely to be a profitable use of your time.

Think back to the example of the businessman in Chapter 3, who was described as being like a surfer on a beach waiting for a suitable wave to arrive. Such a surfer would be very silly if they chose a beach at random and waited patiently for a suitably sized wave to appear. They might find themselves waiting on a beach where the right kind of waves never appear.

Just such a situation might occur if a reader of these hypothetical newspapers randomly read through all the articles waiting for the right idea to come along that just happened to suit their circumstances. It might happen, but it could take a very long time. It would be more sensible to do something intelligent, so as to improve the chances of success.

Here is where the strategy of 'Spread Misere' (Chapter 12 – laying all your cards on the table) can come in very useful. Instead of waiting for an idea or inspiration to come out of the blue you can prompt them to come out by declaring your hand. As an idea comes to you, you can put it down in a letter and send it in to the newspaper for everyone to read.

An entrepreneur might sketch out the details of a business plan. An auteur might explain a particular approach to an e-business solution. An expert might define the limitations of their expertise or describe a new area of interest they were thinking of pursuing. A particular problem can be described. A range of options listed. A letter can be written to spell out exactly the state of the writer's current thinking.

These kinds of articles are liable to spark interest. Responses might expose weaknesses in ideas and plans. New insights might be put forward and unexpected directions or solutions proposed. The situation can be compared to making a stop in the Amazon rain forest to take a compass reading and looking at the positions of the stars. It represents the stop before the next step forward – the end of a generation in an evolutionary strategy and the beginning of another – where stock is taken of current progress before starting out in a new direction: the next stage in an ongoing strategy.

In a steady-state, predictable world, publishing current plans and ideas would be naive and foolish. It would mean presenting competitors with your ideas on a plate. They would be able to use those ideas and plans to gain an advantage at no cost to themselves. But in the volatile, fast-changing, unpredictable environment of e-business, such a strategy would make a lot of sense.

It must be remembered that current plans and ideas in an evolutionary strategy are a snapshot in a continuously adapting and changing solution. The snapshot itself is of limited value unless it is accompanied by the system from which it evolved. This system would belong solely to the writer of the letter, the publisher of the snapshot.

It wouldn't matter if competitors knew any current plans or ideas because they wouldn't be viable for very long; current ideas will be quickly be out of date. Also, any current idea or plan described would be particularly suited to the writer's situation and current knowledge. It would be taking into account the writer's circumstances and range of contacts that were tailored specifically to the writer's unique position. It is unlikely that they would be as suitable to anyone else.

the uniqueness of e-mail discussion forums Using the

metaphor of newspapers, with large numbers of articles written by the readers themselves, puts e-mail discussion forums and newsgroups into perspective. They are valuable sources of information but the signal to noise ratio is low and the volume of messages too high to be able to read all posts and take part in all discussions.

Despite these limitations, they have value in five ways:

1 Skipping through the subject headlines would discover others with similar interests and perhaps reveal different approaches to the same problems.

2 Randomly selecting a few posts to read would provide opportunities for thoughts and ideas to present themselves that would not normally have been considered.

3 As a source of assistance in problem solving.

4 As a means of checking on the validity of current plans and ideas.

5 As a source of valuable contacts.

The first and second values are obtained passively. They simply require time to read through posts. The last three values can only be realized through active participation. It is the nature of this participation that is of special interest because there is no parallel to these internet discussion forums in the conventional business world. They represent an unique opportunity to use communication strategies that had never been possible before the internet came into being.

Internet discussion forums are special; they are unlike any meeting or discussion forums in the world of bricks and mortar. There are similarities with real-life meetings, but real-life meetings have to be held in real time – where no more than one speaker can speak at a time and where the speakers compete with each other for speaking time rather than attention. Emphasis is on putting across views to influence or educate others rather than providing an environment where each person can be concerned only with their own cognitive models.

In a real-time meeting, people haven't the opportunity to choose from a number of concurrent different viewpoints, People aren't able to centre the discussion around their own particular interests. But this is possible in internet discussion groups, where all participants can discuss different things at the same time without conflict or confusion.

A comparison can be made with a technical conference. At these conferences there is usually only one speaker giving a presentation at a time. Everyone has to listen to that speaker and even if there is a question and answer session the speaker is at the centre of attention and the questions asked one at a time. If everyone got up at the same time to ask questions, or started to explain their particular problems, there would be chaos, especially if the audience started answering each other's questions or putting questions to each other. Yet such a situation is possible in an e-mail discussion forum and it doesn't create confusion and chaos.

Similarly, some conferences may have several rooms, occupied by different speakers, giving audiences a choice of different speakers to listen to. It is not possible for anyone to be in all the different rooms at the same time. Yet, in effect, this is what can be done in e-mail discussion forums. Imagine being in two discussion meetings at the same time and a point comes up in one which may best be answered by another group in another meeting. Switching questions across groups isn't possible in real time but it is easily done with e-mail discussions. A point can come up in one forum and without leaving the discussion that point can be taken across to a completely different forum to be discussed simultaneously in a different context – maybe coming back to the original forum with new information to add to the discussion.

The ability for any individual to move an idea around to different discussion forums is a powerful way to develop ideas. This technique would be useful for entrepreneurs who could check out or add to the ideas of the auteurs they had hired. It could be used by auteurs to investigate different possible e-business solutions. It can be used by experts or specialists to enhance their own capabilities and knowledge. It can even be used by members of a conventional managed team to increase their input into a cooperative project. A diagram to illustrate this principle is shown in Figure 15.6.

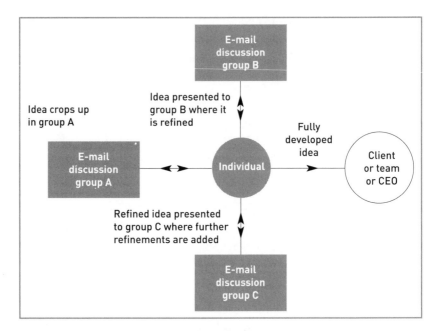

FIG 15.6 Any individual can obtain ideas from e-mail discussion forums, then refine the ideas by introducing them into other forums to get further inputs and perspectives. An idea developed in this way can then be presented to a local group in the world of bricks and mortar

It takes some time to adjust to the idea of participating in several discussions simultaneously, but it can be visualized in terms of the newspaper metaphor where a reader can take a point from one letter in a newspaper and then write a letter to another newspaper to raise the point there. In light of the reader responses to this letter, the idea can be refined and rewritten as a new letter and sent to yet another newspaper to invite further comment. In this way, any subscriber to any newspaper can arrange to be at the centre of a discussion that spans several discussion groups – with the combination of discussions being focused on their own particular problems and cognitive models.

This is what the collaborative model allows. Everyone can take an initiative or take part in discussions and at the same time be in full control to be able to filter out just the messages that are applicable to them. Imagine trying to do this in a real-time discussion group, with everyone trying to focus attention on their personal problems? Imagine trying to do this simultaneously in several real-life meetings that are occurring at the same time?

People often try to compare the benefits of real-time chat and tele-conferencing with those of e-mail discussion forums. But there can be no comparison. They are completely different animals. Real-time chat and tele-conferencing suffer from the same limitations as face-to-face meetings in as much as the discussions are limited to one speaker at a time and the speakers have to share and compete for the same available time.

Real-life, face-to-face meetings and tele-conferencing do have the advantage that there are not the problems associated with information overload – there is no need for individuals to devise strategies to cope with signal to noise ratio problems. But this is why e-mail communication is so different: its value is highly dependent upon the filtering strategy used by the participants.

For anyone to be able to be able to compete successfully in the world of e-business, it is imperative that they adopt a suitable personal strategy to be able to efficiently extract information from the internet environment. An important element in such a strategy will be in making appropriate personal use of e-mail discussion forums.

BRINGING IT ALL TOGETHER

UP UNTIL THIS CHAPTER, THE BOOK HAS BEEN BUILDING UP A CONCEPTUAL VIEW OF THE E-BUSINESS ENVIRONMENT. ALONG THE WAY, A VARIETY OF CONCEPTUAL TOOLS HAVE BEEN INTRODUCED TO THE READER: MOSTLY WITHOUT SPECIFIC EXAMPLES OF APPLICATION. IN THIS WAY A TOOL-BOX HAS BEEN CREATED THAT READERS CAN USE IN A VARIETY OF WAYS TO CONSTRUCT SUITABLE STRATEGIES TO HELP THEM ESTABLISH THEIR OWN PARTICULAR NICHE IN THE WORLD OF E-BUSINESS.

IN THIS FINAL PART OF THE BOOK THE CONCEPTS ARE BROUGHT TOGETHER BY MEANS OF AN EXAMPLE. THE EXAMPLE ITSELF IS TRIVIAL. WHAT IS IMPORTANT IS THE WAY IN WHICH THE PROBLEM HAS BEEN APPROACHED.

THE BIGGEST PROBLEM IN DEALING WITH THE INTERNET IS THAT IT MAKES DEMANDS UPON OUR BRAIN THAT THE HUMAN BRAIN HASN'T EVOLVED TO COPE WITH. WE HAVE EVOLVED MEMORIES AND NEURAL INFORMATION PROCESSING MECHANISMS DESIGNED TO COPE ONLY WITH A LIMITED NUMBER OF PEOPLE AND A LIMITED COMMUNICATION BANDWIDTH.

NOW, THE INTERNET IS GIVING OPPORTUNITIES AND INFORMATION THAT ARE TAXING THE HUMAN BRAIN BEYOND ITS LIMITS. IT IS COMPLETELY OVERWHELMED BY CHANGE, COMPLEXITY AND OVER-CHOICE.

MANY PEOPLE COPE BY LIMITING THEIR USE OF THE INTERNET SO THAT IT DOESN'T OVERLOAD THEIR NATURAL NEURAL SYSTEMS. THEY PLACE STRICT LIMITS ON THE NUMBER OF PEOPLE THEY DEAL WITH. THEY CONFINE THEIR INFORMATION TO FIT IN WITH THE BANDWIDTH THAT NATURE LIMITED THEM TO. BUT THERE IS NO NEED TO LIMIT OURSELVES TO THE CAPABILITIES OF OUR NATURAL HUMAN BRAIN. WE HAVE COMPUTING POWER THAT CAN SELECTIVELY ENHANCE ITS ABILITY TO DEAL WITH LARGER NUMBERS OF PEOPLE AND AN INCREASED BANDWIDTH.

AS AN EXAMPLE OF THE WAY IN WHICH COMPUTERS CAN ENHANCE THE ABILITY OF THE HUMAN BRAIN TO COPE WITH COMPLEXITY, WE NEED THINK NO FURTHER THAN THE SPREADSHEET PROGRAM. THIS HAS MASSIVELY ENHANCED THE CAPABILITY OF THE HUMAN BRAIN TO HANDLE MATHEMATICAL CALCULATIONS AND LOGICAL MODELLING.

THIS FINAL PART DESCRIBES A WAY OF USING THE COMPUTER TO DO FOR THE HUMAN BRAIN IN COMMUNICATIONS WHAT THE SPREADSHEET DID FOR IT IN MATHEMATICS AND LOGIC – AN ENHANCEMENT THAT PROVIDES SUPERHUMAN POWERS TO COPE WITH EXTENSIVE COMMUNICATION, UNCERTAINTY, COMPLEXITY AND INFORMATION OVERLOAD.

THE DIFFERENCE, THOUGH, IS THAT A SPREADSHEET DEALS ONLY WITH LOGICAL REASONING AND KNOWN QUANTITIES. FOR MOST PROBLEMS IN E-BUSINESS WE NEED TO BE ABLE TO DEAL WITH THE ILLOGICAL, THE UNEXPECTED AND THE UNKNOWN.

16

THE CAFÉ – A CASE STUDY

the third dimension of e-business

To pull all the chapters together needs a real-life example. For this, it seems only appropriate that I should use a case study where I have been personally involved. What better example could I use than the writing of this book? It may seem a million miles away from e-business, but in fact it demonstrates exactly what e-business is all about. E-business doesn't have to be centred around a website; e-business is primarily about using the internet intelligently.

E-business is commonly divided into two categories: business to business (B2B) and business to consumer (B2C). Stop to think about this for a moment. Are these really the only two categories that e-business can be divided into? Isn't there another, more important category: person to person (P2P)? As soon as you add in this third category, it opens up another dimension on e-business that brings with it the realization that most e-business is not based around a website, but is about people. It is about people communicating with each other, people exchanging information, cooperating and collaborating together.

Seeing e-business in only two dimensions (B2B and B2C) is a consequence of looking at the internet environment through Industrial

Age eyes. The focus is on a tangible entity – a company – that can be designed, shaped and controlled. Individuals are subservient to this main entity; their behaviour is specified and monitored; their personal niches are predetermined.

The reality, though, is that the internet isn't a suitable environment for these Industrial Age concepts of business. The entities that survive and prosper are not organized companies, but self-organising systems. E-businesses cannot be planned and controlled, they have to be set free to self-adapt. This is anathema to conventional corporate thinking because it isn't covered by any of the business models in the textbooks.

The same also applies to products and services in the information environment. They cannot be designed, planned, monitored and con-trolled: they have to be grown organically. This again is quite outside of the concepts of conventional corporate thinking. To this mindset, the idea that you can just let a product or a service grow by itself, without careful planning and strong management, is inconceivable.

> THE ENTITIES THAT SURVIVE AND PROSPER ARE NOT ORGANIZED COMPANIES, BUT SELF-ORGANIZING SYSTEMS

This is why this book is a good example of product development in the Information Age. The corporate mindset would see the author of a book as needing to be an authority on the subject matter: knowing all the answers. It would see the knowledge as having to be distilled and organized before the writing commences. The corporate mind would think it imperative that the conclusions should be established from the outset.

But what would the corporate mind make of an author who started a book with no pre-planning? With no idea of what the content would be and not even a guiding framework of chapter headings? What if the author began a book without any preconceived idea as to what the conclusions would turn out to be? Would that make any sense to the corporate mind?

Yet that is the exactly the way in which this current book – and its fore-runner, *The Entrepreneurial Web* – was written. This chapter explains the process by which they were created. The mental trick is not to see these books as records of the past, but as exploratory adventures into the future – with notes being taken along the way.

the publishing business
As a background to discussing the strategy for the writing of this book, it will be useful to take a cursory glance at the book publishing industry in general.

1 the product A book is as much of a product as anything else. It requires time and cost commitments to create and is intended to produce a profit.

2 the entrepreneur The entrepreneurial function is carried out by the publisher, who arranges the funding and sets up the infrastructure for the marketing, manufacture and distribution of the books. Most publishers became established long before the internet came into being and their sales and production facilities are run in typical Industrial Age fashion with permanent managed teams to arrange advertising and marketing, organize production and take care of logistics and distribution.

However, book publishing, like any e-business, is in a highly volatile and competitive marketplace where there are many critical unknowns regarding the success of the products. Long experience has proved that the creative side of the business doesn't fit neatly into any business plan, therefore, very few publishers attempt to create books in-house.

Publishers have found it to be far more cost-effective to spread the risks associated with content by putting the creative side into the hands of a variety of independent authors. They do not have to rely on any single book being successful; all they need is sufficient of them to succeed to cover the overall cost of publishing a number of them.

This is a typical game theory strategy used in conditions of uncertainty, where it is virtually impossible to predict the success of any particular move (or product). The content of books cannot be specified in detail, authors are simply commissioned to write within a defined area. They may be given a few guidelines but by and large the results are left largely to chance. Of course, there will be several ways in which authors and contents are selected to improve the chances of success, but the bottom line is that before a book goes on sale nobody can predict whether or not the content is liable to result in a best seller.

The same strategy is used in the fashion industry, the film industry and the music industry. A permanent infrastructure is set in place and the results determined by a probability that at least some of the products that are produced will succeed to pay for the losers and so result in an overall profit.

3 the auteur Creativity is in the hands of individual people – the auteurs – who use their ingenuity to produce a competitive product. Auteurs are selectively chosen by the entrepreneurial body who will usually base the selection upon an auteur's past record, or a realistic and convincing proposal. For books, the auteur will be the author (or authors). In the film-making business, the auteurs will be directors; in the fashion industry, they will be designers; in the pop music industry, they will be bands or artistes.

4 degree of uncertainty Most entrepreneurial bodies will try to cut down on risk and uncertainty as much as possible. They will watch carefully for developing trends and follow these wherever possible. This works for early movers but risk increases when saturation starts to set in once a trend becomes fully established.

Most entrepreneurial bodies will employ a mixed strategy where they follow trends up to saturation point to provide bread and butter income, but continuously speculate on more risky products to give them a chance of being an early mover in any new trend. The proportion of investment in trend following as opposed to speculation is characteristic of the particular style of the entrepreneurial body.

This can be likened to the strategy of the businessman described in Chapter 3, where there is not a single gamble on a fixed idea, but a number of different possibilities are tried out simultaneously. Profit is made through concentrating on the successful and dropping those that fail. In book publishing, the books showing promise are reprinted. In the fashion industry, the more popular garments are repeated; in the music industry, more CD pressings are made of the hits; in the film industry, more performances are put on of the successful films. In essence, these situations are identical to the strategy I used in my button badge-making business, where a collection of uncertainties evolved to produce a reliably profitable outcome by carrying through successes to the next generation and dropping out the failures.

Successful e-business strategies are likely to proceed along similar lines, with entrepreneurial bodies spreading the risks of their funding across a range of uncertain possibilities. It will involve trying to spot and follow successful trends and at the same time experiment with novelty to have the advantage of being the first or an early mover in new trends.

The essential difference, though – between the old established industries that are following trends and looking for new opportunities and e-businesses looking for profitable solutions – is that the unknowns and uncertainties involve more than just the content of the product. In e-business there is not such a reliable infrastructure in place to provide a stable base from which to work. Marketing, production, distribution and logistics are often as changeable and unpredictable as the products themselves.

This happens because the environment is chaotic owing to the fast-changing nature of the technological background. Most investments will be speculative with trends too quickly becoming saturated and more often than not leading to dead ends. This quite dramatically differentiates the nature of e-business from conventional business, because not only does the product content need an auteur's strategy, the whole business infrastructure needs one as well.

It is worthwhile, then, to examine in more detail the way in which auteurs work. As their strategies are likely to have much in common, quite independent of the subject area, it will not make much difference what type of auteur we choose to take as an example. Thus, the strategy of a book author is likely to be fairly representative of all others.

similarities between different players in the game The

idea that entrepreneurs, auteurs, experts and specialists could all have similar strategies is not obvious. Their worlds and their ways of working would seem to be totally different. But if you strip away the details of their activities, you'll find they are each playing the same kind of competitive game: involving investment, risk and future rewards. This process of stripping away the details is known as abstraction and it is at this level that the framework of games theory can best be observed.

By comparing different niches at this abstract level – isolating the game-playing aspects of the people involved – there are remarkable similarities. It is not surprising therefore that individual strategies for game playing, in a fast-changing, highly competitive environment, will be almost identical for most people.

An author of a book is partly an entrepreneur and partly an auteur. The proportions are very much dependent upon the chosen strategy of the author. As an entrepreneur, the author will be risking his or her time and effort for an uncertain and indefinite reward. This reward will come in the form of a small percentage of the sales. As an abstraction, this is the way most entrepreneurs work: a lot of initial effort for a future financial benefit.

Publishers will usually give authors a small advance on future royalties. This advance is based upon the minimum expected sales: usually calculated as the basis of the author's royalty expectation on a first cautious print run. This is a risk because many books do not earn out their advance and both publishers and authors lose out. This could be the equivalent of an entrepreneur getting a loan to start a business, or a small business getting seed capital. But it is more than this; it is also a move in a game of tit-for-tat between one player and another in a non-zero sum game.

An author of a book is also in a similar position to experts and specialists. He will invest a lot of time in study and research before being in a position to use his knowledge profitably. Like the entrepreneur, experts and specialists will have to invest much time and effort before they are able to benefit.

Although most books are not profitable for their authors, authors may have more than just financial rewards as an incentive to write. An author can gain in several other respects:

1   In technical and specialist subjects, the writing experience can provide a learning exercise, where the author becomes proficient in an area of knowledge as a result of the research put into the writing.

2   The author can enhance his or her credibility, the book providing evidence of their competence in a particular area.

3   The book can be a step up a ladder of a career as an author. Like any other profession, the first step is always the hardest. Publishers want to reduce risk as much as possible and they are always reluctant to speculate on unknown quantities. This invariably means that authors have to write for small publishers, in unprofitable niche markets, before being given an opportunity to write for larger publishers who have substantial marketing and distribution resources.

4   It can generate valuable contacts.

Similar to the non-financial reasons an author might write a book, directors might produce films for nothing, fashion designers might work for pittances and bands might play for expenses only. In the world of high technology, where credibility is initially hard to come by, solution providers, programmers, musicians and graphic designers might all start out by working for small fees – or even on a favour basis.

On a larger scale, this principle is carried over to products and services in the world of e-business, where attention and credibility are perhaps even more difficult to come by. Most e-businesses are forced to start off by offering exceptionally good value: perhaps provided at a loss or even given away for free to be able to get their foot in the door of a massively competitive environment.

advantages of a personal website

Just as an author might write a book for the above-mentioned non-financial reasons, so an individual or a company might create a website.

Taking a macro view of the information environment, there is the glaring problem of establishing an identity and creating relationships based upon trust. This was covered to some extent in Chapter 12 where it was suggested that trust in the environment of the internet is best thought of in terms of risk and probabilities within a game theory framework.

Even though this may seem logical, it doesn't dispel the notion that such a basis of trust cannot entirely replace the conventional understanding of trust – which is a mixture of tangible evidence and intangible emotion. Since trust is important to any kind of business association, it is worth looking at it in further detail.

The areas where trust will be an essential consideration would include:

1 an investor investing in a project;

2 a funding organization providing money to explore an idea;

3 a venture capital body sponsoring an entrepreneur;

4 any form of loan arrangement;

5 an entrepreneur hiring an auteur or solution provider;

6 prime movers engaging the services of subcontractors;

7 subcontractors taking on work;

8 freelancers working in collaboration;

9 firms hiring employees;

10 employees accepting positions;

11 any kind of partnership or profit-sharing scheme;

12 acceptance of advice or information.

These are just some of the many situations that arise in the course of regular business activity that require a strong element of trust present before they can take place. This is about credibility.

Unless a person is known to you by universal reputation or through trusted referral, how can you have any means of judging whether or not a person is who they say they are? How can you ascertain whether or not they are trustworthy, reliable, honest, competent, etcetera?

If you visit somebody in their office or place of work there is much visual evidence that can lend credence to what they have to say. This may not be in any tangible form, but it makes a great deal of difference as to the credibility you give them. This contrasts sharply with the credibility you might give to that same person if you only dealt with them by telephone.

It may seem that the internet suffers from the same handicap as the telephone in that there is no visual communication. However, this is not only untrue, it misses the whole significance of the web. A website can provide the vital ingredient necessary for engendering trust and credibility. It can provide the same kind of effect that a visual appearance provides in the world of bricks and mortar.

When you see your next-door neighbour, you can make many subjective judgements as to their personality and character: by the way they dress, the friends they have, the car they drive, the job they have. All these clues provide a background to any conversation you might have with them. If you visit them in their house you might look at their bookshelves to see what books they read and if they invite you to their place of work you will gather all kinds of information that will build on the mental picture you have of them.

> **MANY COMPANIES GET THE IDEA OF A WEBSITE COMPLETELY WRONG**

In a similar way, such information can be available on a person's website. It may have a photograph of them. It might give an indication of their interests, hobbies and professional activities. All kinds of tangible and intangible clues might be gleaned from a person's website – sufficient to give much depth and substance to any communications or business dealings you might have with them. It is this background information that promotes meaningful and valuable communication links, providing strong foundations for partnerships and cooperation.

Many companies get the idea of a website completely wrong. They look at it simply as an advertising medium or a place to do business. They seldom view a website as the reflection of their company's heart and basic philosophy. Yet, in the world of the internet this is their image and if it reflects only an obvious push for sales this image will be cheapened.

Many experts and specialists have realized the value of a website for establishing an online identity. Some of them spend years creating a useful information source, or a library of free downloadable software, music or illustrations. This is not just an act of altruism; these efforts result in an indication that they are competent in their field and are willing to share knowledge freely. Isn't this just the kind of person one would want to collaborate with?

In this way, a website can do for any individual what a published book can do for an author. It isn't necessarily about money and reward. It is about establishing an identity.

discovering that it is a fast-changing world

There are two main categories of writers: writers of fiction and writers of non-fiction. One deals with fantasies and dreams, the other deals with facts. In between these two extremes is a less definable region: an area that deals in ideas and speculations.

Authors who deal in dreams and fantasies can be identified with the providers of internet and web-based entertainment and amusement. They create for eyeballs and attention and are not especially concerned with facts or knowledge. Authors who deal in facts are the algorithmic strategists; they provide specific information gained from past experience and proven or irrefutable facts. Their strategies are more closely associated with those of conventional Industrial Age businesses, where the main goal is reduce to a minimum uncertainties and ambiguities.

Authors who write in the area of ideas and speculations can be more closely associated with the providers of e-business solutions. The focus is on an uncertain and unproven future, rather than a certain and known past.

My own involvement in writing about e-business came as a direct consequence of the kind of unpredictable changes that occur so often in information technology. I'd lost most of my money in a naive rush into CD-ROMs when they first came out. Along with thousands of others I was caught out when the expected boom fizzled out. I came away from that experience poorer but wiser – or so I thought.

Looking for a place to pick up the pieces and start in something new, I was attracted to writing books on programming. This appealed to me because it allowed me to work from home, experiment with new programming ideas and write about the experiments as I went along. It seemed a great way to earn a living – that was until the realities of the unpredictable electronic world caught up with me once again.

At the end of 1998 I had two books published. One I'd spent two years working on (*Magical A-Life Avatars*) and the other was a new edition of a successful programming book I'd written three years previously (*Lingo Sorcery*). Within two months of these being published, a major revision of the programming language I'd been using was announced. To my dismay, it was incompatible with some of the programming examples I'd used in the books. Although these books were written to be read by non-programmers as well as programmers, the examples were proofs of concepts. The fact that some of them now no longer worked greatly reduced the credibility of the author.

This shock forced me to take my head out of the box to see what was happening in the wider world. The experience was much like a soldier spending a lot of time digging a nice deep trench on the front line and then looking over the top to find that while being engrossed in the digging the front line had moved several miles further away.

It didn't take long to figure out that wherever I dug my trench (subject matter I wrote about) the front line would be continuously moving away from it. I soon noticed that this was a trap that many had fallen into. The constantly changing technology had created an unstable environment where the front line was constantly on the move. Change that can be anticipated isn't a problem, but these changes were unpredictable.

As I looked to see how others were coping with the volatility, my attention was drawn to the world of e-business. There it was plain to see that billions of dollars were being lost through the same kind of problem that had wasted a couple of years of my life writing about computer programming. Day after day, businesses were digging expensive trenches on the front line only to find the front line moving away from them.

It was then that I discovered a more interesting game to play than experimenting with computer programming. I could try to work out how best to make use of the information environment of the internet to overcome the problems of complexity and uncertainty: a strategy to keep abreast of the moving front line.

the background

Having had a technical education in electronics and systems control, I had a broad understanding of the technology. I'd also spent 15 years in the volatile world of the fashion industry where that whole business is about coping with constant and unpredictable change. On top of that I'd spent 10 years in multimedia, specializing particularly on the programming side. It wasn't a bad base to start from.

Additional to this, the programming books I'd written had two main themes: object-oriented design and intelligent agents. Both of these themes had as their main purpose the handling of complexity. Object-oriented design involves the splitting up of complex systems into small units; the intelligent agent stuff was about using evolutionary principles to design smart systems.

The second of my two programming books I'd named *Magical A-Life Avatars*. Unfortunately, I'd used that name without realizing that avatars and A-Life were two quite specific areas of interest and research that were totally different from my intended meanings.

Avatars were being associated with the graphical representation of people when they interacted on websites. They were named after the human-like manifestations created by the Indian deity Vishnu who sent them down to earth to mix with humans. I'd come across the word in a different context, where it was explained that these manifestations had been created by Vishnu out of an infinite number of components that were available to him in the heavens.

It struck me at the time of reading that this ancient religious culture had devised a pretty good approximation of genes and a gene pool. Didn't humans manifest in the same way – as a selection of components (genes), chosen from an infinite source of components (the gene pool)? As the intelligent agents I was working on were based upon this same principle – the mixing together of modules of computer code – it seemed reasonable to me at the time to call these creations avatars even though they had no tangible graphical form.

The term A-Life is an abbreviation for 'artificial life'. Its broad meaning is the recreation of biological systems in other media. Mostly though, the term is used to refer to systems that use computer software to emulate the essence of the dynamic processes that underlie complex biological phenomena. It is a fascinating and extensive field of research. My interest in this field was to find ways to artificially extend the capabilities of the human brain to cope with complexity: enhancing human ability to be able to take advantage of the new challenges thrown up by advances in communication technology.

In particular, I was interested in the way in which the human brain was coping with the problem of information overload and its ability to extract useful information from the gargantuan mountain of knowledge represented by the internet and the web.

I'd likened this ever-expanding mountain of knowledge to a vast library, where all the books were randomly placed on shelves and the librarians couldn't keep up with sorting and classifying all the new books that were coming in each day. In such a scenario, it would be a hopeless task to go into this library to try to find a specific piece of information. A more sensible strategy would be to go into the library café to see if there was anyone in there who'd come across the information that was wanted.

The internet represented such a café. It contained millions of people who had been rooting around in various parts of the web looking for information. If there was any particular knowledge that needed to be known, there was a fair chance one of them would have come across it. The trick was to find out which one. Such a task would require a game theory strategy rather than a logical planned approach. I needed to create software that would help me deal with those millions and find just those who would be able to help me when I needed any particular information.

I started by creating an on-screen representation of the café that would be of a more manageable size. I knew I couldn't list everyone on the internet, but I could list all the people I knew. Looking at my e-mail address book, I found this numbered around 500 people. These included close personal friends and many people with whom I'd had regular e-mail dialogue. Mostly though, the names and e-mail addresses were of people I'd corresponded with briefly as a result of my e-mail discussion group activity and book writing.

As I glanced through the list of 500 names, I realized that I couldn't remember much more than a tenth of the people listed. Some names rang a bell, but I had no idea in what context I'd had correspondence with them and couldn't place who they were. All I was aware of was that they came from all parts of the world and they represented a vast range of different speciality knowledge.

Selecting only those whom I could remember, I ended up with a list of about 50 people. As I went over this list, it struck me that these 50 were probably a random sampling of the total list of 500. Statistically, these 50 would represent pretty much the same characteristics as the whole list: people from all over the world with a vast range of different speciality knowledge. Most likely they would have lists of contacts and associates similar to mine. I then realized that being in contact with 50 people was probably just as effective as being in contact with 500. This would allow me to create a café of a more manageable size.

This can be appreciated by seeing the situation in terms of the small-world cluster effect. The 50 would probably be in contact with 50 others themselves; this meant that I was within two links of 2,500 people. These would be directly linked to 625,000 others. I soon realized that through a small café of 50 people I'd have indirect access to thousands.

This led to a design of a café consisting of a main list of 500 people, with 'seats' in the cafe for a specially selected 50: those with whom I was in more regular contact. A schematic of the café software I created is shown in Figure 16.1.

In the book *Magical A-Life Avatars*, I'd expanded on this basic café model

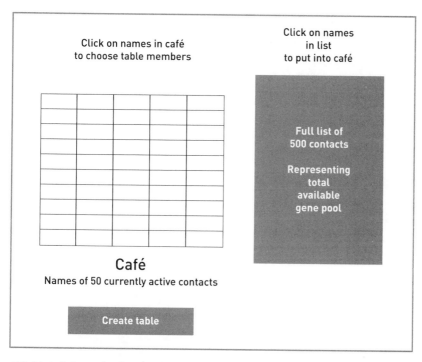

FIG 16.1 Schematic of café software representing a list of 500 casual contacts and a method of selecting from these to put some of them into the café. Any of those in the café can be selected, singly or as a group, to sit at a table for discussion

to include software that would allow people to represent themselves as clones. The idea was that people could exchange these clones with acquaintances and contacts so they could appear in each other's cafés. The clones were created by means of a simple questionnaire that asked various pertinent questions about career and range of knowledge and interests. By making use of these clones – reading in the information they contained and attaching it to the name in the café's database – café owners wouldn't have the problem of forgetting the relevant details of the many people they corresponded with on the internet.

After I wrote the book, I invited all the people in my list of contacts to take part in an online discussion forum to explore the possibility of putting these ideas into practice. Unfortunately, it didn't work out as intended. Everyone wanted to approach the project in a different way and instead of a cooperative project, it developed into heated exchanges with the e-mail correspondence descending into disorganized chaos.

To cope with this problem, I used the café software and put all the people who were subscribed to the discussion forum (again about 500 people) into the café's database. I then selected from this list the 50 most active posters to place in the café. From these, I could selectively choose small groups to make it possible to have more productive e-mail discussions.

I mentally visualized this as a café with tables, where I could select people to join me at a table for a private discussion. This might be one person, two, three or more – about eight participants seemed to be the

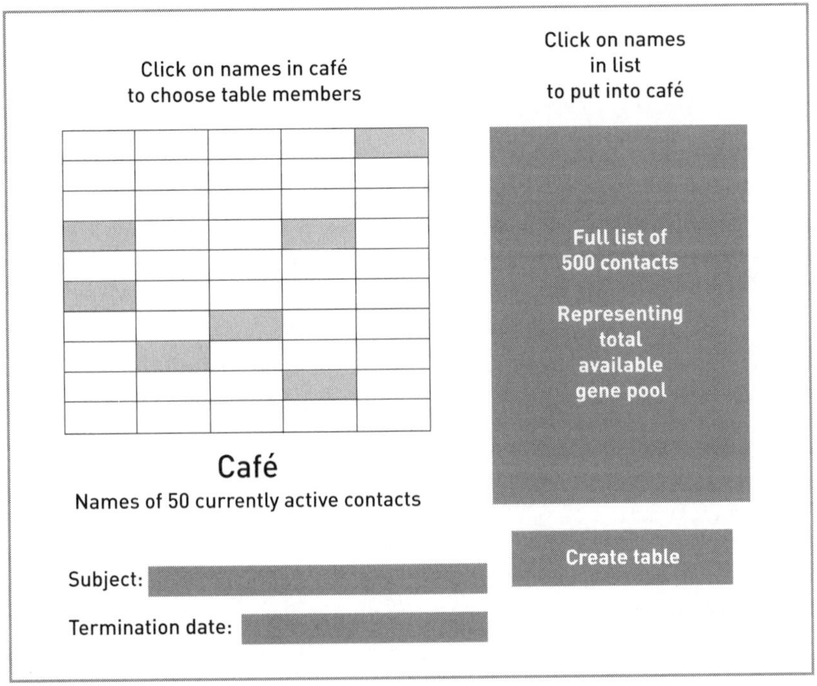

FIG 16.2 The screenshot shows a café with seven people being selected from a café of 50 people to have a private discussion around a virtual table

optimum number for a manageable discussion. The café selection technique for choosing seven people to join me at a virtual table is illustrated in Figure 16.2.

Selecting a group of people for discussion was then arranged simply by clicking on the names, which would be highlighted when selected. I arranged for a subject line to describe the nature of the discussion and a termination date to set the length of the discussion. The table could then be created by clicking on the 'Create Table' button.

When the 'Create Table' button was clicked, the program would then take all the names selected, together with the content of the subject line and the termination date, and create a text file as shown in Figure 16.3.

The table record was stored in such a way that it could be recalled at any time by clicking on a table number, and the table details (similar to those shown in Figure 16.3) would be put into the computer's clipboard ready for pasting into an e-mail.

These table details could then be used as the footer to any e-mail messages sent to the people listed as being at the table. The names could be entered into the 'To:' line of the e-mail, so that everyone at the table would receive a copy. The subject line would be entered in and, as every subject line contained a unique name for the created table (in the example this is ['UGP2M']), correspondence from different tables wouldn't get mixed up.

When everyone received a copy of the e-mail, they'd know that to reply to the table they'd have to copy the subject heading and the names from the footer into the 'To:' line of their e-mail. In this way each table resulted in the creation of a mini e-mail discussion forum with everyone sending in their responses to the same small group of people. A typical table e-mail is illustrated in Figure 16.4.

The café proved to be extremely versatile. It could be used to select single names for regular one-to-one e-mail dialogues or any number of people, according to the subject area. The different kinds of table that can be created are shown in Figure 16.5.

To: Peter Small ‹peter@genps.demon.co.uk›, Daria@schoolhouse.edu›, Jill
Green ‹jgreen@somewhere.co.uk›, John Brown ‹jbrown@aplace.com›, Bill
Smith ‹bsmith@anotherplace.com›, Jean White ‹jwhite@university.com›.
Bob Redhat ‹bredhat@acom[any.com›, Capt Kirk ‹ckirk@enterprise.org›

From: Peter Small ‹peter@genps.demon.co.uk›

Subject: [Table UGP2M] Reading chapter 14

Cc:

Bcc:

X-Attachments: ch14 ugb.html

Hellor Table UGP2M,

Attached is chapter 14.

I await your comments and discussions with interest.

peter

Please use the subject heading below in your responses to the table
and paste this footer to the bottom of all posts

Subject: [Table UGP1M] Reading chapter 14
Table termination date: 24th June 2000
Reason table called: Reading and commenting on "The Ultimate Game of Strategy" book
Number at table: 8‹‹
People at table: Peter Small ‹peter@genps.demon.co.uk›, Daria@schoolhouse.edu›,
Jill Green ‹jgreen@somewhere.co.uk›, John Brown ‹jbrown@aplace.com›,
Bill Smith ‹bsmith@anotherplace.com›, Jean White ‹jwhite@university.com›. .
Bob Redhat ‹bredhat@acom[any.com›, Capt Kirk ‹ckirk@enterprise.org›

FIG 16.3 Example of the text file created when the 'Create Table' button is
clicked

The unique advantage of e-mail discussions over real-life discussions,
chat lines or tele-conferencing is that it is possible to take part in many
discussions simultaneously. In the context of the café, it means that the
café owner can create several tables and sit at all of them at the same
time. This is illustrated in Figure 16.6.

As discussed in a previous chapter, when explaining the advantages of
being able to hold simultaneous discussions in different online discussion

Table record

Please use the subject heading below in your responses to the table
and paste this footer to the bottom of all posts

Subject: [Table UGP1M] Reading chapter 14
Table termination date: 24th June 2000
Reason table called: Reading and commenting on "The Ultimate Game of Strategy" book
Number at table: 8‹‹
People at table: Peter Small ‹peter@genps.demon.co.uk›, Daria@schoolhouse.edu›,
Jill Green ‹jgreen@somewhere.co.uk›, John Brown ‹jbrown@aplace.com›,
Bill Smith ‹bsmith@anotherplace.com›, Jean White ‹jwhite@university.com›.
Bob Redhat ‹bredhat@acom[any.com›, Capt Kirk ‹ckirk@enterprise.org›

FIG 16.4 E-mail showing how café details are entered as a footer. Names are put
into the 'To:' heading and the identifiable subject line copied in

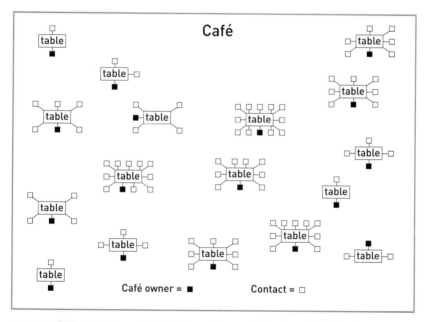

FIG 16.5 Different types of table that can be created in the café. This diagram
shows how the tables can be made up from a selection of 1 to 12 people (it can go
up to 50 but the efficiency starts to go down over 12). All these tables can be
running simultaneously

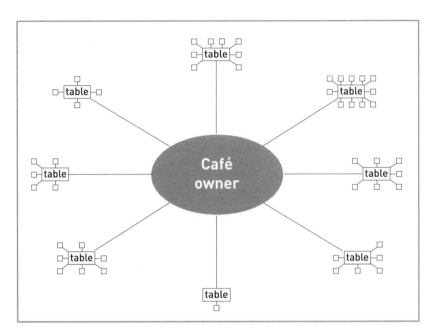

FIG 16.6 The owner of a café can create several tables for different discussions and sit at them all at the same time

forums, ideas can be developed by moving them around to different tables. This is illustrated in Figure 16.7.

Suitably choosing different mixes of people at the tables, and switching an idea between tables, the café can be used as a sophisticated idea-processing device. The idea can be exposed to different groups who might look at it in different ways. Although this may involve only a limited number of people in the café, the small-world cluster effect can effectively call upon the knowledge and influence of hundreds.

The café can be used with paid advisers or employees sitting at the tables. It can be used amongst peers: experts and specialists, working in the same field, who help each other out with the exchange of information and ideas. Indeed, it can include a mixture of all three, as would often be the case in a real-life e-business situation.

Figure 16.8 shows how auteurs might use a café to design e-business

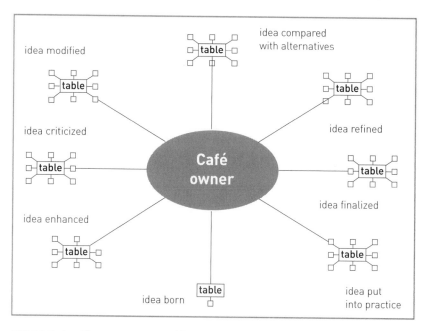

FIG 16.7 A café owner can move ideas around to different tables, to get various different opinions and viewpoints. With the right groups of people in the café, an idea can be developed from conception to implementation

solutions. They'd have a direct connection to their main employer, the entrepreneur or client. They have a table to talk jointly with key representatives of the producers of the core product. They'd have tables to discuss marketing, hardware requirements, website design, back-end databases, fulfilment and logistics, etc. They'd probably have tables set aside to have discussions with various other people whom they'd know from internet discussion forums: peers who work on similar problems to themselves.

Notice, in Figure 16.8, that none of the collaborators in the auteur's café need be employees. Neither need they work as a managed team. Some could be paid, others could be contributing on a tit-for-tat basis. An auteur can call tables into action on a discontinuous basis, for short periods at a time. Also, the auteur can call several tables into action concurrently and

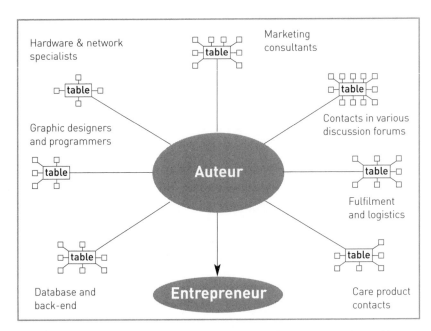

FIG 16.8 An auteur, working on an e-business solution, might set up a café to organize all the collaborators who are involved in the project

be able to sit in on all of the discussions at the same time – perhaps swapping information from one table to another where applicable.

Similarly, entrepreneurs might arrange their business organization through a café. They may have tables to discuss financing with investors, advertising and marketing with consultants, legal matters with lawyers, core product matters with producers. They may take the precaution of using several auteurs to work independently on the same e-business solution, to make sure they do not get locked into an inferior approach. Such an entrepreneur's café may take the form illustrated in Figure 16.9.

The use of a café is not confined to entrepreneurs and auteurs. Any executive working in a conventional business environment could also use the internet and a café to organize his functions and responsibilities. Figure 16.10 illustrates how an executive manager who reports only to the CEO might organize the functioning of his or her responsibilities.

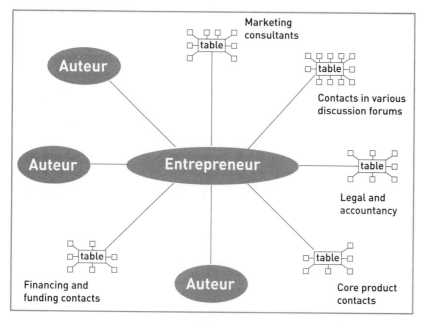

FIG 16.9 A café set up by an entrepreneur, who covers the risk of getting locked into an inferior solution by using several auteurs to work independently on the same e-business solution

Instead of sitting in on endless rounds of time-consuming real-life meetings, they could run all meetings concurrently and be able to sit in on them all at the same time without leaving their office. Because of the unique way in which e-mail discussions work, they would not have to wait through hours of inconsequential detail before coming to the crucial issues that need their attention. In the virtual world of e-mail discussion, the most vital aspects can be isolated to concentrate upon.

Notice in Figure 16.10 how the executive manager is shown as having a separate café set up to have discussions with customers or clients. This allows him to have a uniquely valuable perspective when he takes part in discussions at the various departmental tables.

The CEO might not even be aware of the methods by which the executive manager is organizing his functionality through the internet

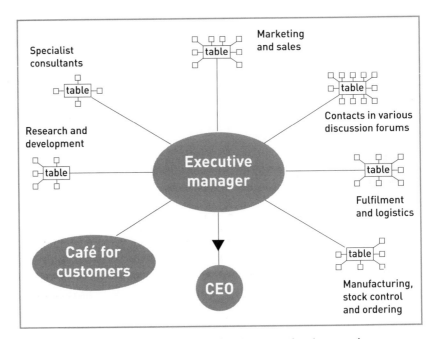

FIG 16.10 Cafés can be set up by executives in conventional companies. By means of the internet, they can monitor and control a variety of different departments and obtain feedback from customers or clients

and a café. It would probably be a mystery as to how everything in the organization was running so smoothly.

the interaction of cafés and tables

It might seem that the café owner would be in an advantaged position. It may be hard to see why anyone would want to sit in somebody else's café and help them out with their problems. It is only when you realize that anyone in a café can have their own café that it begins to make sense. Figure 16.11 shows how a table in a café might consist of a table of café owners. A little bit of mental manipulation lets you understand that the cafés are fixed but that the table might be in any one of the owners' cafés.

It makes a great deal of sense for anyone setting up a café of collaborators to encourage the people in their café to form a café of their own. This

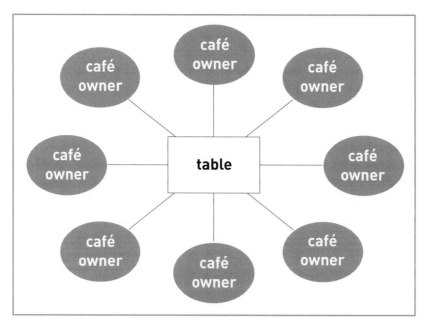

FIG 16.11 People in a café can be café owners themselves. This would mean a table could be made up of café owners who could each call on the expertise within their own cafés to help solve a problem at the table. It would also be possible for people to move in and out of each other's tables on a tit-for tat-basis

multiplies the value of each collaborator and makes it easier to exchange favours on a tit-for-tat basis, i.e., 'You sit in my cafe to help me solve my problems and I'll sit in your café to help you solve yours.'

Once you start to think about café owners moving in and out of each other's cafés, the boundaries of the cafés start to merge. Instead of each café being a closed network of communication, they become part of a larger whole where information can flow from any table in one café to any other table in another.

This is illustrated in Figure 16.12, where people having an e-mail discussion at one table are also having an e-mail discussion at another – perhaps in different cafés. Other tables can be linked indirectly to this central table by any of the people in the network taking part in a discussion at a table in another café outside the network. Figure 16.12 shows how a table outside

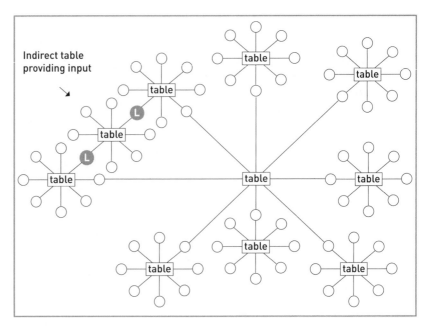

FIG 16.12 Tables in different cafés can be linked by people being part of more than one table discussion. Information arising at any one table can be passed on to any of the others. Because such linking can extend beyond table boundaries the system of communication is open rather than closed

a communication network of directly connected tables can have two independent links to it through two people being connected to both.

The transparency of café boundaries as information flows from one table to another is due to the small-world cluster effect. This is illustrated in Figure 16.13 where person 'A' might have several communication paths that can filter through some important information that person 'B' brings to a table quite remote from person 'A'. Person 'A' is then able to introduce this important information brought up at a remote table by person 'B' to their own table.

This is the power of the internet, to disseminate any important information rapidly through a community. A good or bad report on a product or service can flow around the world, going from one group to another in a matter of hours.

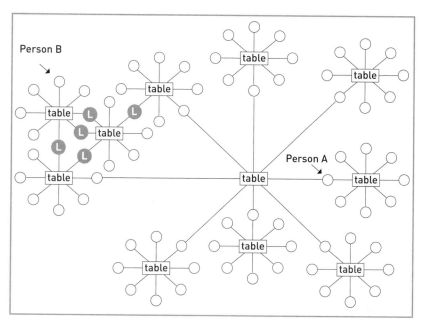

FIG 16.13 An important piece of information, announced by person 'B' at one table discussion group, can rapidly transfer to a remote person 'A' via several other discussion groups at other tables

Not everyone is good at transferring information from one discussion group to another. Sometimes this is deliberate. It is quite common within large companies for people to build power bases for themselves by withholding information. This can be done if there is a hierarchical system of management where information flows from top to bottom. Anyone imposing a block in the flow of information in such a hierarchical system can give themselves a distinct advantage over anyone below them in the chain. Communication by way of e-mail discussion groups can easily bypass information blockers as illustrated in Figure 16.14.

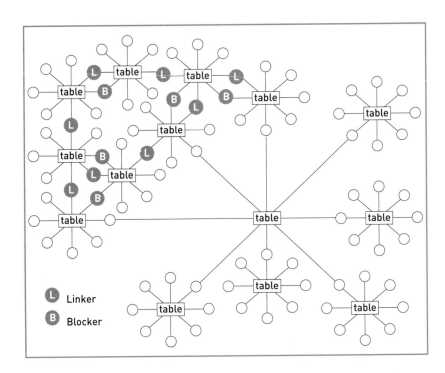

FIG 16.14 With people being able to take part in more than one discussion group it is very hard for anyone to block information flow. Whether blocking is through poor communication or deliberate intent, there are usually many different ways these blocks might be circumvented. How many routes can you find around this network to avoid blockers?

17

CUSTOMERS AS PRODUCT DESIGNERS

panning for gold

Several readers of the draft chapters of this book had been puzzled as to why it had not included website design, marketing techniques, the use of banner advertising and getting the attention of search engines.

The short answer is that if these were the routes to creating a successful e-business solution this book would never have been written. I'd have been spending my time in sunny climes with nothing to concern myself with but how to spend my riches. Common sense tells you that if these really were the way to produce a successful e-business solution then there would be many examples of these successes and everyone would be concentrating upon these issues.

If you spend any time on e-mail discussion forums that discuss these attention-getting techniques it doesn't take long to realize that the only people who are benefiting are the people selling these kinds of services. Just as in any gold rush, it is the people making the shovels who profit first. The real miners shouldn't be concerned about the shovels until they've first decided where to dig.

This book is for the kind of miner who doesn't just buy a shovel and dig where all the others are digging. It is for the kind of miner who first explores the landscape, looking for essential clues. These kinds of miners don't start with the shovels, they start with a pan to pan the river beds. They look for specks of gold that have accumulated in the hollows.

The miners with their pans are scorned by the miners with their shovels, who pass them by as they head towards the places where everyone else is digging. Why bother collecting specks of gold when there are rich seams up in the hills waiting for somebody to find them?

The miners with their pans smile, as they see other miners following each other into the hills with their shovels. The blind leading the blind. The miners with the pans have a better way of finding the gold. They know that if they find a river with a few specks of gold it must have passed through a part of the hills that was leaching gold. If they find some specks and follow the trail upstream it will lead them to where the gold is.

This whole book, up to this chapter, can be thought of as the e-business equivalent of the smart miner searching for rivers and specks of gold. The river is a river of people on the internet – potential customers. The specks of gold are the needs and wants of these people. The trick is to learn how to pan. This has been what this book has been about and this final chapter is about taking that final journey upstream to find the gold.

> **THE IDEA THAT AN E-BUSINESS SOLUTION CAN BE CONCEIVED AND DESIGNED WITHOUT A DETAILED BUSINESS PLAN AND A STRONG MANAGEMENT TEAM IS TOTALLY FOREIGN TO THE BUSINESS MIND OF THE INDUSTRIAL AGE**

the only designers who know what to design

In e-business, there are too many variables to be taken into account, too much uncertainty, too many unknowns and knowledge gaps. Products and services in e-business cannot be planned and designed in the same way as they could be in the Industrial Age. But the idea that an e-business solution can be conceived and designed without a detailed business plan and a strong management team is totally foreign to the business mind of the Industrial Age.

Examples of the failure of business plans and strong management teams abound in the world of e-business, as evidenced by the spectacular failures of some of the early dot-com startups. Failure was often blamed upon poor business planning and lack of sound management, but this was only the judgement made in retrospect. At the time these companies got their funding, they all appeared to have sound business plans and good management. This must be so because it is usually the basis upon which any venture capital is granted or IPO (Initial Public Offering) investments made.

The real truth is that conventional business methods are unworkable in the fast-changing world of communication technology. Plans are made to look bad and management made to look poor because the approach is all wrong from the start. Time and time again, people and companies have produced e-business solutions that are fully planned and developed before being exposed to potential customers. Success happens before a product or service goes to market, but it happens only in the heads of the designers. When it becomes time for a product or service to face up to the reality of the marketplace, almost invariably it is found wanting. What seemed certain to lead to a profitable e-business in the design stages produces nothing but disappointment when it is presented to the real world.

There is only one type of specialist that can design products and services that do not meet this fate, and this type cannot be organized and managed – it is the customer. Customers know what they want and what they don't want and if they can be part of the creation process they can produce far better results than the cleverest of designers or market researchers.

One of the readers in the café of people reading the drafts of the chapters of this book, Anette Standfuss, grasped the idea neatly. She commented to her table:

From my point of view the main point of Chapter 16 is collaborative work and building dynamic networks around ideas and projects and the main point of Chapter 17 is collaborative learning and problem solving.

Comments on Chapter 16. Here I see two main points regarding the café technology:

1   Using the café technology for creating and managing new e-enterprises. As said before, this is about building dynamic networks, working collaboratively using effective communication strategies to manage information overload and the dynamics of the environment.

2   Using the café technology in enterprises of the world of bricks and mortar. In this case the main question is, how will the use of such a technology change the organization? As is said in this chapter, such a technology is a possibility to bypass information 'blockers' and break up hierarchies.

Comments on Chapter 17:

I love this chapter. There is a very interesting point mentioned. It is said that the author is using the café concept as a planning tool and (see Fig. 17.4): 'The principle was very simple, you start from any point and through a process of steps, proceed towards a satisfactory solution. At the end of each step, stock is taken and a new direction is taken.'

Customers can ... become integrated in the development process by including them as members of the development team.

> **INVOLVING CUSTOMERS IN THE DESIGN IS SOMETHING QUITE DIFFERENT FROM CUSTOM DESIGN**

Involving customers in the design is something quite different from custom design. Too many companies assume that if they offer a customer a whole range of options and allow him to choose from these options (or fit options to a customer profile), this will automatically form a sound basis for an e-business solution. They quite forget that they are in a constantly moving and highly competitive environment. How can they be sure that the range of options they have on offer will cover customers' rapidly changing needs and expectations? They can't, unless their customers are actively involved. This involvement should not be limited only to the selection of options. Customers should be included as an integral part of the system that produces the products. They provide the guidance.

Before the advent of the internet, the involvement of customers at the initial design stages of a product or service was largely impractical. The nearest that got to this was market research, but this is expensive and is only a very crude approximation of what can be achieved through involving potential customers by way of the internet.

The internet now makes it possible to get customer help in guiding the development of a product or service at every step of the way: from conception to final design. But the definition of a final design in a fast-changing competitive environment isn't the same as it was in the Industrial Age. In the Industrial Age, a final design implied a frozen state: a state where the product or service has achieved a condition of acceptable permanence.

Such a state of permanence is not viable for long in a fast-changing world. The final product has to take the form of a system, a system that is flexible and adaptive. This kind of final design will never reach a state of permanence and will continuously need to involve customers as an integral part of the system to keep it on track. They must always be on hand, to guide evolutionary changes as the product responds to the fast-changing needs and competition of the marketplace. Products and services can then be shaped by the customers – through their feedback, contributions and suggestions. It is in the ability to tap into and include this design source in a system that most often leads to success in the world of e-business.

This is the single most successful strategy used in e-business: getting customers involved at the design stage. You don't have to guess what people want, they will tell you and help you provide it if you set up a sufficiently interesting or rewarding situation for them to participate.

a café as a guidance device

A conceptual jump can now be made to see how the café can be used as a guidance system that steers a café owner towards a goal, or – using the gold-prospecting simile – to follow the specks of gold up a river. Again we'll use the guided missile metaphor, but when this metaphor was used previously, a vital factor was missing: the question of uncertainty. In the previous metaphor, the missile was seen as homing in on a single identifiable target. In the world of e-business, goals are not so easily identifiable. Uncertainty and unknowns have the same effect on a person seeking an e-business solution as a missile seeking to lock on to a target when there are a large number of possible targets and these are in the midst of a cloud of decoys. This greatly increases the complexity of the problem.

A guided missile handles this problem by tracking a number of targets simultaneously. It will approach them as a group, carrying out tests on each to try to eliminate the decoys. When it is near to the group it will have to choose just one of them to pursue. It will probably be the nearest.

This is virtually the same strategy of the businessman compared to the surfer waiting on a beach for the right wave to come along. There are many possible business niches to exploit, just as a surfer might see many waves and the missile might see many targets and decoys. The business-man will be tracking many possible niches and trying to eliminate the red herrings and dead ends in exactly the same way as the surfer will be looking for the largest waves and the missile will be eliminating the decoys. Businessman, surfer and missile will all have to make a single final choice: the businessman will go for the most viable, the surfer will go for the largest and the missile will go for the nearest.

What they all have in common is a necessity to discriminate between the possible targets and avoid the decoys. It is in solving these problems that the café can be called into use. The modified missile metaphor is illustrated in Figure 17.1.

In Figure 17.1, the guided missile metaphor is showing how the café is used as a device to discriminate between possible goals and avoid dead ends and red herrings. It shows how a café might be used by an auteur to create a business solution with the aid of a café. However, as an abstraction, it is difficult to relate this to a real-world situation without an example.

For this example, we can continue with the way the author wrote this book. It was written under the guidance of a representative group of potential future readers: customers who were included as an essential part of the design process. They were the river and specks of gold that led to the conclusion of this book. It is not a pure e-business, because the product that evolves – the book – is sold mostly through outlets in the bricks and mortar world. But most e-business products are like this: hybrids that make use of the environment of the internet for real-world needs.

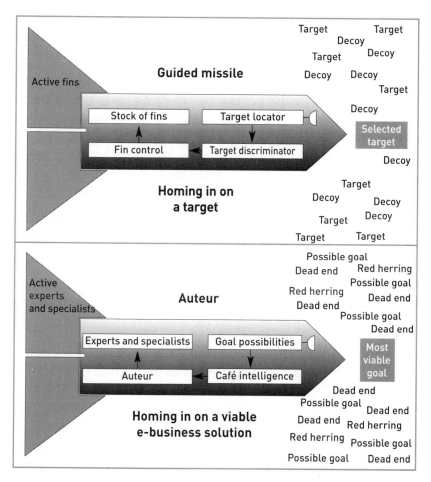

FIG 17.1 Guided missile metaphor illustrating how the café can be used to discriminate between targets and decoys

the dilemma

After I'd written *Magical A-Life Avatars,* I worked for several months on refinements to the café software. I created an intelligent database that could pull up details of a list of contacts to be able to bring the right combination of people together at a table to solve any kind of problem. It could be used by entrepreneurs, auteurs, specialists, experts, freelancers, executive managers, team leaders and managers. I had in mind that this could form the basis of a viable e-business.

When I'd finished the prototype, I started to think about how I could market this software. This is when I discovered that creating a product is only a small part of creating a viable e-business. How would it be financed? How would it be marketed? What competition would there be? Would somebody copy my mousetrap and come up with a better version backed up by millions of dollars of investment capital? It was then that I took a serious look at the world of e-business and came up with a list of problems similar to that list of initial assumptions described in the introduction.

The more I thought about e-business, the more paradoxes I discovered. It was a world of uncertainty and change and even if I raised a million dollars in venture capital there would be no guarantee of success. This was an environment that I had never before encountered.

Then the thought struck me that the café I'd been working on for months was supposed to be able to solve any kind of problem. Could I use the café to solve the problem of how to create a viable e-business? It had to be in the form of a strategy. How could I use the café to create a strategy? How could I use the café to understand the internet and the e-business environment?

It was in puzzling about how I could use the café to develop an intangible concept such as a strategy that the idea of a book came to mind. Whereas trying to focus café discussions on a vague concept like a strategy might be difficult, it would be easy to focus discussions on the content of a book. For this I could use potential readers to give me guidance.

the problem of content

At first, it appeared I had a catch-22 situation. I couldn't get café discussions going without content and I couldn't get content without discussions. Then I remembered the strategy of evolutionary design. You could start with anything and go through a process of evolution to find a solution. Could I use this same process to create a book that explained how to approach the creation of an e-business?

I thought about the material I had to start with. I'd had 10 years' involvement in the technological world from the beginnings of CD-ROM, through the advent of the first HTML browsers and the take-off of the internet and the world wide web. I didn't know the details of all the technologies involved but my experience with computer programming gave me a valuable insight into the underlying principles. I'd had an extensive experience in the entrepreneurial world of the fashion industry. Could I capitalize on this past experience to play the role of an auteur in an evolving system that produced a book on e-business?

At the time, The Financial Times Publishing Company, with their experience of producing books for business, were combining with Addison-Wesley, who were renowned for their speciality in producing computer books – both companies are owned by the media giant, Pearson Education – and were planning to bring out a new series of books aimed at e-business. The idea was to combine business theory with computer communication technology. This new series was to go under the imprint of FT.COM.

When I approached them with this idea of creating a book using an evolutionary design technique they were interested because conventional business strategies weren't able to deal with the problems that were cropping up in the e-business world. On the strength of my past experience and the two technical programming books I'd written, my proposal for the book *The Entrepreneurial Web* was accepted.

creating the café
The first thing I did was to mail all my list of contacts asking if any of them would like to read and comment on the chapters of a book as I wrote them. About 40 agreed to take part. I then added to these a number of people from various e-mail discussion forums that I belonged to: those whom I knew were actively involved in one way or another in the e-business world. I then had a full café of readers and randomly divided them up into six tables with about eight to each table.

The people in the café were an ideal cross-section of the type of readers the book would be aimed at; they were about as mixed as it is possible to get. Not only were they typical of the readership, they also each had unique knowledge that could contribute valuable input to the book. They included application developers, programmers, entrepreneurs, website designers, database specialists, hardware specialists, marketers, business executives, technical writers, teachers, students. They were a random selection of people who weren't all e-business experts but in one way or another worked or studied in the e-business environment. The only thing they had in common was experience in using e-mail discussion forums.

In effect, the café consisted of six small-world clusters where the members of each cluster had extensive links to a large number of areas in the world of e-business.

the café as a problem solver

When I first explained the idea of the café to the readers, many were under the impression that the content of the book would be a joint effort – where all the readers provided input and between us we'd decide what were the best ideas and meld those into a strategy by common agreement. This concept is illustrated in Figure 17.2, where each table is seen as discussing ideas separately, then for these ideas to go into a common pool where everyone could take part in deciding which were valid and which were not. This strategy would be similar to conventional ways of working, which involves combining the outcomes of special project groups or think tanks.

This system, of inputting many different ideas and using the combined experience of many to decide amongst them, works well in a stable environment – when there are not too many unknowns and uncertainties. In a situation involving more knowledge than any single person can possess and including many unknowns and uncertainties, it is difficult to obtain any consensus. Usually, the discussions break into irreconcilable factions. Worse still, when the subject matter is largely intangible – about thinking and strategy – there are usually as many different opinions as there are people and it is difficult even to agree about what it is that has to be decided upon.

The use I had in mind for the café was quite different from most people's expectations. I saw the café as a problem-solving device, with the role of

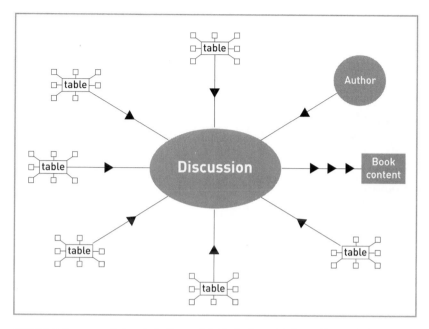

FIG 17.2 Some participants in the café initially thought the café was designed to generate ideas that would be selected through joint discussion and decision making

the author being that of a catalyst in a self-evolving system. The author would introduce ideas and information into the system by means of book chapters. These would be passed, one at a time, to each table separately – for each person to contemplate individually. With each chapter, everyone would speculate upon what was implied and where it was leading. They would collaborate by writing down their own impressions and let others comment on their observations. All these comments and discussions would then form the basis for writing the next chapter. This system is illustrated in Figure 17.3.

This is much in line with the process of collaborative learning described earlier. The readers weren't meant to convince each other of the validity of their own thinking, they were collaborating by each offering up their thoughts so that others might compare them with their own. This can be

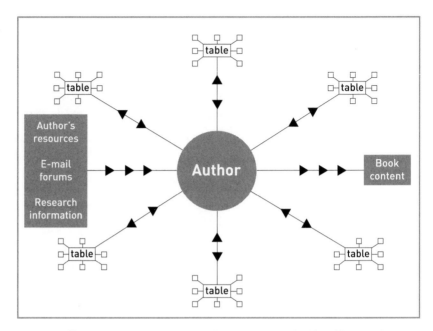

FIG 17.3 Chapters are passed separately to a number of tables. The people at the tables collaborated by applying this knowledge to themselves as individuals and sharing these thoughts with the others at their table

likened to the technique of collaborating by soliloquizing as described in a previous chapter. In fact, this led to more than soliloquies, it sparked off many informative discussions, where people at the tables often changed or modified their original viewpoints and perspectives.

It was this element of collaborative learning that maintained the review readers' interests. Once they discovered it wasn't just about commenting on and criticizing a book, but an exercise where they could expand and develop their own thinking, it grabbed their imaginations. Instead of simply reading an author's views they were part of a system that was developing a solution.

What was very hard for most people to adjust to, though, was that it wasn't intended that they should have to have a common agreement on the validity or applicability of the chapter contents. They each had to give an opinion as to how it affected or influenced them personally. They each had unique situations, unique experiences and knowledge; it couldn't be expected that they would all agree on a common viewpoint.

What was required was for each person at the tables to give some indication as to how the information was affecting their own individual conception of the e-business environment – explaining to the others how it related to their local situation, where it was leading their thinking and what knowledge gaps it was exposing.

At the beginning, most people in the café wanted a synopsis of what the book was about and a few signposts to indicate the direction the book would take. They were a little bemused when I explained I had no idea what the book would contain until it was finished as the content would evolve as it went along. All I could give them was a description of the final goal: finding a way to think about the environment of the internet to be able to make full and profitable use of it.

Not surprisingly, they were somewhat alarmed when I told them that I didn't have an answer to this problem yet, but this evolutionary approach to writing a book was designed to find out. Some of the café members dropped out at this stage. It seemed pointless that they should read and comment on the chapters of a book where the author seemed to know even less than they did.

Others were more sanguine about the project; although they weren't sure how it would turn out they decided to stick with it for a while to see what happened. There were also several people who had read my previous books and were familiar with my evolutionary approach to problem solving. They had a little more faith.

The principle was very simple; you start from any point and through a process of steps, proceed towards a satisfactory solution. At the end of each step, stock is taken and a new direction explored. In this way, there is a relentless progress towards the intended goal. This is the same method as would be used to move towards a destination when travelling through an uncharted rain forest. The steps in this book-writing process

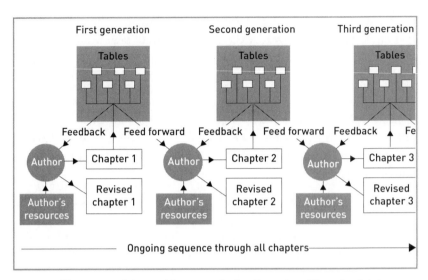

FIG 17.4 The approach to reaching a conclusion through writing a book is by means of a number of chapters. These chapters act as a set of ideas that evolve over a number of generations

are chapters, each equivalent to a generation in an evolving system. This is illustrated in Figure 17.4.

Understanding how the process of evolution takes place is not intuitive. As one scientist famously remarked, 'Evolution has been around for so long that most people think they understand it.' The reason why evolution is so hard to understand is that account has to be taken of progress that takes place in the future.

> THE REASON WHY EVOLUTION IS SO HARD TO UNDERSTAND IS THAT ACCOUNT HAS TO BE TAKEN OF PROGRESS THAT TAKES PLACE IN THE FUTURE

Think of the conventional way a book might be written. The author will write the draft manuscript, then this draft will be sent to reviewers for their comments and criticisms. In light of those comments and criticisms, the author will make changes and corrections. It would be unusual for the author to say, 'Hey, those comments gave me an idea to write a different kind of book, I'll start again.' Imagine now, instead of the author sending out a whole manuscript to reviewers, it is sent out a chapter at a time. And at each new chapter the author thinks, 'Hey, those comments gave me an idea to write the book a different way, I'll change direction in the next chapter.' This is what happens when a book is written with an evolutionary strategy.

This is illustrated in Figure 17.4, where an author submits each chapter to the tables in the café and gets feedback and feed forward. Conventional feedback allows changes to be made to the current chapter being read. These changes correct only factual errors or improve clarification; this conventional feedback is not used to alter the main content. For better or worse, the original content is retained because it represents a record of the thinking processes at that chapter. This cannot be changed because the following chapter builds upon it. Changes in thinking or direction emanate from the feed forward; this affects not the current chapter, but the following chapter that has yet to be written.

Figure 17.4 shows each chapter representing a new generation in an evolving solution. At the end of each generation – or chapter – the author takes the next step in a direction highly dependent upon the feed forward from the previous generation. Altering the previous chapter in the light of feed forward would make as much sense as the evolutionary process going back in time to modify a previous generation. Evolution acts by changing future designs, not by acting retrospectively on the past.

This evolutionary process used for book writing means that ambiguities, doubts, uncertainties, knowledge gaps and differences of opinion expressed by readers are not used to modify the chapter to which they apply. They provide a starting place for the next chapter and are answered there.

Making corrections in future chapters allows the book to progress in much the same way as species evolve in a biological ecosystem: a gradual progression towards a solution to a problem. In the case of a species, the solution is in answer to the problem of success and survival in a highly competitive biological environment. In the case of this particular book, the solution is in answer to the problem of success and survival in the highly competitive e-business environment.

the café as a guidance system
Figure 17.5 illustrates the activity at the end of each chapter (the pause times between the generations of an ongoing evolutionary process). The chapter content is sent to each table in the café. Each person at a table responds to the content by posting comments and opinions to all others at their table. Often these responses will trigger a discussion with several people joining in.

An author, using this system to write a book, will effectively be sitting at each table and receiving a copy of all posts. This intelligence will be divided into two categories: feedback and feed forward, with the feed forward directing the new direction of the book in the next chapter. This can be compared directly with the guided missile metaphor described at the beginning of this chapter – see Figure 17.1 – with the intelligence received being used to discriminate between different goals and avoid decoys (dead ends and red herrings). It is this intelligence that is guiding the author as the book progresses towards a conclusion.

In effect, the café acts like the compass and the celestial observations of the traveller trying to make a journey through a rain forest. It acts like the target selection software of the guided missile. The difference is that

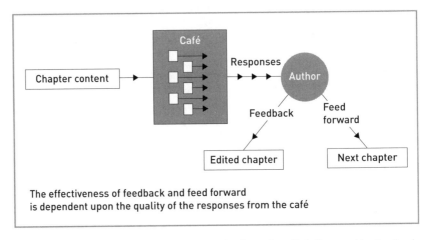

FIG 17.5 The direction and content of the book are heavily influenced by the feed forward of the responses from the people at the tables in the café. This acts as an intelligent control system to drive the direction of the book

the café guidance system is not an algorithmic set of rules – it is an organic system that can be made to evolve.

an organic intelligence system

In thinking about the progression of ideas as a book passes from chapter to chapter, it is easy to think of the evolution taking place at the level of the book content. These evolutionary changes are obvious for all to see. However, as far as the authoring is concerned, there is another, more important place where evolution takes place: in the café. The content is being driven by the readers in the café; if this café can be made to evolve, it can become progressively more efficient at guiding and influencing the content.

This can be compared to the evolution of humans. It is common to think of human evolution as taking place at the physically observable level: shape, size and form. In fact, evolution takes place at a much lower level of organization: the genes. Although the physical form may be constantly changing and adapting to an environment, it is the genes that are being selectively reconfigured. Figure 17.6 illustrates the biological equivalents of the café, the table and the people at the tables.

The author's guidance system – the café – can thus be viewed as an organism, with the responses from this system being a result of its gene activity. Just like any organism, the responses and behaviour can be varied by varying the genes. In other words, an author can control the system that is guiding the writing of the book by reconfiguring the people at the tables in the café.

Here we come to the very essence of the theory of evolution – and also the fundamental basis of evolutionary design strategies. An organism proceeds from one generation to the next by preferential selection and reorganization of its genes. Genes and gene arrangements that perform well in one generation are selected to go forward to the next. Those that perform badly are not carried through to the next generation.

This means there is a very simple, single heuristic rule that drives the evolution of the stem. It is applied to every gene and gene combination in a generation: survive and breed lets you stay in, if you don't you go out.

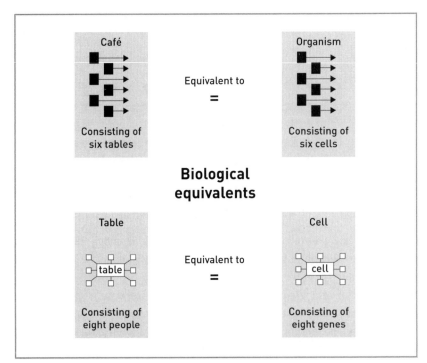

FIG 17.6 The biological equivalents of the café and its constituent parts. It can be likened to an organism that has six cells, each cell having eight active genes

The café can be arranged to evolve towards more efficient operation using exactly this same principle. In this case though, the heuristic rule that is applied doesn't relate to survival and reproduction. It relates to how well genes perform as an intelligent source of author guidance: guide well and you go through to the next generation, if you don't you go out. The difference is that in biological evolution the selection is automatic; in the café it will need human intervention.

reconfiguring the café

In a genetically evolving café, selection and rearrangement of people at the tables have to be arranged through heuristic rules. These rules, as explained in a previous chapter, are rules of thumb: rough and ready rules that really amount to no more than the application of common sense.

The most obvious first rule is that people not commenting on the chapter contents are evolved out. It makes no sense to keep them in because they would be reducing the efficiency of the café to provide guidance. They are removed after two or three chapters of failing to respond, so that they can be replaced by others.

The second common sense rule is that people who respond well to each other's comments should be kept together. This involves organizing the arrangement of the table in groups of people rather than on an individual basis. This corresponds with the method of splitting up genes at a point – as was mentioned earlier in the section describing genetic algorithms.

The third rule concerns the organization of the café as a whole. It doesn't make sense to have all the tables in a café reacting in the same way, any more than it makes sense for all cells in a biological organism to function identically. For greater efficiency, it is far better for tables to be arranged to specialize, functioning to complement each other.

This can be arranged by designating tables to play particular roles in the guidance system and selecting appropriate people to sit at those tables. For example, one table can contain people who concentrate on feedback while other tables contain people whose responses are more in the nature of feed forward. Some tables can specialize in being critical, others in being enthusiastic. There are a number of different ways in which the appropriate mix of people can affect the way in which a table responds to chapter content.

The fourth rule is to put negative first responders at the same table – because some people have a natural tendency to respond quickly with a negative viewpoint. This is often because they skim too rapidly through the content and take things out of context. After running many generations of these tables, I've discovered that the mood and opinions of tables are disproportionally influenced by first responses. If the first response is negative, it can inhibit responses that are valuable for feed forward.

It is an often observed characteristic of groups that they are easily influenced into a common mindset. There is an experiment, often mentioned in psychology, that demonstrates this phenomenon. It revolves around an optical illusion that a single stationary spot of light in a darkened room can appear to move. If a group is sent into a room and asked to determine whether or not the spot is moving, the group nearly always decides it is or it isn't according to the first opinion voiced.

This leads to a fifth rule that runs counter to some of the other rules: keep changing around the people at the tables so that a common mindset doesn't become fixed. Unlike the situation in conventional organizational structures, the tendency for a group to form a common mindset is not beneficial in discussions involving unknowns and uncertainties. It is just as easy for a group to agree upon a wrong conclusion as a right conclusion. Such agreements form early in discussions and often inhibit views that might look at other viewpoints.

Changing people around at each new chapter can also counter bias. For instance, discussions at two tables might come to totally different conclusions owing to the bias of some of the early discussion leaders. In the following chapter (where probably both viewpoints have been taken into account), people are switched between the tables. This has the effect of keeping everyone fairly open minded because they are continuously being exposed to different perspectives.

This is how an evolutionary strategy was used to write this book. Although it was written by the author, the writing was guided and kept on course by the people in the café. They had access to hundreds, perhaps thousands of other people's views through their personal world of contacts. It was this community, helped along by a few heuristic rules, that kept the book on course to home in on the main goal – of finding a suitable way to establish a personal niche in the world of e-business.

from book writing to e-business
Although the above strategy was used for writing a book, there is every reason to believe that a similar strategy would be applicable to projects or goals in any niche – be it in the world of conventional business or in the plethora of different niches

that make up the world of electronic communications. The connectiveness of the internet environment has vast potential to improve efficiencies and its full potential can only be realized through imaginative communication strategies.

The first flurry of excitement about the potential of e-business was based upon looking at the internet and the world wide web through the eyes of conventional, Industrial Age philosophies. Its main focus was on the website. This was seen to be the prime scene of the action. Many ignored the real power of the internet: the ability to organize and communicate with people. The internet was often seen as an inconvenient hurdle that had to be crossed to get to where the real business was thought to be: at the portals and the places that attracted eyeballs.

Billions of dollars were poured into website-oriented businesses, which were designed and constructed using Industrial Age business models and management techniques. At first there was surprise when some of them failed. Then, as the failures escalated, people began to question the principles upon which the new online businesses were based. People started asking sensible questions, such as 'How is this investment going to make a profit?'

At the height of the speculative bubble in dot-com start-ups, it suddenly began to dawn on people that there was more to e-business than setting up a grand, all-singing, all-dancing website, even if it incorporated a sophisticated back-end. The real game was about providing better value and increased efficiency. If the final product or service to the customer or client didn't deliver those, then all the technology in the world wouldn't help make a viable e-business.

Many are still trying to cling on to the old ideas, the methods of the past. Sharp salesmen are still cashing in on the unrealistic dreams of naive investors. Advantage is still being taken of businesses unfamiliar with internet technology to provide them with useless websites at exorbitant costs. Billions of dollars are still being squandered on hopeless schemes, which a grain of common sense would banish to the trash can.

The stark reality is that e-business isn't about technology, it is primarily about communication efficiency. This involves separating useful communication signals from a background of noise. Communication creates noise, but this isn't something to be avoided, it is something to be tackled.

One of the first weapon research labs I worked in had developed a system for measuring the surface temperature of the sea from a low-flying aircraft. It wasn't designed to measure the absolute temperature, it was designed to measure only the randomly fluctuating temperature variations as the waves mixed erratically with the air above.

By applying suitable filtering to the random noise produced by the heat sensors measuring these small variations in temperature, they could sometimes detect a discernible pattern: the pattern of a submarine as its progress disturbed the water at the surface. Out of the noise a valuable order could be discerned. This is what e-business is really about: filtering through the noise of communication to reveal valuable patterns. Figures 17.7 and 17.8 illustrate this concept.

It may seem strange to think of filtering out a pattern of people to create an e-business niche, but isn't this the way all business niches are created? Team leaders filter out people to create a team. A salesman filters out a list of valuable contacts. A contractor will filter out a collection of subcontractors. An expert will filter out a group of peers to share knowledge. An auteur will filter out a group of collaborators, an entrepreneur will filter out a number of investors, an investor will filter out a set of advisers.

All business niches rely on the filtering out of sets of key contacts that together form a viable system. The internet is a vast sea of possible contacts. All it needs, to create any kind of a niche, is to apply an intelligent filtering system. This was the main message in the fore-runner to this book, *The Entrepreneurial Web*, where the value of a person was considered in the context of an object-oriented world. In this world, everyone has a value that is the sum of their own abilities and knowledge plus the ability and knowledge of their contacts. People do not act alone, they act as part of a self-created group. The more accomplished this group, the better the individual will be able to perform.

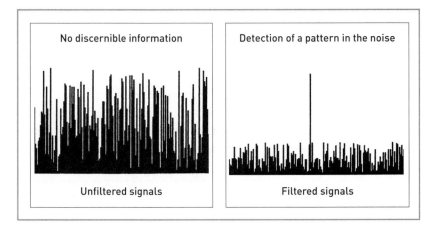

FIG 17.7 Random signals are received by temperature sensors. When these are suitably filtered they reveal the presence of a submarine

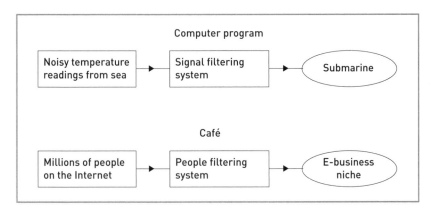

FIG 17.8 Like the way in which a computer can filter out a distinctive pattern in noise to detect a submarine, so a café using a genetic algorithm strategy can filter out a pattern of people for an e-business niche

final conclusion

At the beginning of writing this book, I had no preconceptions as to how it would all come out. I was that businessman in Chapter 3, who was looking at the waves, waiting for a suitable surfing wave to come along. The problem then was that even if a good wave had come along I probably wouldn't have been able to recognize it, neither would I have known how to ride it – because I hadn't yet learned to surf.

In the course of writing *The Entrepreneurial Web* and this current book I've picked up many useful ideas and learned from the experiences of countless other people – thanks go to the people in the café and the many others from various e-mail discussion forums. I've benefited also from e-zines, newsletters, websites and discussion forums – not to mention many face-to-face discussions and meetings in the real world.

The collected input from all the people directly or indirectly involved have produced a book of conceptual ideas. These can be considered to be tools, which can now be included in the tool-box of concepts that the reader will use to establish his own particular niche in the world of e-business. Some of these tools may be redundant, some of them useless, some of them non-applicable. But, hopefully, there will be enough useful tools included in this book to justify its purchase.

For me, the most important conclusion I got from putting this book together was that e-business is not simply a matter of creating a product or service and then marketing it to customers or clients. It involves something much more interesting: it is about creating a dynamic system of interdependences.

In the world of e-business, products cannot be definitively described, designs can never be frozen, customers cannot be satiated. E-businesses have to be given an independent life of their own so that they can self-adapt to the rapidly changing environment and competition. This is my own most important learning from this book-writing exercise: e-business isn't about designing a product or a service. It isn't about technology or marketing. It is about designing an adaptive system.

Now to put my tool-box and learning to the test. For details please read the epilogue which has been written just as this book goes to press.

THE NEXT BOOK:
WEB PRESENCE

THE FORE-RUNNER TO THIS BOOK, *The Entrepreneurial Web*, looked at the internet environment as a whole: trying to find an appropriate mind-set to make strategic use of the internet and the world wide web. This second book *The Ultimate Game of Strategy* creates a tool-box of conceptual models to use in a strategy to establish a personal niche in the world of e-business.

These demand a third book, a book that demonstrates how these theories and conceptual tools are used in real-life situations.

As this book goes to press, I begin this third book: provisionally entitled *Web Presence*. The intention is to use the mindset created in the first book, and the tool-box of concepts described in the second, to create one or more actual e-business systems – and write about the experience as I go along. The core product or service of the e-businesses will be of small consequence because it is the strategy that is important. Such a strategy should have universal application.

In keeping with the conclusions of the first two books, I begin with no fixed idea and no plan. I start with no capital and intend working without any management system or business structures based upon teams and leadership. According to the dogmas of established twentieth- century business practice, such a strategy will lead to certain failure. I need to confound that prediction in order to validate the conclusions of the first two books.

The premise of starting with a good business idea, a business plan and a strong management team is useful only as a means of obtaining funding. Unfortunately, after the funding has been acquired, this premise becomes a serious handicap – a millstone round the neck. It is therefore my intention to skip over the idea of attracting funding at an early stage and concentrate upon what should be the principal purpose of any e-business – creating wealth. This can only come about through finding a way to improve efficiency somehow. Improved efficiency is the sole source of wealth creation.

The conclusions of the first two books overwhelmingly come out in favour of e-business being about communication between people rather than the communication-enhancing technology itself. This focuses attention upon the creation of collaborative associations as being the key elements in any e-business strategy. If these collaborations result in an improvement of efficiency in some way, this will create wealth – which can then be shared among the collaborators. In other words, e-business is about creating non-zero sum games where all the players can win.

It is not quite as straightforward as it sounds. Without planning and management, something must be put in its place to provide stability and continuity. A self-regulating system has to be created: an adaptive system, of mutually collaborative associations where everyone is dependent upon everyone else. The paradox is that to be survivable, such systems must contain duplication and expendability, such that no part of the system is critically important. This includes the prime movers.

This current book ended with a description of the café being used to write a book. It will now be used to create e-businesses. Whether it ends in success or failure, either way it will be an interesting adventure and should make interesting reading.

The progress of these explorative e-business ventures for the next book will be obtainable from my website at: http://www.avatarnets.com

Peter Small

INDEX